The Hidden Power of a Surrendered Life

Compelling Lessons of Influence from the Life of Esther and Other Yielded Lives

GLENDA MALMIN

CITYBIBLE
PUBLISHING

Portland, Oregon, U.S.A.

Published by City Bible Publishing

9200 NE Fremont, Portland, Oregon 97220

Printed in U.S.A.

City Bible Publishing is a ministry of City Bible Church and is dedicated to serving the local church and its leaders through the production and distribution of quality restoration materials.

It is our prayer that these materials, proven in the context of the local church, will equip leaders in exalting the Lord and extending His kingdom.

For a free catalog of additional resources from City Bible Publishing please call 1-800-777-6057 or visit our web site at www.citybiblepublishing.com.

The Hidden Power of a Surrendered Life

ISBN: 1-886849-82-X

Table of Contents

Esther 3

I would like to dedicate this book to my beloved partner, hero, and friend, my loving husband Ken. As odd as it may seem to dedicate a book to a man when the primary character of the book is a woman, I know of no other person who lives a more surrendered life to the will and purposes of God than this man. No one I know exemplifies more the lesson, "What I am a part of is more important than the part I play," than this man. He goes out of his way to make others successful, as well as safe and secure in their callings, never promoting himself and always encouraging others. He is sacrificial and loyal, both in word and deed, to those whom God brings his way, regardless of their station in life. He has crossed the threshold of personal sacrifice on behalf of others more than once in his ministry career and has always done so with complete abandonment to the cause of Christ.

Thank you, Ken, for being my hero, my confidante, my mentor, and my constant source of encouragement. Thank you for the yielded life that you live, not only out of principle, but out of a surrendered heart. I will be forever grateful for your unselfish love and faithful devotion.

Acknowledgements

I give honor and thanks to my Lord and Savior, Jesus Christ, for giving me salvation as a precious and personal gift. Thank You for keeping me on the pathway of the surrendered, especially at those times when my heart was prone to wander toward easier paths that required less sacrifice. Your way is best, though the twists and turns never cease to amaze me. Thank You for being You and allowing me to be me. What a great and mighty God You are!

I would like to thank my family for being there to politely read the first manuscripts and offer encouraging words and wise suggestions. Thank you for the lives you live and how you impart them to me.

I would also like to thank Mrs. Edie Iverson for being my ministry mentor and friend. Many lives have been touched and changed because of the power of your surrendered life to the will and purposes of God. Some people will never know, until they arrive on 'the other side,' what you have surrendered on behalf of their success. What a bright star you are in God's kingdom! Thank you.

Acknowledgements and a very sincere thank you to my personal prayer partners, Phyllis Brown, Kathy Taylor, Mary Henderson, Donna Chesnutt, Linda Amundson, Detta Vasak, Donis Meier, Robert and Donna Jameson, Aryn Hires, Jana Brott, Matt Rogers, and Fred, Lynn, and Andrea Whaley. You are indeed testimonies of those who live surrendered lives daily, abandoning yourselves in prayer and in practical service. Thank you for your prayers and encouragement. I pray that this book will honor the hours of prayer that you have invested.

I would also like to thank my incredible editor, Kathy Tanksley, for challenging me and stretching me. Thank you for the hours of sacrifice and the wisdom you offered. I salute you and your husband, Dr. Steve Tanksley, who is currently serving our country in the war against terrorism. You are truly walking testimonies of the power of surrendered lives.

*All illustrations are used with permission.

*The New International Version Bible is used for quotation unless otherwise noted.

Foreword
By Barbara Wentroble

The ways of God conflict with the ways of the world! The world tells us we are to hold onto what we have if we want to have enough. God's Word tells us to give to others, and He will give back to us more than we gave away (Luke 6:38). The world says we should get even with those who have wronged us. God says we are to forgive (Matt. 6:14-15). The world tells us to speak our minds and not let people take advantage of us. God says a soft answer will turn away wrath (Prov. 15:1).

Glenda Malmin captures the paradox of God's ways in her book, The Hidden Power of a Surrendered Life. She powerfully illustrates the emotions that seek to hinder us as we transition into new seasons and new relationships in our pursuit of the Lord. She eloquently describes thoughts that could have been in the heart of Queen Esther as she pursued her destiny in the Lord. Glenda reveals the path of a similar destiny that God has given us for today. An important key in apprehending our destiny involves learning to see the Lord in each circumstance of life. Apprehending the grace of God in these circumstances will strengthen us as we face tragedies, storms of life and difficult relationships.

I love the way Glenda emphasizes that a life of humble surrender is a life living life for others. Living life for others is amazingly foreign to many people. We are bombarded with clichés such as "Take care of #1," or "You deserve a break today." In other words, "self is more important than others." Contrary to a life of self, Glenda paints a picture of the surrendered life. She shows the wisdom of God in taking whatever may seem shattered in our lives and using those things for His glory. God makes use of a surrendered life to even touch future generations. When we understand the power of a surrendered life to impact not only our generation but also future generations, our hearts can rejoice in the wisdom of God.

I highly recommend this book for those seeking a greater revelation of their purpose in life. The Hidden Power of a Surrendered Life is destined to propel many people into their God-given destinies!

Preface

Have you ever wondered about the direction your life has taken and pondered the "whys" of the pathway? Have you ever felt trapped by the decisions that you have made for your life? Have you ever desired to make a marked difference but wondered how to go about it effectively?

If you have ever grappled with such feelings, there is a young woman of antiquity named Esther who can relate to your question-laden journey. In fact, you will be astonished at the parallels as you gaze across the generations through the windows of her pilgrimage. You will find that God, in His sovereignty, connected Esther with others who would influence her journey; their very lives will begin to look familiar to you, as you see in them the godly characteristics of those who impact your own life.

Esther was much like an average teenage girl in our own culture. She had hopes and dreams, plans and desires. She had the opportunity to either surrender her will and make the best of the challenges presented to her, or to be unbending and risk the lives of others, as well as her own. But Esther was never an island unto herself. She lived with a constant awareness that her influence would affect others.

Rather than charting her own course through life, Esther constantly found that her path was laid out for her. She often found the need to surrender to the decisions of others, rather than make the choices she might have preferred. Surely, there were times when she felt trapped by her circumstances and yearned to break free of them. Yet she found peace as she surrendered, not to the circumstances, but to the God who was in charge of the circumstances. Her lot in life was to die to herself so that others might live. It was in dying that her influence came. Yes, her roadway was paved beforehand by the Master Builder, but it was made up of many bends and turns, many choices that she herself had to make.

She must have been continually amazed at the remarkable interventions of God in her life. Have you ever hoped that an extraordinary God would intervene in your very ordinary life? Do you trust that you will surmount the hills and the valleys of your life and reach your desired destina-

tion? Are you willing to remain surrendered to the will of the One who charted your journey? If so, you are destined to forge ahead in your pilgrimage and make a difference.

At the beginning of each chapter in this text, you will find a quoted portion of Scripture from the book of Esther. Then, in story and monologue format, you will be introduced to Esther and the other main characters of the book as though they were telling you a part of their own journey. Granted, there is a measure of poetic license taken as the ponderings of their private heart-thoughts and prayers unfold in each chapter, but as the biblical characters come alive, you will find that their experiences hold many keys to help you navigate your own life path.

At the end of each chapter is a list of related Bible verses that may be used for personal or group Bible study.

The primary focus of this book is not as much on exegetical interpretation as it is on the personal application of principles of truth in the quoted verses. I would like you, the reader, to apply the lessons drawn from Esther's biblical personal account to your own life. Let the power of her surrendered life motivate you to reach out to a generation in need.

If you are well versed in Scripture, I hope that you will take the time to read the account again and be freshly challenged by the example that Esther has set for each of us. Resist the temptation of the average Christian reader to skip over the Scriptural text. Read it once again and allow the account of this amazing young woman to penetrate your life in a deep, significant, and motivating way.

If you are unfamiliar with Scripture, I hope that you will glean much from the recorded account of Esther. As you look at her life with me, you will find that this remarkable person of history is a woman with whom you can easily identify today. You will find her to be in need but blessed, apprehensive yet bold, youthful but wise. You will read of her penetrating questions and her unlimited surrender to the will and purposes of the God she served.

Though technology advances and history blazes forward, human nature remains the same. I pray, as you journey with me through the life of this young heroine and those to whom she related, that you will find your own life woven together with the ancients and see their lives in yours. Esther and her beloved mentor Mordecai both had hesitations, concerns, opinions, and deep challenges in their roles, yet they remained surrendered to the will of God. I hope that you will take heart afresh as you see how your life is intimately linked with others across the ages. May you see your life interwoven, not only with Esther and Mordecai, but also with the lives of other courageous contemporaries who surrendered their lives to the Lordship of Jesus Christ.

"These things happened to them as examples and were written down as warnings for us, on whom the fulfillment of the ages has come" (1 Corinthians 10:11). As the apostle Paul says in this New Testament passage, may we learn from Esther's example and consider it carefully. As contemporaries who have stepped into this new millennium, may we be freshly challenged to trust more in the Lord of our circumstances than in what our natural eyes behold. May we humbly submit ourselves to the Master's guidance and leave a rich legacy for the next generation.

My hope, as you read these pages, is that you will be freshly encouraged and motivated to surrender to the purposes of God in your life. If you do so, perhaps you will be among those who rescue a generation from impending doom and brightly reflect the power of a surrendered life.

Ordered Steps

THE HIDDEN POWER OF A SURRENDERED LIFE

God Sets the Stage

"This is what happened during the time of Xerxes, the Xerxes who ruled over 127 provinces stretching from India to Cush: At that time King Xerxes reigned from his royal throne in the citadel of Susa, and in the third year of his reign he gave a banquet for all his nobles and officials...Queen Vashti also gave a banquet for the women in the royal palace...when King Xerxes was in high spirits from wine, he commanded the seven eunuchs who served him...to bring before him Queen Vashti...to display her beauty...Queen Vashti refused to come. Then the king became furious and burned with anger...he spoke with the wise men who understood the laws...Vashti is never again to enter the presence of King Xerxes. Also let the king give her royal position to someone else who is better than she...Then the king's personal attendants proposed, 'Let a search be made for beautiful young virgins for the king....'" (Esther 1:1-2, 9, 10-13, 19; 2:2).

Xerxes, king of the entire Persian Empire, paced the floor of his royal bed-chamber in torturous agony. His pounding step was so determined and hurried that his kingly robes flew behind him with a flurry at each turn he made. The relentless pacing of his feet, though swift and forceful, could not keep time with the racing of his heart. His scepter of authority was discarded on the floor, tucked halfway beneath his bed after being slammed down in fury for many nights now. His crown was tossed aside with disdain, a misplaced token that he would curse in the morning as the sun peaked across the horizon and duties demanded his kingly garb.

Grief and a deep sense of loss plagued his thoughts one moment, as rage and indignation encompassed him the next. The clash of emotion, the struggle between love for his wife and rage for his queen, was more than he could bear. The public rejection of his queen at the pinnacle of his royal celebration had become like the stranglehold of a brutish enemy of late. Initially it had merely stunned him, but now Xerxes was haunted with the suffocating awareness that his attempt to restore his kingly dignity by expelling her was weak at best and left his soul with lonely nights and afflicted days.

"What a grand idea this was," he thought sardonically as he paced the floor in frustration. *"At least it seemed to be at its inception! Winters can be so boring, and an 'open house' displaying the wealth of my kingdom and my own splendor and majesty to the nobles and princes of my provinces had been such a glorious idea. Not only would it honor my leadership at this strategic point in time, but it would also spur on support for the upcoming invasion into Greece. If a little honor was to come my way in the process, well, what harm could there be in that? After all, I am Xerxes, the sovereign ruler. Have I not earned my own noteworthiness? Truly, I am a 'history-maker!'"*

Though he was the supreme ruler over 127 provinces from India to Ethiopia and wealthier than any Persian king before him, Xerxes' thirst for power and influence could not be quenched. He longed for more peoples and more lands to be conquered in his name. He yearned for Greece to bow its knee to Persian authority and respect him as king.

He had been Persia's king for three years now. At the age of thirty-five, he had a very commanding presence; he was tall and handsome, young and virile. It was said of him: *"Of all those tens of thousands of men, for goodliness and stature there was not one worthier than Xerxes himself to hold that command."* [1]

His father Darius I, the former king of Persia, had died in November of 486 B.C. and left the kingdom to him at the age of thirty-two. His mother was Atossa, the daughter of Cyrus, founder of the Achaemenid Persian Empire and king of Babylon. The royal blood in Xerxes' veins ran pure and rich.[2] He had served as the viceroy of Babylonia for over twelve years, prior to his kingship, and did so with such excellence that in 498 B.C. his father had a palace built in his honor. Not only was Xerxes a handsome and dutiful son, he was an intelligent and competent ruler, as well.

In the first three years of his reign as king, Persia had become the dominant nation in the land through Xerxes' many conquests. He was strong in power and influence, and he certainly did not plan on that decreasing in the years ahead. To conquer Greece, however, would require the strength and unity of the entire empire. He needed a plan that would stir all of his provinces to invade Greece and bring it in under his wing. He was the one of whom Daniel had prophesied: *"And now I will tell you the truth. Behold, three more kings are going to arise in Persia. Then a fourth will gain far more riches than all of them; as soon as he becomes strong through his riches, he will arouse the whole empire against the realm of Greece."* [3]

The royal winter palace in Susa was the perfect setting to present his princes and nobles with his newest challenge.[4] While they were feasting and celebrating their wealth and national dominance, he had planned to soften their wills into submission and stir their thirst for the next great conquest. A six-month gala event was designed to underscore to the entire nation and their provincial princes that his leadership and military prowess was worthy of their support. He had been confident that they would all enjoy personal tours of the palace and royal entertainment that only a great king could provide. It was to be an extravaganza that the world would never forget!

The temperatures in Susa at this time of year were mild, and travel was easy for his royal subjects.[5] The crafting of the palace had its beginnings under the reign of his father, but it had recently been completed under his supervision. Its elaborate décor was comprised of precious timber and gemstones from each province.[6] The timber was imported from Lebanon, Gandahara, and Carmania. Gold came from Sardis and Bactria, precious lapis stones from Sogdiana, turquois from Chorasmia, and silver and ebony from Egypt. The ivory was from Ethiopia, Sind, and Arachosia, the stone columns from Elam, and other rare materials were brought from many other provinces. These unique adornments from the provinces were his idea and should have served him well in the eyes of his royal subjects.

Xerxes sunk into a chair and reflected on the magnificent celebration he had thrown, *"The capstone was to be the grand banquet of seven days for all of Susa. What a marvelous idea that was—what planning it entailed! It was impressive indeed—truly a lavish affair like the world had never before experienced or shall ever forget, I'm sure."*

Climaxing the half-year extravaganza with a grand-finale weeklong banquet for all the people of Susa, from the least to the greatest, was meant to be the proverbial "frosting on the cake." While he offered drink and feasting to the men, his queen flattered their wives with even more Persian delectables.

"Ah yes, the women had their party with their 'proper cup of tea,' and we men feasted until we could feast no more. By my command, there was neither watering-down of the wine nor pushing it when it was no longer wanted. Each man's desire was served just as he wished . . . each man but me, that is."

His thoughts shifted to his queen, his magnificent Vashti, *"And then came my final display of the beauty of my kingdom, my queen! Little did I know what calamity awaited me from one simple request! How scandalous was her behavior; she's no queen worthy of regal adornment; she's merely an unworthy wife who brought disgrace to my name!"*

The winter celebration was indeed grand, but as we all know, grand plans do not always come to pass in the manner in which they were intended. In fact, all was well until Xerxes lulled himself into a drunken stupor and his intoxicated thoughts shifted to his own narcissistic greatness, his grand schemes, and his guests' lust for more. It was then that he made one grave error. On the last day of the feast, he made a foolish, drunken order to his courtly and beautiful wife. In turn, he was stunned and shamed by Queen Vashti's irate refusal to parade her beauty in front of him and all the drunken men of Susa.[7] Everyone in attendance was horrified, and as the palace was cleared hastily, speculations began as to which side the justice of the king would stand. The grand palace décor was soon forgotten, and the strategies of war were postponed to a later time.

"What came over her?" Xerxes asked himself in bewilderment. *"Did I require too much? No, impossible! I am the king; she is the one who must bend—not me! Did I not allow her great latitude? She was free to have her own celebrant banquet with the women in the royal palace. She should have been grateful to me for such a privilege. Women have never had it better in all of history! She not only should have come at my bidding, she should have thought of it ahead of time and offered to serve me in any way that would have pleased me."*

He stood abruptly and began pacing again as his anger grew and his heart began to race. *"How dare Vashti not bow to my wishes and do my bidding! How could she be so audacious and shame me in front of my noblemen—and all of Susa?! Who does she think she is?! Granted, I did woo her with romantic illusions of influence and grandeur at times, but every woman should realize her true place—even a queen. She has needed reminding at times, but I never thought her strong mind would become a belligerent one. What was she thinking?! Oh, how my mind races in so many directions!"*

Xerxes' wife and queen, Vashti, was as beautiful as he was handsome. Her beauty had been an alluring and pleasant distraction from his duties. He had adored her and preferred her presence over the countless concubines offered him daily; he had even frequently allowed her to keep him from the affairs of state. Just the sight of Vashti could cause his heart to race and his focus to wander; the mere memory of her exacted the same responses within him even now. However, in recent months he had been so distracted by plans for an extravagant national celebration, as well as his all-consuming strategy for the invasion of Greece, that he had neglected to connect with her. These two distractions were deliberately linked in thought and intention. In his mind it was all very clear—the celebration was the means to bring about the invasion. However, he now wondered if Vashti had not realized his strategy, and thus, had unknowingly foiled his plans. His thoughts were plagued day and night with questions concerning his lack of communication and her lack of submission. He was bewildered by such an extreme reaction from the woman to whom he had shown such favor.

"Vashti knows her beauty brings joy and honor to me, just as my wealth does," he lamented. *"She knows my love for her parallels my love for . . . well, for myself. It wouldn't be right for me to love or honor her more than myself. After all, she is a mere woman, and I am a sovereign. Whether I'm merry with wine or as sober as a rock, who does she think she is not to yield to my wishes and surrender to my commands? How will my provincial princes trust my leadership into the invasion of Greece if they cannot trust the leadership they see in me within my own palace walls?"*

Xerxes' anger toward Vashti began to burn within him once again as he calculated how her behavior assaulted his grand scheme and left only the residue of humiliation in his heart and whispers of degradation within the palace walls. As he stood on the veranda of his personal chambers, hoping to find solace in the beauty of his gardens, his tortured thoughts would not leave him alone, and his mouth could not help but speak to his own soul.

"Such self-importance by a queen should not go unpunished, but what am I to do? What would restore my honor in the eyes of my people and bring justice to Vashti at the same time? I know, I will consult with my wise men; they have always been well able to fashion their astute legal perspectives into shrewd proposals. Yes, I'll go to them."

In the days following the banquet disaster when Xerxes had his "splendor and glory" shattered by his queen, through the providence of God, his musings were saturated in frustration and anguish. The counsel of his advisors was soon to come, but for now he was left to his agonizing self-deliberations.

———•◦•———

While Xerxes was venting and scheming in his chambers, Vashti, too, was struggling with her own plight. Like her "lord, the king," her feet were pacing and her thoughts were racing. A myriad of emotions and thoughts whirled through her mind, one colliding against the other. She looked longingly for solace as she gazed out over the king's gardens from her balcony window. Rather than finding the comfort she sought, she overheard Xerxes spewing venomous statements to the wind in her regard. She instantly felt renewed anger over his ghastly and humiliating order during the banquet, and her indignation escalated nearly to the point of eruption. She pursed her lips tightly, while her head exploded with pain due to her rising blood pressure. Despite the ache in her head, she remained steadfast in the fact that her response to his drunken whim was justified.

"I hear his ranting and raving on my behalf," she declared. *"Let it go with the winter wind and dissolve into the air, just as it should. One minute I am a queen in whom he delights, and the next he threatens to banish me. Who is he to speak in such blasphemous tones of me?! Is he not a mere man in a king's garments?!*

"How dare he ask me to organize and host such a grand banquet reception for so many women and then expect me to respond to his every chauvinistic whim! How humiliating! How can I influence women if they think I am nothing but a servant in my own home?! One minute Xerxes tells me he loves and respects me, that I am a woman of great influence, and the next he expects me to be subservient to his over-inflated male ego, as well as his drunken stupidity!"

She turned from the window abruptly; the garden view did nothing to soothe her raw emotions. She was hurt and disappointed as she thought of her husband, the king she had grown to love. *"How could he be so self-indulgent, so self-focused?! He said we were a team in the romantic quietness of his chambers. He said that we would be an example to the nation of a man and a woman working together for the betterment of the kingdom. How could I have been so blind to his manipulative schemes?! Were there not other times when I was wounded by his momentary insensitivity and lack of obvious respect? Has he not been erratic in his emotions and duplicitous in his behavior at other unexpected times?! What was I thinking? I am stunned at my own lack of genuine discernment, but I will not be duped or used again."*

She stepped over to the mirror and contemplated her reflection. She longed to be recognized, not just for her beauty, but also for her keen insight and strength of character. She was not a mere object to be paraded and admired. She was the Queen of Persia, and she deserved respect. *"I have worked hard to get where I am. I not only put up with all of those humiliating beauty treatments, but I was mentored in political history and policymaking until my mind was weary of it all. I have earned my respect, not only as a woman, but as a partner, as well. If Xerxes thought he could get away with humiliating me and lowering me to the status of a slave in front of the lustful eyes of his loyal subjects, he had another thought coming! I am no mere woman. I have tasted of power, and I have earned the respect that is due me. The eyes of men will no longer ogle me; I care not whether they be nobles, princes, or King Xerxes himself. I will not settle for anything less than what is rightfully mine. The humiliation of his drunken demand is the last straw. I refuse to be treated like this again; I'd rather be banished to the desert than live in the palace of such a duplicitous king!"*

MARKS OF THE HEART

Emotions and egos exploded like unmanaged fireworks this historic weekend in the royal palace. The king's extravagant celebration, designed to arouse the empire to support his springtime military campaign against Greece, ended in an upheaval he could have never imagined. In fact, the halls still echoed with devastating silence rather than strains of rejoicing. The only voices to be heard were the whispers of legal counsel behind closed doors and the reverberations of the ranting and raving of the royal couple in their separate, private chambers.

All had been well until the king made one devastating mistake. He expected his wife to yield to his momentary whims as though she were just another one of his subjects. After all, he was the king; whether it was in the privacy of his own chambers or in front of a crowd of men who had been consuming alcohol and feasting for seven days and longer, his command was his command. It was not a polite petition; it was a command. He was accustomed to both men and women alike bowing to his every command, whether they were in "high spirits" with wine or not. Surrender and obedience was not an option to him; it was a way of life.

Yes, Xerxes was a king who had grown accustomed to people and nations surrendering to his will, but he had met his match in his queen through the providence of God. After three years as king and a six-month display of exorbitant pride and arrogance, he was reduced to a tyrannical reactionary and heartsick lover in one fell-swoop.

Though his dissolved marriage would leave a mark on his heart, as all relationships do, this queen would be banished. Her departure would set the stage for the entrance of another queen. Her exit would reflect the ordering of Xerxes' steps by a God who was unseen to the natural eye. It would also require that the next queen step carefully and in accordance with wisdom.

Vashti stood up to the king in pride to empower herself and was rejected. There was coming a day when a new queen would stand before the king in surrender to empower the lives of others. Both had courage. One was cloaked in pride, the other in humility. One displayed the short-sightedness of rebellion, the other the genius of submission. One sought to empower herself, the other to empower her king and her people. One would succeed where the other had failed.

Not only was King Xerxes arrogant and egotistical, so were his associates. Not only was he temperamental and demanding, so were his closest leaders. Not only was he emotionally unstable, so was the atmosphere of his capital city. Not only did he lack understanding of the providence of God and was in need of a savior, so was his nation.

Perhaps the heart of an egotistical and hardened king could be softened by strength overlaid with meekness.[8] Perhaps evil leaders could be rooted out and a watching and waiting people could be rescued. Only time and the providential intervention of the one true God would reveal the answers.

What truly lies within the power of a surrendered life? In a moment's time, one queen stole a king's confidence to command and brought reproach to his leadership. Could another instill in him the courage to take command once again and rescue a generation? In a moment's time, one queen lost her power and prominence. Could another step into such a place of influence without following in her footsteps? Only time and the surrender of a maiden would tell.

Can you hear the pride, rejection, and dismay of Xerxes cry out across the ages? Can you hear the isolation, outrage, and wounding of Vashti? Can you hear the all-too-familiar voice of the enemy turning gender differences into gender wars? These may be familiar heart-themes in the lives of people around you today, people who have been placed near you by the very heart and plan of the Lord.

Proverbs 21:1-2 tells us, *"The king's heart is in the hand of the Lord; He directs it like a watercourse wherever he pleases. All a man's ways seem right to him, but the Lord weighs the heart."* Was God providentially setting the stage for a rescuer to step onto the scene in Xerxes' period in history? Is He not also setting the stage for you today, as well? Take a courageous look at those around you and see if you can discern whether God is up to something. There is a "turning of the watercourse" because there is a need for rescue.

Have you observed the "heart-atmosphere" of those around you recently? Maybe Queen Vashti did the right thing, and maybe not; numerous Bible scholars debate that fact, even today. What we do know is that her response to her husband and his response to her opened the door for a new queen and a new realm of influence. The stage was set.

BROKEN HEARTS AND CHOSEN VESSELS

As a child, did you ever create a stage in the living room or the backyard to entertain other neighborhood children? I did. I can remember using clothespins to clip up old blankets to set the stage. I wanted my neighborhood audience to be amazed at the "splendor and majesty" that was planned just for them. I can still remember putting the music on and stepping out onto the makeshift stage to pantomime a song while it played in the background. I could organize the show, perform several acts myself, and administrate the punch and cookies.

Those were "the good ole days." My emotions ran high, and I expended all my energy, but the excitement made it worth every creative thought and effort that I put forth. Just to be "on stage" made it worthwhile. The power of influence was energizing and addicting. Watching and waiting for the response of the audience was simultaneously nerve-wracking and exhilarating, even for me as a child.

Though I am a college instructor today and not a performer, I recognize the fact that I am still a visual observer. I tend to look for responses from my students to discern how much they are learning. However, if you have ever been a learner or a teacher, you know that the countenance does not always reflect accurately what is going on in the heart.

Regardless of your station in life, whether it is in a palace or the backroom office of a fledgling company, there are people around you whom God has strategically placed in your life for you to influence. Regardless of the person's position, whether he is a boss, husband, or a small child diagnosed with autism, he has a heart that has been bruised, misguided, or in some simple yet profound way prepared by God for you to influence. And regardless of the response, whether it is an outward, overt expression or a quiet, demure reply, the audience at hand is watching, waiting, and observing you.

While you may be totally unaware of the fact, these people may be incapable within themselves of receiving your influence without your humble surrender to them. Yes, surrender. Whether the "stage" is big or small, your yielding to the will of the Father above, as well as the sincere hearts of your "audience," will be impacting.

Sometimes people have so many layers of bruising, wounding, shame, or rejection that the only familiar feeling they have left intact is their pride. They know well that it is a distorted pride, but nevertheless, it's theirs. So they hang onto it obstinately until it pushes others away.

Sadly, often the ones they push away are the ones they love the most. The only way anyone can cut through the gruff exterior is through the anointing of kindness and humility. For it is through surrender that humility shines and releases kindness to heal broken hearts. When broken hearts are healed, the rescue of a generation is set in motion. God is always "setting the stage."

> "For it is through surrender that humility shines and releases kindness to heal broken hearts."

Prideful, wounded, and reactionary "kings" come in a variety of shapes and sizes. One young woman, who I met at a Bible college in India, was born into a Roman Catholic family. Unlike the increasing respect and fellowship between Catholics and Protestants in America, there is much prejudice and disdain between the two groups in India. When a family member converts to Protestantism from Catholicism in India, it brings great shame and reproach to the family.

This young woman was one of eight children. She received Jesus Christ as her Lord and Savior at a street meeting and converted to Protestantism. While her mother was alive, she was somewhat sheltered from her father's wrath. But then her mother died, and her seeming protection was gone. After this young woman's mother died, her father attempted to murder her numerous times. He beat her, attempted to poison her, and utterly rejected her.

One day, when she was in her bedroom, he poured kerosene on the windowsills and the doorway of her room with the intention of lighting it on fire while she was inside. He was unable to successfully strike a match to the kerosene before she pushed her way out of the door. From there, she ran to a pastor's house for refuge.

The next day her father and brother came to get her. Upon their arrival, her father beat her in front of the pastor, dragged her into the street, and threw her into the back of his jeep. Halfway home, the father and brother stopped for tea, and she jumped from the jeep and ran through the jungle back to the pastor's house.

The pastor immediately arranged for her travel to the Bible college where I met her. At this school, she would receive training for a year and would then be sent out with another young woman to evangelize and disciple a group of believers in a nearby village. Within a year or so, a new church would be established. The two girls could then return to the Bible college to have a marriage arranged for them or to be sent out again to help establish another church.

Psalm 27:10 says, *"Though my father and mother forsake me, the Lord will receive me." Verses 11-14 go on to say, " Teach me your way, O Lord; lead me in a straight path because of my oppressors. Do not turn me over to the desire of my foes, for false witnesses rise up against me, breathing out violence. I am still confident of this: I will see the goodness of the Lord in the land of the living. Wait for the Lord; be strong and take heart and wait for the Lord."*

David proclaims in this Psalm that even when those whom God has ordained to protect and nurture us turn away, the Lord will take care of us. He is always "setting the stage" for something greater than we are able to see within the momentary circumstances.

Whether this angry and disappointed father wanted to be used by God or not, he was and continues to be. Through the surrender of his daughter to the lordship of Jesus, his story, too, is being proclaimed for the Gospel of Jesus Christ. His rejection, though it wounded her, only inspires Jesus to draw this daughter closer to His heart. He will use this father's ignorant arrogance and pride to "set the stage" and accomplish His will. Christ will heal the broken heart and multiply the scattered hopes into a field that will bear fruit for His kingdom.

A daughter rejected is a vessel chosen. God is in the business of mending broken vessels ever so gently and using them ever so mightily.

His promise to her, as she has boldly faced her "King Xerxes," has

> *"God is in the business of mending broken vessels ever so gently and using them ever so mightily."*

been this verse: *"For you have died, and your life is now hidden with Christ in God. When Christ, who is your life, appears, then you also will appear with him in glory"* (Colossians 3:3, 4).

Even though it is never God's will for a father to beat, burn, or reject his daughter, if he chooses to do so, God will hear the cry of that daughter and rescue her. In doing so, He will "set the stage" for her, not only to be rescued, but also to be fruitful in His kingdom. He will mold and shape the "rescued" into a "rescuer." God does not waste anything or anyone. All He asks for is a surrendered heart and the willingness to go.

———◆———

Was God setting the stage for the rescue of a generation to come through a humble, unsuspecting young girl so long ago in ancient history? Yes, He was. Was He orchestrating events in history to do so? Yes, He was.

Because of Queen Vashti's position of influence and her refusal to obey the king's command, the recommendation of Memucan, the king's counselor, to the broken and baffled King Xerxes was *". . . let the king give her royal position to someone else who is better than she"* (Esther 1:19). And so the search began.

The world will always appraise levels of influence and compare candidates, but it is God who sets the stage.

Is He turning the watercourse in hearts today and setting the stage for the rescue of a generation? Yes, He is. Proverbs 16:9 says, *"In his heart a man plans his course, but the Lord determines his steps."*

Will there be humble vessels within view, those who are willing to die to self-focused ambitions? Will there be vessels who are willing to surrender their own backyard stage for the platform of a King? That is up to you and me. May you and I be counted among those yielded lives. May we see within our generation the providential hand of God move, not only through the hearts of kings, but through the *power of a surrendered life.*

Ordered Steps

2 SAM. 22:37 *"Thou hast enlarged my steps under me; so that my feet did not slip." (KJV)*
"You broaden the path beneath me, so that my ankles do not turn." (NIV)

PS. 18:36 Same verse as listed above

PS. 37:23 *"The steps of a good man are ordered by the LORD: and he delighteth in his way." (KJV)*
"If the Lord delights in a man's way, he makes his steps firm." (NIV)

PS. 37:31 *"The law of his God is in his heart; none of his steps shall slide." (KJV)*
"The Law of his God is in his heart; his feet do not slip." (NIV)

PS. 85:13 *"Righteousness shall go before him; and shall set us in the way of his steps." (KJV)*
Righteousness goes before him and prepares the way for his steps." (NIV)

PS. 119:133 *"Order my steps in thy word: and let not any iniquity have dominion over me." (KJV)*
"Direct my footsteps according to your word; let no sin rule over me." (NIV)

PROV. 4:12 *"When thou goest, thy steps shall not be straitened; and when thou runnest, thou shalt not stumble." (KJV)*
"When you walk, your steps will not be hampered; when you run, you will not stumble." (NIV)

PROV. 16:9 *"A man's heart deviseth his way: but the LORD directeth his steps." (KJV)*

"In his heart a man plans his course, but the Lord determines his steps." (NIV)

JER. 10:23 *"O LORD, I know that the way of man is not in himself: it is not in man that walketh to direct his steps." (KJV)*

"I know, O Lord, that a man's life is not his own; it is not for man to direct his steps." (NIV)

1 PETER 2:21 *"For even hereunto were ye called: because Christ also suffered for us, leaving us an example, that ye should follow his steps:" (KJV)*

"To this you were called, because Christ suffered for you, leaving you an example, that you should follow in his steps." (NIV)

NOTES

1 "According to Herodotus (7.187), Xerxes was tall and handsome: 'Of all those tens of thousands of men, for goodliness and stature there was not one worthier than Xerxes himself to hold that command.' Although he was not an active soldier as his father had been, he was no doubt trained in military skills. Prior to his accession, Xerxes served as the viceroy over Babylonia for about a dozen years. As early as 498 B.C. we have a reference to the building of a palace at Babylon for 'the king's son.' After Darius's death in November 486, Xerxes succeeded him as king. He was about thirty-two years old." Edwin M. Yamauchi, *Persia and the Bible* (Grand Rapids: Baker, 1990), 193.

2 "He is known to us in history outside the Bible as Xerxes, which is the Greek form of his Persian name. This Xerxes reigned over the Persian empire from 485 to 465 B.C. . . . The name of the son of Darius which deciphered as *Khshayarsha*, which, when translated into Greek, is *Xerxes*, and which, when translated into Hebrew, is, practically letter for letter, *Akhashverosh*, that is, in English, *Ahas-uerus* . . ." J. Sidlow Baxter, *Explore the Book*, Vol. 2 (Grand Rapids: Zondervan, 1960-1973), 2:262.

3 Daniel 11:2

4 "Susa (the Greek name), or Shushan (the Hebrew name), was an ancient capital of Elam which Darius I rebuilt as the winter capital of the Persian Empire." John C. Whitcomb, *Esther: Triumph of God's Sovereignty* (Chicago: Moody Press, 1971), 33.

5 "During the winter the area is pleasant and Susa was used then as a residence by the Achaemenid kings. Rains in January and February create lush pastures for the shepherds. The area, however, is intolerably hot for six months of the year, particularly in July and August when temperatures reach 140 degrees Fahrenheit." Edwin M. Yamauchi, *Persia and the Bible* (Grand Rapids: Baker, 1990), 280-281.

6 History tells us that this palace was built by Darius I, Xerxes' father, and completed by Xerxes. It was extravagant and its décor was representative of many of the provinces of the kingdom. "The cedar timber, this—a mountain by name Lebanon—from there was brought . . . The *ya-ka* timber was brought from Gandhara and from Carmania. The gold was brought from Sardis and from Bactria . . . The precious stone lapis-lazuli and carnelian . . . this was brought from Sogdiana. The precious stone turquois, this was brought from Chorasmia . . . The silver and the ebony were brought from Egypt. The ornamentation with which the wall was adorned, that from Ionia was brought. The ivory . . . was brought from Ethiopia and from Sind and from Arachosia. The stone columns . . . a village by name Abiradu, in Elam—from there were brought." R.G. Kent, *Old Persia*, 2d ed. (New Haven: American Oriental Society, 1953), 144; see also F.W. Konig, *Der Burgbau zu Susa nach dem Bauberichte des Konigs Dareios I* (Leipzig: J.C. Hinrichs, 1930); R.G. Kent, "The Record of Darius's Palace at Susa," JAOS 53 (1933): 1-23, originally from Edwin M. Yamauchi, *Persia and the Bible* (Grand Rapids: Baker, 1990), 296.

7 "Since Persian modesty required women to be veiled in public, it appears that the king was asking her to degrade herself to satisfy his drunken whim. She refused to be displayed, thus greatly angering the king." William MacDonald, *Believer's Bible Commentary* (Nashville: Nelson, 1995), 498.

8 "Archaeologists excavating at Susa have unearthed inscriptions in which this king refers to himself as, 'The great king. The king of kings. The king of the lands occupied by many races. The king of this great earth.'" Charles R. Swindoll, *A Woman of Strength & Dignity, Esther* (Nashville: Word, 1997), 24.

A Chosen Perspective

"Now there was in the citadel of Susa a Jew of the tribe of Benjamin, named Mordecai son of Jair, the son of Shimei, the son of Kish, who had been carried into exile from Jerusalem by Nebuchadnezzar king of Babylon, among those taken captive with Jehoiachin king of Judah. Mordecai had a cousin named Hadassah, whom he had brought up because she had neither father nor mother. This girl, who was also known as Esther, was lovely in form and features, and Mordecai had taken her as his own daughter when her father and mother died" (Esther 2:5-7).

As Esther sat leaning on one elbow, enjoying her late morning tea, she felt contemplative, almost pensive, in regard to her history lessons from earlier in the morning. It wasn't so much that she had questions, or even further dialogue, for that matter. It was just that she felt a deep need within herself to understand the ways of God more intimately. Somehow, understanding the history of her ancestors and how God worked in their behalf seemed linked to her future. She could neither express her speculative thoughts in words nor in the questions with which she had commonly pelted her beloved mentor Mordecai. It was simply something that she felt.

How thankful she was for Mordecai. He never seemed to mind her unending questions or her periodic pensive moods. As a young woman, she was indeed blessed to have someone in her life so knowledgeable of

God's ways. Mordecai instructed her as other fathers and teachers of the law instructed their sons. He never belittled her or implied that she was less astute simply because she was a woman. In fact, he not only schooled her in Jewish history and law, but he had the elder servant women train her in the practicalities of being a godly woman, as well.

Although Cousin Mordecai was extremely knowledgeable, he was always kind and entreating as he taught her. His demeanor was such that she could engage him in open dialogue quite easily. Given her inquisitive personality, she was thankful that he was not only knowledgeable, but patient and gentle, as well. He was definitely strong-minded in his opinions, but he was always wise in how he delivered them. In fact, he had spoken with her often about the need to be not only knowledgeable, but perceptive and discerning, also. She could say, without doubt, that she had never known him to be less than wise in word or action. As a curious girl growing up, she had discretely watched and listened in on numerous deliberations he had had with his peers. She doubted that anything could disrupt his controlled demeanor. If so, she certainly had never seen it. He walked softly but had great influence among the Jewish people. For that and many other reasons, the respect and regard she felt for him had always been great.

This morning in their lessons, Mordecai had sat before her in his patriarchal robes of lapis blue and ivory. The subtle color of his garments and the gentleness of his gestures as he spoke soothed her heart and invited her responses. Though his deep brown eyes could always read her every thought and penetrate her heart, they forever communicated the kindness and openness of a beloved father. As an eager student, she had sat nearby with her wooden schoolboard covered in a fresh glaze of wax and a clean metal stylus in hand ready to take notes. The special notations she made would be inscribed on parchment later.

Today Mordecai rehearsed segments of the history of the Jews during times of captivity and times of freedom. He spoke of their fate being directed by the one true God. He reminded this one-person captive audience of the careful, loving hand of the mighty God of Israel as He had created streams in the desert for His chosen people in times of desolation and wellsprings of refreshing in seasons of blessing. Esther had heard similar lessons before; Mordecai had methodically led her through the lessons of the sacred scrolls, the Torah of Moses, in measured increments every three years since she was six years old, as any good Jewish mentor would. Though these stories were familiar, for some peculiar reason, they affected her differently today.

She was now growing in understanding as a young woman rather than a simple child; although, according to Cousin Mordecai's repeated commentary, she had never really been a child with simple thoughts or questions. She believed him, for he spoke to her as a trusted father. He was, in fact, the only father that she had really known. She often wondered why she constantly longed to study and understand more, rather than being concerned about household décor and creative recipes like the other girls her age. *"Was I born before my time? Do I have a man's mind trapped in a woman's body? What kind of destiny could God have in mind for a girl like me?"* As her late-morning tea grew cold, these questions and many more plagued her mind as they had on numerous other days.

The history of her people fascinated her, but their future captivated her thoughts even more. Her speculations on that topic alone could keep her mind spellbound for many hours in a day. Mordecai taught that the Jews were a chosen people—chosen by the one true God. While she could see and understand this historically, she wondered how that truth would affect her personally, today and tomorrow. She was but a simple hand-maiden, well versed in history perhaps, but as a woman, she had little hope for a truly exciting future. She could see no burning bushes or parted waters in her future. *"How will my ancestral heritage truly connect with my future?"* she mused.

Esther continued to mull over her thoughts as her tea grew colder still, her fruit browned, and her morning biscuit grew stale. She leaned back against the large linen pillow behind her and whispered, *"Jehovah, You are the one true God. I thank you for my beloved mentor, Cousin Mordecai. Even though my father and mother are lost to me in this life, I shall look forward to meeting them one day on the other side of this life. In the meantime, please know that I am forever grateful to You for my dear 'father' Mordecai. I rejoice in your goodness to me and I place my trust in You afresh today. I know that you have ordered my steps and I thank you for the privilege of being counted among your chosen people. Although we have been scattered like seed and our identity as a people has been shaken to it's very core, I stand in awe of You."*

It had been many years since Esther and Mordecai's ancestors had been exiled to Babylon by Nebuchadnezzar's army. Nebuchadnezzar and his mighty army broke into Jerusalem and the towns of Judah and burned their walls and buildings to the ground. They removed everything of value, utterly destroyed the city, and then took as prisoners anyone whom they deemed a possible threat. In 605 B.C., the third year of the reign of Nebuchadnezzar, he deported *". . . some of the Israelites from the royal family and the nobility—young men without any physical defect, handsome, showing aptitude for every kind of learning, well informed, quick to understand and qualified to serve in the king's palace. . . . They were to be trained for three years, and after that they were to enter the king's service."*[1] In 597 B.C., *". . . he carried into exile all Jerusalem: all the officers and fighting men, and all the craftsmen and artisans—a total of ten thousand. Only the poorest people of the land were left."*[2] There were two other times when Nebuchadnezzar deported thousands more from Jerusalem in 586 and 582 B.C., while executing anyone whom he suspected might be zealous enough to raise up a rebellion among the people.[3]

Mordecai's ancestors could be traced as far back as his great grandfather Kish, who had been carried off to Babylon with his family and other countrymen in Nebuchadnezzar's initial siege. His grandfather was a man named Shimei, and his father was Jair.[4] Though Esther was too young to remember him, she knew from Mordecai's family history lessons that her uncle Jair was a young adult during this initial siege some fifty years ago.

As Esther stared blankly at the wall, lost in her thoughts, she wondered, *"What would it be like to be totally uprooted from your home and dropped into a foreign kingdom? What would it be like to be expected to become a functioning part of a new society, never knowing if there were traitorous eyes watching your every move?"*

Once the exiles were in captivity in Babylon, Nebuchadnezzar wanted to benefit from the ethnic distinctiveness of each conquered group, so he allowed them to live and worship according to their own customs. Therefore, the Jews who were exiled from Judah did not live in poverty and despair in Babylon but were allowed to prosper and become influential citizens as long as they honored the authority of the land.

Because the Jews had no temple in which to worship and offer sacrifices in Babylon, their worship focused primarily on prayer, fasting, confessions, and the study of the written scrolls, the Torah of Moses. It was commonly known that many of the Jews did not pray for a messiah who would suffer and die for them; they prayed rather for a warrior king from David's lineage who would deliver them. God did, indeed, have their deliverance in mind, but it was not as some might have supposed.

Esther pondered the promise of a messiah for her people, *"Lord, when will the promised messiah come for your people? What does a true 'rescuer' look like, a sacrificial lamb or a majestic lion?"*

When Cyrus seized Babylon in 539 B.C., he already controlled Asia Minor, stretching from Sardis in western Asian Minor to Susa in Persia. From central Persia, he occupied the trade route between Europe and the Far East. By the time he took Babylon, he ruled as far as Egypt. Though he did allow the Jews to continue their worship as they saw fit, he did not stop the worship of false gods in Babylon. This, of course, was a disappointment to the Jews; however, God would soon address Cyrus through a prophet and give them an opportunity to return to their homeland.

According to the scroll of Ezra, God did just that. *"God, You are truly amazing!"* Esther mused as she continued to rehearse her history lessons in her mind.

During the first year of his reign as king of Persia, Cyrus received a word from God, spoken to him through Jeremiah the prophet. He was to allow as many Jews as desired to return, to go to Jerusalem to build a temple. Cyrus selected Zerubbabel, a descendant of one of Judah's former kings, to lead some forty thousand Hebrews back to Jerusalem.

Soon after, during an expedition to conquer yet more nations, Cyrus died, and Cambyses, his son, succeeded him. Cambyses was not sympathetic toward the Jews, and though the reconstruction work of the temple had begun, it was soon stopped. His reign did not last for long, though, as his thirst to expand the borders of his rule kept him away from his throne in Susa for three years. When Cambyses returned to Persia, Darius, a member of Cyrus' extended family, had won the hearts of the Persians and assumed rule. Cambyses is said to have committed suicide in shame soon after his return.

Differing from Cambyses, Darius felt sympathetic to the Jews and had the work resumed on the temple in Jerusalem. It was completed and rededicated in 515 B.C. He spent his later years enjoying the ethnic expansion of his empire and is said to have had a harem of women of various races in his palace in Susa. In 486 B.C., he died at the age of sixty-four and was succeeded by Xerxes, his son.

Many of Mordecai and Esther's Jewish compatriots had returned to Jerusalem when the Lord stirred the heart of king Cyrus to release them to return, and more returned under the rule of Darius. Mordecai and Esther had talked about this together many times.

Mordecai had prospered so in the capital city of Susa that he, along with numerous others, had decided to stay. Even though some forty thousand had decided to return to their homeland, their numbers had multiplied much beyond that in their seventy-year captivity. Esther didn't mind staying in Susa. Since she had been born and raised in Persia and both of her parents had died there, she really knew no other life than that which she had had with her cousin Mordecai. He was like a father to her now. She could not possibly consider leaving him to return to a homeland that was more foreign to her than Persia.

Even though Mordecai and Esther had chosen not to return to Jerusalem, they felt secure in their knowledge that the presence of Jehovah would continue to be with them in this foreign land. Because He had proven to be so faithful during the years of captivity, they both felt confident that He would not depart from them now. *"After all,"* Mordecai had said many times, *"A Jew is a Jew, whether he or she resides in Jerusalem or in Susa."*

Mordecai had told her that he found it beneficial to take on a Babylonian name. Even though his name was derived from the name of the Babylonian god Marduk[5], he was convinced that the Lord had led him to make this identification with the Persian culture and that it did not indicate any loss of heart or desired identity with his Jewish ancestry. When he gave Esther her Persian name, a name derived from the goddess Isthar, he said that he had a strong sense that this was the wisdom of Jehovah, as well. She was just a child at the time and had no real voice in the decision, but she trusted implicitly in Mordecai's wisdom. He told her often that she *"would always be his little Hadassah,"* her given Jewish name. However, what he had not told her was how strongly he felt, through prophetic wisdom, that something more was on the horizon for this chosen little Jewess. *"Surely,"* Esther thought, *"this identification with the Persian culture will not ultimately rob us of our distinguishing ethnic characteristics and beliefs, as some say. Or will it?"*

Esther continued to contemplate God's provision for His people. She never questioned the decision to remain in Susa rather than returning to Jerusalem; that decision had been made in her own heart already, regardless of what others thought. She found within herself a burning desire to make a difference to her people right here in the middle of the Persian Empire. Unlike some of her friends and their families, she did not feel a need to return to Jerusalem. As she deliberated with herself, she openly voiced her thoughts to the Lord, *"Though we have not returned to Jerusalem along with so many of our kinsmen, I am confident that You have a purpose for me in this world and that I am chosen of You. Surely, You will lead us in the days that lie ahead. You are forever faithful!"*

Overwhelmed by the emotion that began to stir within her, Esther moved from her reclining position at her tea table and began to kneel. She then buried her head in the linen pillow and earnestly petitioned

Jehovah on behalf of the Jews of Persia. *"Lord, I pray in earnest on behalf of my people, and yet . . . I am too ashamed and humiliated to lift up my face to You, my God; for our iniquities have risen higher than our heads, and our guilt has grown up to the heavens. Since the days of our fathers to this day we have been very guilty, and for our iniquities we, our kings, and our priests have been delivered into the hand of the kings of the lands, to the sword, to captivity, to plunder, and to humiliation, as it is this day. And now for a little while grace has been shown from the Lord our God, to leave us a remnant to escape, and to give us a peg in His holy place, that our God may enlighten our eyes and give us a measure of revival in our bondage. For we were slaves, yet our God did not forsake us in our bondage; but He extended mercy to us in the sight of the kings of Persia, to revive us . . ."* [6]

She could feel her heart begin to literally ache as tears began to fall from her eyes to her pillow. Her spirit cried out as she reached her arms up toward a loving Father, pleading, *"Jehovah, teach me how to pray. For I too desire a 'measure of revival in our bondage.' Do come and 'revive us,' even here in Susa. Oh God, hear my prayer today. Let Your presence be shed abroad in Susa and remember those of us who are here as your representatives. Use us as bright stars that shine in the darkness. We are Your chosen ones in a far and distant land. Do not forget us; I implore You to set watch over us."*

TRUSTING GOD THROUGH PREJUDICE

Yes, Mordecai and Esther had remained in the capital city of Susa while many of their people returned to their homeland. Some scholars feel that they were out of the will of God in doing so. They feel that any Jew who did not return to their homeland did so out of rebellion, pride, and stubbornness. These students of history interpret the book of Esther as a book about unfaithful Jews who were delivered by the grace of God in spite of their sins, not a book of courageous people who were in harmony with the will and purposes of God.

Ezra 1:5 says, *"Then the family heads of Judah and Benjamin, and the priests and Levites—everyone whose heart God had moved—prepared to go up and build the house of the Lord in Jerusalem."* This seems to indicate that God did not move on every Jewish heart at this time to return to their homeland, but that He purposed for some to remain in their captive land to be a testimony and witness for Him.

This is worthy of mention because it demonstrates some of the prejudice that Esther may have faced in her day. Just as some contemporary students of history judge her motives today, so too, some of her own peers may have sat in judgment in her day, as well. Because Mordecai and Esther did not choose to return, some may have ostracized and accused them of losing heart for their native land and of becoming too attached to the prosperity of Susa.

Sadly, this type of rejection, when it happens to you and me, can affect our sense of identity and security, and in turn, affect our freedom to walk in the knowledge of God's will and purpose for our lives. We must never forget that deliverance is an issue of the heart, not of geography or of circumstances.

> "We must never forget that deliverance is an issue of the heart, not of geography or of circumstances."

I was told a number of years ago of a science experiment that illustrates this very point. A group of college students were told to test a group of white mice by timing them as they ran through a prepared maze. They were told that the mice had been previously tested and that a designated group of them were slower than the others. In actuality, the mice had been tested previously but had all been timed with the ability to run at approximately the same speed. However, when the mice ran through the maze during this set of tests, they ran according to how the students believed they would run, with the designated group running slower than their counterparts.

These scientists then conducted a similar experiment in the classroom with a group of student teachers. They told the student teachers that certain students were slow learners and could not perform to the equivalent academic standards of the rest of the class. Again, as previously tested, these students were actually as academically and mentally sound as the rest of their classmates. However, while these particular student teachers taught them, they performed with less aptitude than normal.

This is a simple, yet frightening, illustration of how we tend to perform according to others' perceptions of us. We can actually be affected by what others believe about us. This experiment also demonstrates that what others think is not always accurate. This principle can apply in a spiritual sense, as well. What others think about our abilities or our decisions is not always in alignment with God's perspective. We must be careful to derive our sense of identity, purpose, and knowledge of our abilities from God's perspective and not limit ourselves to what others think.

Esther knew that her people were chosen by God to do His bidding in the earth. Mordecai had probably recounted that calling to her from the time that she was a small child. Deuteronomy 14:2 says, *"For you are a people holy to the Lord your God. Out of all the peoples on the face of the earth, the Lord has chosen you to be his treasured possession."* It was important for her to remember this, regardless of what others may have thought.

Did God tell Ezra or Nehemiah that all of the Jews had to return to Israel at this time? No, He did not. Does He direct every individual today in the same way within his or her unique family or ethnic grouping? No, He does not seem to do so. If He did, we would all be doing the same thing in the same geographic area and the Gospel would never reach the ends of the earth. Sometimes I think it can be our own selfishness that keeps us within our own walls instead of sharing the light of Christ.

God was not done with Susa yet. I am convinced that just as He called some of His people to return to their homeland, He also left a remnant in Susa purposely to be a testimony and witness for Him. I personally do not take the stance that He was a weary God who was irritated with the people who remained and rescued them simply out of pity.

Lamentations 3:21-23 says, *"Yet this I call to mind and therefore I have hope: Because of the Lord's great love we are not consumed, for His compassions never fail. They are new every morning; great is Your faithfulness."* He is a compassionate God. His compassion flows even in the midst of unbelieving or disobedient people, and His compassion also flows out of humble, trusting, and faithful people. However, it rarely flows out of an absence of people. God loves to use people to accomplish His will and share His love and mercy.

In fact, the last words Jesus spoke to His disciples before He returned to heaven were, *". . . you will be my witnesses in Jerusalem, and in all Judea and Samaria, and to the ends of the earth"* (Acts 1:8). Witnesses cannot witness if they are not present. It is up to each individual to determine if he or she is to be a witness within his or her own city, nation, or the far reaches of the earth.

Sometimes those whom we judge for not making the same choices we make turn out to be instruments of God's grace in our lives or in the lives of others in remarkable ways. I suspect that if we would spend more time loving and encouraging one another and less time judging one another, we could probably be more effective in our witness for Christ.
It is actually a wonderful thing when God's people are scattered throughout society, doing His bidding in the marketplace as well as in the house of God. Whether you are a minister in a church, a student in school, or a retired gardener, you are chosen.

Psalm 110:3 (Amplified) says, *"Your people will offer themselves willingly in the day of Your power, in the beauty of holiness and in holy array out of the womb of the morning; to You will spring forth Your young men who are as the dew."* What a beautiful picture this is. Just as the dew in the early morning hour is on every crevice and bump of God's earthly creation, so we are to be. We are a scattered people, but we are chosen to rise up and offer ourselves to the Lord in the day of His power.

I heard a story once of a little boy who lived in a small town in America during the Great Depression of the 1930s. He and his family had very little money with which to live, so he had virtually no toys. One day he made a little boat out of a piece of wood, some string, a stick, and a piece of paper. He played with it every day in a nearby stream. One day, much to his dismay, the current of the stream captured the boat and carried it away.

Not many days after this, he was walking downtown and noticed his little boat in the window of a secondhand store. He went in and said to the storeowner, *"That's my boat you have in your window. It's mine. I made it."*

The storeowner replied, *"Son, I paid a price for that boat. If you want it back, you'll have to pay for it."*

The boy worked for many days, doing every kind of odd job that he could to earn the pennies that it would take to buy back his boat. Finally, he had earned the required amount. He went back to the store, and there was his boat, still in the storefront window. He excitedly went into the store and purchased it.

He then went back to the stream to play. As he gently put the boat back into the water, he said to it, *"I made you and I paid for you; you're twice owned."*

Isn't that what the Master has done for you? He made you, and He paid the price of His Son for you; you're twice His. He has not only redeemed you, but He has also chosen you for a special purpose—a unique destiny. Surely, just as it was with Esther of old, He has a purpose for all that He has invested in you.

ACCEPTING YOUR DESTINY

1 Peter 2:9-10 says, *"But you are a chosen generation, a royal priesthood, a holy nation, His own special people, that you may proclaim the praises of Him who called you out of darkness into His marvelous light; who once were not a people but are now the people of God, who had not obtained mercy but now have obtained mercy."*

If you have received Jesus Christ as your personal Savior, you have a familial tie to other Christian believers; you are part of a generation chosen by Him for His purposes. Yet, like Esther, you also belong to a people who are scattered. They are scattered throughout neighborhoods, cities, and nations, hidden like dewdrops in the forest and on blades of grass in your own backyard. Regardless of your circumstances or station in life, you have a destiny in God that is linked to this generation and time.

You and I must recognize and accept the sense of destiny that God has for women in these days. We must have an ever-expanding vision of our destiny in Him. Yes, Mordecai was chosen by God, but so was Esther. Mordecai had a purpose and destiny in which to walk, but Esther did, as well.

> *"Regardless of your circumstances or station in life, you have a destiny in God that is linked to this generation and time."*

From L. E. Maxwell's book *Women in Ministry*, I quote:

> *[Christian] women, do not forget your heritage. You are the spiritual descendants of the Sarah's, the Deborah's, and the Hannah's of the Old Covenant. Your line is renewed again in the New Testament in Mary, who gave birth to Jesus Christ; Elizabeth, who mothered His great forerunner; in Mary of Bethany, who anointed His precious head and feet; in Mary Magdalene, who was last at His cross and first at His empty tomb; in the host of women, who in early gospel days, gave their hearts, homes and deepest toil to the cause of the Master. Your line is again renewed in church history, until for faithfulness, devotion, heroism, martyrdom and all else that pleases the heart of the great Christ, woman has led the way, borne the brunt, shared the vigils, preached with life and lip, and handed the cause on to the next age with its banners proudly breasting every gale of opposition. . . ! Remember then, sisters, your marvelous heritage, and your amazing responsibility.*[7]

Esther's Persian name means "star" or "good fortune." This was truly a prophetic name for this young maiden, as she was destined to be a star that would shine brightly in a dark season of the history of her people in

Persia. Her Hebrew name, "Hadassah," means "myrtle." In ancient Greece, the myrtle was highly esteemed as sacred and its leaves were used for crowns of victory. It was a Greek symbol of triumph and victory. Truly, this was another prophetic name for the heroine of our story.

Isaiah 41:19-20 says, *"I will put in the desert the cedar and the acacia, the myrtle and olive. I will set pines in the wasteland, the fir and the cypress together, so that people may see and know, may consider and understand, that the hand of the Lord has done this, that the Holy One of Israel has created it."*

If Esther (Hadassah) were to fulfill the meaning of her names, she would need to keep within her heart **a chosen perspective**. For in the days that lay ahead of her, there would be a palace that had the appearance of a lush garden on the outside but was a desert within. Would this be the planting of the Lord for her, *". . . so that people may see and know, may consider and understand, that the hand of the Lord has done this"* (Isaiah 41:20)?

A year ago I heard a story of a young woman who was learning to rock climb. In spite of her natural fear of the sport, she put on her gear, tied on the rope, and started up the face of the designated rock with the rest of the group.

When she got to a ledge where she could catch her breath, the person holding the rope at the top of the cliff accidentally snapped the rope against the side of her face, causing one of her contact lenses to fall out of her eye. With hundreds of feet below and several feet still above, she suddenly had to cope with blurry vision. She prayed that the Lord would help her to find her lens nearby, but she searched to no avail.

When she got to the top of the cliff, she asked a girlfriend to examine her to see if the lens had been lodged into the corner of her eye somewhere. There was no contact lens to be found.

She sat down and waited for the rest of the party to arrive at the top, looking out across the mountain range. As she looked, she thought of the verse, *"For the eyes of the Lord run to and fro throughout the whole earth, to show Himself strong on behalf of those whose heart is loyal to Him"* (2

Chronicles 16:9a, NKJ). She prayed silently to herself, *"Lord, You can see all these mountains. You know every single stone and leaf on these mountains, and You know exactly where my contact lens is."*

When the time came to go back down the mountain, the group hiked down the trail. Just as they got to the bottom, there was a new party of rock climbers coming along. As one of them started up the face of the cliff, she shouted, *"Hey, you guys! Anybody lose a contact lens?"* She had noticed the contact lens as it moved slowly across the face of the rock, borne on the back of an ant.

What does that say to you about God's providential guardianship, about the little things in our lives, even the little ants in our lives? Know this: God cares and He is watching.

The father of this young woman is a cartoonist. When she told him this incredible story, he drew a picture of the ant carrying the contact lens with the thought-words written over his head, *"Lord, I don't know why You want me to carry this thing. I can't eat it, and it's awfully heavy. But if this is what You want me to do, I'll carry it for You."*

Jesus taught, *"Indeed, the very hairs of your head are all numbered. Don't be afraid; you are worth more than many sparrows"* (Luke 12:7). As humorous as that picture is, I somehow believe that if He cares about hairs and sparrows, He cares about contact lenses and ants, too. If God orders the steps of ants so carefully, I can only thankfully imagine how He orders your steps and mine, just as He did Esther's.

Chosen to be a star in the midst of darkness and to wear a crown of triumph and victory, this was to be her destiny, as it is ours today.

You are *C**hosen*

DEUT. 7:6; 14:2 *"... The Lord your God has chosen you out of the peoples on the face of the earth to be His people, His treasured possession."*

PS. 105:43 *"He brought out His people with rejoicing, **His chosen ones** with shouts of joy."*

ISA. 41:9 *"... **I have chosen you** and have not rejected you."*

JOHN 15:19 *"... you do not belong to the world, but **I have chosen you** out of he world ..."*

ROM. 11:5 *"So too, at the present time there is a remnant **chosen by grace**."*

EPH. 1:11 *"**In Him we were also chosen,** having been predestined according to the plan of him who works out everything in conformity with the purpose of His will."*

1 THESS. 1:4 *"For we know, brothers loved by God, that **He has chosen you**"*

Benefits of Being Chosen

JISA. 42:1 *"Here is my servant, whom I uphold, my chosen one in whom I delight; **I will put my Spirit on him** and he will bring justice to the nations."*

ISA. 44:2-3 *"This is what the Lord says—He who made you, who formed you in the womb, and who will help you: Do not be afraid, O Jacob, my servant, Jeshurun, whom I have chosen. For **I will pour water on the thirsty land**, and streams on the dry ground; **I will pour out my Spirit on your offspring, and my blessing on your descendants.***

ISA. 49:7 *"... **Kings will see you and rise up, princes will see and bow down**, because of the Lord, who is faithful, the Holy One of Israel, who has chosen you."*

ISA. 65:9 *"I will bring forth descendants from Jacob, and from Judah those who will possess my mountains; **my chosen people will inherit them**, and there will my servants live."*

ISA. 65:22 *"No longer will they build houses and others live in them, or plant and others eat. For as the days of a tree, so will be the days of my people; my chosen ones **will long enjoy the works of their hands.***"

MARK 13:20 *"If the Lord had not cut short **those days**, no one would survive. But for the sake of the elect, whom He has chosen, **He has shortened them.**"*

LUKE 18:7 *"**And will not God bring about justice** for His chosen ones, who cry out to Him day and night? ..."*

ACTS 22:14   *"... The God of our fathers has chosen you to know His will and **to see the Righteous One and to hear words from His mouth**."*

ROM. 8:33   *"Who will bring any charge against those whom God has chosen? **It is God who justifies**."*

JAMES 2:5   *"Listen, my dear brothers: Has not God chosen those who are poor in the eyes of the world **to be rich in faith and to inherit the kingdom** He promised those who love Him?"*

REV. 17:14   *"They will make war against the Lamb, but the Lamb will overcome them because He is Lord of lords and Kings of kings—and with Him will be His called, chosen and faithful followers."*

Responsibilities of Being Chosen

GEN. 18:19 *"For I have chosen him, so that he **will direct his children and his household after him to keep the way of the Lord by doing what is right and just** ..."*

DEUT. 18:5 *"for the Lord your God has chosen them and their descendants out of all your tribes **to stand and minister in the Lord's name always.**"*

ISA. 43:10 *"You are my witnesses, declares the Lord, and my servant whom I have chosen, so **that you may know and believe me and understand that I am He.** Before me no god was formed, nor will there be one after me."*

COL. 3:12-17 *"Therefore, as God's chosen people, holy and dearly loved, clothe yourselves with compassion, kindness, humility, gentleness and patience. Bear with each other and forgive whatever grievances you may have against one another. Forgive as the Lord forgave you. And over all these virtues put on love, which binds them all together in perfect unity. Let the peace of Christ rule in your hearts, since as members of one body you were called to peace. And be thankful. Let the word of Christ dwell in you richly as you teach and admonish one another with all wisdom, and as you sing psalms, hymns and spiritual songs with gratitude in your hearts to God. And whatever you do, whether in word or deed, do it all in the name of the Lord Jesus, giving thanks to God the Father through Him."*

NOTES

1   Daniel 1:3-5

2   2 Kings 24:14

3   Ezekiel 1; Jeremiah 52

4   "Mordecai's line of descent is traced from a certain Kish, carried off by Nebuchadnezzar in B.C. 598—the year of Jeconiah's captivity—who was his great-grandfather. The four generations, Kish, Shimei, Jair, Mordecai, correspond to the known generations in other cases . . . The age of Mordecai at the accession of Xerxes may probably have been about 30 or 40; that of Esther, his first cousin, about 20." F.C. Cook, ed., *Barnes Notes: The Bible Commentary*, Heritage Edition, 14 vols. (Grand Rapids: Baker, 1996), 492.

5   What made Esther's name significant was its connection to the great Babylonian goddess "Isthar." The name Mordecai comes from the god Marduk. Both Isthar and Marduk were deities of Babylon at this time. Since some Jewish exiles, such as Daniel and his friends, bore Babylonian names, it is quite possible that Mordecai's name is the equivalent of the common Babylonian personal name, Mardukaia, which contained the name of Marduk, and Esther's name could be linked with Ishtar also. Study thought derived from Merrill C. Tenney, ed., *The Zondervan Pictoral Encyclopedia of the Bible* (Grand Rapids: Zondervan, 1977), 377.

6   Ezra 9:6-9, New King James. The book of Esther chronologically occurs between the six and seventh chapters of Ezra. Even though Esther's personal yearnings may have been inclined to the heart-attitude of Ezra's prayer, she and Mordecai would not have been knowledgeable of it at this time, as Ezra had not yet made this particular petition in prayer.

7   L.E. Maxwell with Ruth C. Dearing, *Women in Ministry, A Historical and Biblical Look at the Role of Women in Christian Leadership* (Wheaton, Ill.: Victor, 1987), 149; citing J.G. Morrison, *Satan's Subtle Attack on Woman* (Kansas City, Mo.: Nazarene), 7, 22-23.

The Planting of the Lord

"Later when the anger of King Xerxes had subsided, he remembered Vashti and what she had done and what he had decreed about her. . . . When the king's order and edict had been proclaimed, many girls were brought to the citadel of Susa and put under the care of Hegai. Esther also was taken to the king's palace and entrusted to Hegai, who had charge of the harem" (Esther 2:1-8).

It had been a disastrous three years since King Xerxes had his palace celebration three very long years.[1] The campaign into Greece had been unsuccessful and exhausting. He was glad to be home, back in his winter palace in the citadel of Susa. Yet without the distraction of war, being back in the palace stirred within him a deep desire to have a queen by his side. Everywhere he looked he seemed to see couples; even within the palace hallways he continually noticed the alluring glances that passed between guards and maids. The simple fact was that he missed Vashti.[2]

Three birthdays had passed since his queen was banished. There had been no celebrations because there was no one who genuinely cared about him; so he spent each passing birthday in the loneliness of a drunken stupor. Numerous concubines feigned interest, but he was no longer interested in them, nor they in him.

He didn't need an acquiescent concubine to seduce him; he needed a queen in whom to confide. He needed a wife to care for him the way that only an affectionate companion could. He didn't want cold submission and obedience; he longed for warm conversation and intoxicating embraces.

Subduing the revolt in Babylon and then leading the invasion into Greece had been troublesome and exhausting.[3] There was no measure of fulfillment in it. The battles were wearisome and lonely, not to mention unsuccessful. Now that he was back in Susa, he was tired, bored, and hungry for love. He longed to pour out his soul and receive the response that could only come from the heart and perspective of a loyal spouse.

His attendants were proposing that a great search be made of the most beautiful virgins in all of his provinces. He had gone along with the idea and appointed commissioners in each province to bring their most beautiful girls into the awaiting harem.[4] This plan certainly appealed to him; however, waiting another year without a queen seemed unbearable.

His anxious mind inquired from within, *"Why couldn't it be someone within the very city limits of Susa? Why do I have to wait for the search to be made and the beauty treatments to be completed? How will I busy myself in the meantime?"* He so longed for a queen—not just a woman, but a queen.

DAYS OF JOY AND MOMENTS OF WONDERING

For Mordecai, the past three years had been pleasant ones. They had been days of joy as he watched Esther grow and literally blossom into young womanhood. She was a continual breath of fresh air to him. The atmosphere in Susa, however, had changed; darkness seemed to permeate the very air they breathed. Since the king had dismissed his queen and was virtually losing his campaign against Greece, the climate of Susa was one of tension. But to come home each day to his precious Esther was to step into a warm and welcoming place of refuge. She had become like a daughter to him, and he adored her. Truly, she was the fulfillment of her Hebrew name "Hadassah" and her Babylonian name "Esther." She was both his little "myrtle tree" destined for triumph and greatness and his bright "star" in the midst of the darkening cloud over the city.

Esther loved to sit in Mordecai's presence and listen to the stories of her ancestors. His instruction brought sheer joy and delight to her heart. She truly was being fashioned as a piece of fine art under his tutelage. She could feel the richness of her heritage soaking into her spirit and shaping her perspective each time Mordecai prayed and each time he lovingly posted another bit of Jewish history onto the doorpost of her heart.

At times her spirit seemed to reach across the ages and tap into the song of Hannah of old. Although it seemed a mystery to her, she could feel such affinity with Hannah's song. *"My heart rejoices in the Lord; in the Lord my horn is lifted high . . . He raises the poor from the dust and lifts the needy from the ash heap . . ."*[5] These words seemed to ring within her very soul.

At other times her spirit seemed to soar into the distant future and adhere to the melodious words, *"My soul glorifies the Lord and my spirit rejoices in God my Savior, for He has been mindful of the humble state of His servant . . ."*[6] The words sounded so unique, and yet so connected.

Could it be that the one true God was a great weaver at the shuttle of her soul, intertwining the past with the present and the future? While these moments of prophetic contemplation did not frighten her, they did puzzle her at times. She didn't presume to understand them, but she did trust in Jehovah, for truly He was the only wise God.

Not only had Esther grown into a gracious hostess and strikingly beautiful young woman, she was a bright, articulate, and intelligent one, too. Not only was she a breath of fresh air to Mordecai, but she also truly had the ability to encourage and lighten the heart of almost anyone with whom she came in contact. She continually amazed his guests with her gracious hospitality and the ability to articulate her knowledge of her Jewish heritage, as well as the current issues of Susa.

Esther so enjoyed the mutual and friendly bantering between her and Mordecai when they spoke of the heritage of their people and the current issues that faced them. Even though she felt that she had developed a rather keen sense of the lines of justice, injustice, and divine providence, Mordecai warned her often that these were treacherous days and that she must be careful about voicing her opinions too openly. Though he had taught her to reason and process the questions of her heart through the grid of Jehovah's wisdom, he openly expressed concern and fear that she spoke too openly of her opinions at times.

There was coming a season of change. Esther could sense it in her very being. She wondered, *"Will the turning of the leaves in my heart be lush and blossom into the beauty of springtime, or will they fade and wither away as a leaf falling from a tree preparing for winter?"* There was both a sense of excitement and a sense of dread in her spirit at the same time. *"What is this paradox of emotion, this dichotomy?"* She walked in peace, and yet at times, she sensed almost a rending of her heart from within.

"What does the future hold?" she mused. *"Where is the next bend in the road in my personal journey, and how is it connected to the past and to the future?"* At times her youthful desires yearned to run headlong into the next milestone of her life, and at other times she felt overcome by the very spirit of restlessness that seemed to pervade all of Persia at this time.

Mordecai had told her of the great search for a new queen for King Xerxes. His associates in the king's court had warned him that she might catch the eye of those responsible for the search. Although the king's men would search throughout all of his provinces for the most beautiful virgins to be found, Esther had a natural beauty that would be difficult to hide when the king's men came looking. She perpetually captured the eyes of onlookers in the marketplace and was known for her comeliness.

While the thought of being part of such a grand beauty pageant sounded exciting to many of Esther's peers, she didn't think it was appealing at all. If a maiden didn't win the contest, it was well known that she would end up with all of the other concubines who belonged to the king and would probably never really know love. If she did win, she would be married to a king who didn't know God and was known for being temperamental, moody, and often angry. The question bolted to the forefront of her mind, *"Could there be true love with any man like that, much less a preoccupied king?"*

Esther desired true love, not slavish obedience. Wasn't it slavish obedience that King Xerxes had required of Vashti? And she was rumored to have been the most beautiful queen of all time, one whom he loved dearly! It was frightening to think of being married to someone who could have someone banished just as quickly as he could see her coming down a corridor. It didn't sound like the kind of life she desired at all. Her girlfriends could wish that upon themselves, if they so desired, but she preferred to stay outside those palace walls.

Esther realized that God had blessed her with some physical attributes that appealed to the eyes of the men in the nearby marketplace as well as to some who came to visit her cousin Mordecai. Though they might desire her, she refused to let her heart respond to any man's wistful look, for she also knew that she would only allow her heart to be given to the man that Jehovah and Mordecai selected to be her husband. She could easily surrender to their choice; she trusted them.

She was, in fact, thankful that God and Mordecai would do the choosing. She thought that surrendering to Mordecai's wisdom would be far wiser than trusting the dictates of her own heart on such an important issue. She only hoped that whoever was chosen would love and appreciate her for the person whom God had formed her to be. Mordecai had told her many times that natural beauty fades but a pure heart illumines true love and brings light to many, and she believed it. She hoped to marry a man who would treasure the purity of her love, and she wanted their marriage to be a light to many.

DESPERATE PETITIONS

Those were the musings of yesterday. Today the loneliness she felt was more than words could express, deeper than the deepest well. It clouded her judgment by day and encompassed her sleep at night. She felt restless, emotionally exhausted, and frightened. She could still hear the fateful knock of Xerxes' men at Mordecai's door. The sound of that knock rang in her ears both day and night. She wished it had never come. It haunted her hour after hour. Whether her eyes were open or closed, her ears still heard the heavy *knock, knock, knock* of the dreaded moment of her captivity.

This was not the life Esther had had in mind. What a surprise it was to find herself in the king's palace, entered into a beauty pageant of which she had no desire to be a part. The initial meditations and questions of her heart were many and varied, one colliding against the other. As she sat in her dreary chambers somewhere within King Xerxes' palace walls, the questions of her heart came spewing out to the God who had chosen her and ordered her steps, the God who had allowed this confusing uprooting to take place in her life. *"Jehovah, what am I doing here? Surely I am in the wrong place! This queen-hunting absurdity is not for me; I am content with my singleness. Please, God, let this be a mistake; awaken me from this nightmare. Allow one of my dreamy-eyed friends to awaken in the morning to this pageantry proposition in my place. Mordecai and I are in no rush to find me a husband. At the very least, I am a Jewish girl in need of a Jewish husband, not a Jewish girl in want of a Persian king. Oh God, how could this be your plan?!"*

Esther felt despair clutching her heart; desperation filled her petitions. She stood and began to pace back and forth. *"Am I to be relegated to the hall of concubines, neither married nor single for the rest of my life? Am I never to taste of true love?"* Her colliding emotions surged. *"Surely You do not desire me to be yoked to a heathen king. Surely this would not be Mordecai's desire, or Yours. Oh, let this not be Your choosing for me! How could there possibly be divine planting in the midst of this uprooting of my soul?*

"I don't want to be in this revolting pageant, focusing on natural beauty, all for the sake of a narcissistic and pretentious heathen king. Mordecai has taught me all my days that inward beauty is more important than outward beauty. What does that truth have to do with this royal parade of vanity?! And why has Mordecai instructed me not to tell of my lineage after he taught me to be so proud of it all these years?"

As Esther plopped down on the cushion nearest her dressing table, her unrestrained emotions began to subside, though her thoughts continued. *"I have to admit that the thought of being a 'chosen' one is exciting indeed. To be chosen by a handsome, wealthy man of my own kindred would be wonderful, but to be chosen by a churlish heathen king, how could that be Your will for any Jewish girl?! Surely You do not want me to be planted in the garden of such a king. I will be but a small lily in this vast garden, rather than the 'myrtle tree' that was once 'destined for triumph and victory.' How could any 'star' be seen in such overwhelming darkness?"*

As Esther continued, now more familiarly postured on her knees, a surrender and calmness began to come into her soul. She continued her conversation with her very present God as she tuned her ear to His voice. *"Yes, Lord, 'trust' and 'surrender' are engraved within my heart. I do trust You, and I will surrender to You and Your purposes, but is it possible for a heathen king to usurp Your will in my life? What triumph, what victory could be in any of this? Yes, I do believe that my steps are ordered by You. I have always held to that belief. Each day I have trusted You. I have trusted that You and Cousin Mordecai would find just the right husband for me at just the right time. But could this possibly be Your choosing, Your planting, Lord?!*

"Help me to fulfill all that You have destined for me, Father. Let Your planting be mine, and mine, Yours. Plant me as a tree or as a fragile flower, but plant me well. My trust is in You."

THE COST OF SURRENDER

Can you hear the prayer of Esther cry out across the ages? Does the ultimate cost of total trust and surrender ever cross your mind? Does the possibility that uncaring believers or unbelievers could usurp God's will for your life ever cause hesitation within your own heart?

Perhaps you cannot identify with being taken from the comforts of your home and placed in the largest beauty pageant ever known, to parade before a king. However, you may be able to identify with the questions of God's literal planning and planting in your life. Why has He placed you in your particular family, church, and place of employment? Just as Esther may have felt like a small lily in a vast garden, you may also feel insignificant and unnoticed in the garden in which God has planted you. Just as Esther was destined to be *"like a lily among thorns"* (Song of Solomon 2:2), so are you.

Everything about Esther's life had been a planting from the Lord. God foreknew that His people in Susa would need a deliverer from a wicked enemy. He had uniquely planted Esther into her Jewish lineage, into Mordecai's home, and into the king's palace. Her permanent place was never meant to be within a natural lineage or geographic boundary; it was meant to be in God alone. She had been blessed and protected in order that she might be a blessing.

You have also been uniquely placed in your family, ethnic group, and geographic region for a reason. God has even uniquely designed your physical features and personality type. He desires for you to use all of these characteristics for His purposes. **You have been blessed to be a blessing.**

WHEN DESTINY KNOCKS

There is another woman in the Bible who was born into a designated family and ethnic group and was in a certain geographic region at a specific time by the will of God. She was not a Jewess, but she was also a rare *"lily among the thorns,"* the desert thorns, that is. She too moved more than once in her life, but destiny found her in the right place at the right time by the planting of the Lord.

Her name was Jael, and her story can be found in Judges chapter 4. Her name means "climbing," and God strategically planted her in a valley and gave her a unique mountain to climb. She was married to a man by the name of Heber, who was part of a seemingly insignificant wandering tribe of nomadic people, known as the Kenites.[7] The Kenites were descendants of Jethro, the Midianite father-in-law of Moses. They were known to be excellent metal smiths and craftsmen,[8] and also acted as excellent guides through the desert for the Israelites.[9] Although they were not known as fierce warriors or prominent judges, they were loyal friends of the Israelites.

Heber, Jael's husband, evidently decided that he had been a nomad long enough and wanted to settle down and pitch his tent in Zaanannim under a grove of oak trees in the upland valley of Kedesh.[10] As much as Jael may have wanted to settle down, to settle under a tree in Zaanannim, away from her family and kinsmen, must have seemed totally outside an environment where she could ever do anything very significant.

During this time in history, the nation of Israel was on a spiritual roller coaster. At times they served the Lord, and at other times they were apostate. During this particular season, Israel was in a backslidden state, and the Lord had allowed Jabin, the king of Canaan, to subdue them.

Jabin's capital city of Hazor was a very prominent city, a metropolis in its day. Due to its *"enormous size, its large population, and its strategic location on the main road between Egypt and Mesopotamia,"* it was considered to be one of the most important fortresses in the region.[11]

Sisera was the general of Jabin's army. He lived in a place called Harosheth, a nearby city in a well-known timber district.[12] It was here at Harosheth that many Israelites had been enslaved, felling timber and preparing it for transport to Zidon. Everyone in Harosheth knew of the great general Sisera.

The strength of Sisera's army was nine hundred iron chariots. At this time in history in this particular region, Sisera's army was considered to be a huge military machine. The Israelite oppression by King Jabin and General Sisera had lasted twenty years, the longest and most severe period of oppression that Israel had yet experienced. Thus, they were awakened from their sin, viewed this oppression as punishment for their rebellion, and sought the Lord for their deliverance. Judges 4:3 says that Sisera had *"cruelly oppressed"* the Israelites, and *"they cried to the Lord for help."*

Knowing that the battle was not many hillsides away, Heber took off and left Jael alone to fend for herself. Whether he went scouting for the

Israelites or searching for food or for minerals to smith, Scripture does not say. We just know that he was away from the tent, and Jael was home alone. It was this day that God had chosen for destiny to knock on her door.

The Israelite general, Barak, led ten thousand men in pursuit of Sisera. Judges 4:15 (Amplified) says, *"And the Lord confused and terrified Sisera and all his chariot drivers and all his army before Barak with the sword. And Sisera alighted from his chariot and fled on foot."* The man, Sisera, who showed up on Jael's doorstep, was one of the most feared generals and important men in the known world at this time. This simple maiden, living a seemingly insignificant life, planted by the Lord under a small grove of trees in a tent, suddenly found herself at a turning point in history.

Why Jael? Why was she given this opportunity? While the prophetess and judge, Deborah, was well known, lived in a prominent place, and was sought by many for guidance, Jael was known by no one except her kins-men. No one was seeking her insight or wisdom concerning anything in her tent or under her tree, not even her husband. Why would anyone think she would know anything about how to stop the great enemy forces of General Sisera?

Jael simply stood outside the door of her tent, the place where the Lord and her husband had planted her, and destiny came knocking. This planting was not just some romantic idea of lakefront property under the shade of an oak tree that she and Heber had dreamed up; it was the sovereign planting of the Lord. If Jael had moved to another location, outside the will of God, she would have missed the greatest opportunity of her lifetime and one of the greatest events in the history of her people.

It was this day, in a humble tent-home under a tree, that she beck-oned to the enemy Sisera to come in, to treat his palate and rest his eyes. Little did he know that this seemingly insignificant little tent-dweller could and would do a mighty act for God. After he fell asleep and snug-gled under a blanket with warm milk in his stomach, Jael grasped a tent peg and drove it soundly through his head. She fulfilled the prophecy of Deborah, and found herself in the middle of a sovereign, miraculous victory, orchestrated by God.[13]

Through her humble surrender to the planting of the Lord, destiny came knocking on her door. With humility and courage in her heart, she joined forces with others throughout the ages who were rescuers of their own generations.

Another day would come in the future when another enemy named Haman would stand outside another maiden's door. He would also wait for her to beckon him to a feast for his palate. There would be no rest for his soul, either. Just as Jael drove a tent peg through Sisera's head and brought him to his doom, so would Esther drive the sword of the Lord through Haman's schemes and bring him to a hangman's noose. Just as Jael's courage brought deliverance to the Israelites from a cruel oppressor, so Esther's courage would release them from the onslaught of the enemy once again.

Two little maidens, planted among a small tribe of insignificant people in unsuspecting dwelling places, were used mightily of the Lord to accomplish His purposes. Whether it was in a valley with a mountain to climb or in a palace of darkness that needed a star to shine, remaining where the Lord had planted them was a crucial key to victory for God's people.

DEEDS OF KINDNESS

Some of the most insignificant people walking through life, joyfully planted in the will and purposes of God, can accomplish some of the greatest deeds for Christ. They did so in ancient history, and they still do so today.

Two such people, who had their individual lives securely planted in the will of God and who were about to weave their lives together in the garden of His compassion, were a lovely couple, Ralph and Colleen.

Ralph and Colleen met each other in 1998 in Redding, California, while ministering to the poor and homeless. God had individually and uniquely

> *"Some of the most insignificant people walking through life, joyfully planted in the will and purposes of God, can accomplish some of the greatest deeds for Christ."*

placed them both at this particular time and station that many poor and needy people could be rescued from hopelessness and introduced to Christ. They fell in love and made plans to be married.

As they prepared for the wedding day, they made decisions that would literally plant the seed of their new marriage into the hearts and lives of those for whom Christ had died. They had been blessed to be a blessing. This reality existed in the very conception of their relationship, and it would be birthed anew at their wedding celebration.

Ralph and Colleen had become the friends of many of the poor and homeless to whom they ministered and wanted to invite them to their wedding to help celebrate their special day. They desired their wedding day to be a day of generosity and miracles, just as the wedding had been in Cana, where Jesus did His first earthly miracle. Just as Christ's love had been planted in their hearts, they desired to see His love planted in the hearts and lives of others who were in desperate need of His grace and mercy.

Because they wanted this very special day to be a day of blessing, not just for themselves, but for all those who attended, they requested that anyone who wished to give a wedding gift would instead purchase needed items for their homeless friends, such as sleeping bags, coats, hats, and gloves. These gifts would then be given to the attendees-in-need at the reception. The bride and groom also served all their guests, rich and poor alike, a wonderful and complete dinner.

This was such an amazing deed of compassion that the local newspaper sent a reporter and photographer to cover the event. They published a picture of the bride and groom, serving food to the needy in a tuxedo and wedding gown, on the front page of the Sunday edition of the newspaper. Next to the picture was an article describing the wedding, the needy crowd, and the involvement of two participating churches.

While the article represented a wonderful testimony to the community, the reporter had missed another story that took place behind the kitchen doors. This was an answer to the prayers of the bride and groom that miracles would be released that day and that the perishing would be rescued.

One needy man and woman, who were passing through the area,

stopped by the church to get in on the free wedding meal. The man struggled to walk and was in obvious pain. The ministers of the ceremony spoke with the couple and discovered that the man had cancer and had been given two to three years to live. He had braces on each wrist due to carpal tunnel syndrome, a brace on his neck because cancer had destroyed the muscles that upheld his head, and hip replacement surgery had left him walking with one leg shorter than the other.

After the couple had eaten the wedding dinner, the pastors invited them into the church kitchen to receive prayer. As the pastors prayed first for the man's wrists, he became free of pain. They then prayed for his leg to be lengthened and asked his wife to watch, knowing that the healing would increase her faith, as well. One pastor reports that *"both his leg and her faith grew quickly."* Next, they prayed for his hip, and he walked across the kitchen with no pain or hindrance. The man then removed his neck brace and they prayed for a creative miracle of redeveloped muscles. By this time, others began to come into the kitchen and join in prayer, including a medical doctor who also believes that healing miracles are for today. He placed his hands on the man's neck and prayed for the cancerous lumps to be removed and for the specific weakened neck muscles to be restored, and as he prayed, it happened. The man's doctors' reports have since confirmed that all cancer is gone. He now jogs every morning.

On the following Sunday morning, the man gave his testimony in church, saying, *"I walked in here a cripple; but God gave me my life back!"* The man and woman, who had wandered into the wedding to eat a meal, received a feast from the Lord. They both received Christ as their personal Savior as a result of the miracles performed that day.[14] The Lord made Ralph and Colleen's day a successful "rescue" for others through their compassion and through the prayers of the pastors in the kitchen.

It is always so amazing how God is on the move in so many miraculous and unseen ways. May He open our eyes to more of His numerous wonders! The story of this beautiful wedding reception indeed captures the heart and spirit of truly surrendered lives. It also demonstrates the purpose of blessing—to pass on blessing to others.

"WHEN DESTINY KNOCKS, WILL IT FIND YOU HOME?"

Mordecai had been given to Esther as a gift in days that were now gone by, but his voice of wisdom and intercession would continue to ring in her ears in the days just ahead. She had been blessed in his house, and now there was another house and a people for her to bless. Whether she was in Mordecai's house or the king's palace, she was in the presence of the Lord, *"under the shadow of His wings"* (Psalm 17:8; 36:7).

Just as Esther, Jael, and Ralph and Colleen were blessed in order to be a blessing, so too are we. Wherever the Master plants us, whether in a palace, a tent, or a wedding chapel, it is with purpose and intent. Within that planting, there is a day when destiny will come knocking, and any blessings He pours over us are to be poured out in return for the sake of others.

Jael's welcoming tent and warm milk brought death to the enemy and blessings of freedom from persecution to her people. Ralph and Colleen's wedding day was a blessing that warmed the hearts of many and brought about a healing miracle in a broken vessel. The discovery of Esther's blessing in the king's palace in the citadel of Susa is yet to come in our story, but her planting was sure. Each day was a day of destiny for all involved and each was determined by the planting of the Lord. Each brought about the rescue of those who were perishing.

> *". . .there is a day when destiny will come knocking, and any blessings He pours over us are to be poured out in return for the sake of others."*

Just as these individuals' lives have reached across the ages and have been united in calling and purpose, each one first discovered the blossoming of his or her faith in the planting of the Lord. Each of them saw this faith arise in the lives of those they touched in destiny. Each one, tucked away in the planting of the Lord, was a powerful tool in the hand of God. May we too be as obedient as these shining examples and be participants in the rescue of a generation.

The Planting of the Lord

PS. 1:3   *"And he shall be like a tree planted by the rivers of water, that bringeth forth his fruit in his season; his leaf also shall not wither; and whatsoever he doeth shall prosper."
(KJV)*

PS. 92:13   *"Those that be planted in the house of the LORD shall flourish in the courts of our God." (KJV)*

JER. 12:2   *"Thou hast planted them, yea, they have taken root: they grow, yea, they bring forth fruit: thou art near in their mouth, and far from their reins." (KJV)*

JER. 17:8   *"For he shall be as a tree planted by the waters, and that spreadeth out her roots by the river, and shall not see when heat cometh, but her leaf shall be green; and shall not be careful in the year of drought, neither shall cease from yielding fruit." (KJV)*

ISA. 61:3   *"To appoint unto them that mourn in Zion, to give unto them beauty for ashes, the oil of joy for mourning, the garment of praise for the spirit of heaviness; that they might be called trees of righteousness, the planting of the LORD, that he might be glorified." (KJV)*

ISA. 60:21   *"Thy people also shall be all righteous: they shall inherit the land for ever, the branch of my planting, the work of my hands, that I may be glorified." (KJV)*

JER. 24:6   *"For I will set mine eyes upon them for good, and I will bring them again to this land: and I will build them, and not pull them down; and I will plant them, and not pluck them up." (KJV)*

JER. 32:41   *"Yea, I will rejoice over them to do them good, and I will plant them in this land assuredly with my whole heart and with my whole soul." (KJV)*

EZEK. 17:22   *"Thus saith the Lord GOD; I will also take of the highest branch of the high cedar, and will set it; I will crop off from the top of his young twigs a tender one, and will plant it upon an high mountain and eminent:" (KJV)*

EZEK. 17:23   *"In the mountain of the height of Israel will I plant it: and it shall bring forth boughs, and bear fruit, and be a goodly cedar: and under it shall dwell all fowl of every wing; in the shadow of the branches thereof shall they dwell." (KJV)*

HOS. 2:23   *"And I will sow her unto me in the earth; and I will have mercy upon her that had not obtained mercy; and I will say to them which were not my people, Thou art my people; and they shall say, Thou art my God." (KJV)*

AMOS 9:15   *"And I will plant them upon their land, and they shall no more be pulled up out of their land which I have given them, saith the LORD thy God." (KJV)*

MATT. 15:13   *"But he answered and said, Every plant, which my heavenly Father hath not planted, shall be rooted up." (KJV)*

N O T E S

1　The six-month celebration in the citadel of Susa was held in the third year of King Xerxes' reign (Esther 1:3). Esther was not brought before the king until the tenth month of the seventh year of his reign (Esther 2:16).

2　"The war with Greece straggled on, while Xerxes more and more lost energy—the victim of life in his harem, which seems to have been the dominating interest of his life . . ." D. J. Wiseman, ed., *Peoples of Old Testament Times* (London: Oxford Univ. Press, 1975), 326.

3　"Even before his expedition against Greece Xerxes had to suppress a revolt in Babylonia, when two rebels successively assumed power and had tablets dated by their names. The king's general Megabyzus crushed the revolt, and Babylon was severely punished. Its fortifications were demolished, temples destroyed, the golden statue of Marduk melted down, and estates confiscated and given to Persians." D. J. Wiseman, ed., *Peoples of Old Testament Times* (London: Oxford Univ. Press, 1975), 326.

4　"So the resolution was to put Vashti away, and to give her dignity to another woman. But the king having been fond of her, he did not well bear a separation, and yet by the law he could not admit of a reconciliation, so he was under trouble, as not having it in his power to do what he desired to do: but when his friends saw him so uneasy, they advised him to cast the memory of his wife, and his love for her, out of his mind, but to send abroad over all the inhabitable earth, and to search out for comely virgins, and to take her whom he should best like for his wife, because his passion for his former wife would be quenched by the introduction of another, and the kindness he had for Vashti would be withdrawn from her, and be placed on her that was with him. Accordingly, he was persuaded to follow this advice, and gave order to certain persons to chose out of the virgins that were in his kingdom those that were esteemed the most comely." William Whiston, A.M., trans., *Josephus Complete Works*, (Grand Rapids: Kregel, 1960), 238.

5　1 Samuel 2:1, 8

6　Luke 1:46-48

7　"[KEE nights] (metalsmiths)—the name of a wandering tribe of people who were associated with the Midianites <Judg. 1:16> and, later, with the Amalekites <1 Sam. 15:6>. The Kenites lived in the desert regions of Sinai, Midian, Edom, Amalek, and the Negev. The Bible first mentions the Kenites as one of the groups that lived in Canaan during the time of Abraham <Gen. 15:19>; their territory was to be taken by the Israelites <Num. 24:21-22>. The Kenites were metal craftsmen who may have traced their ancestry to TUBAL-CAIN <Gen. 4:22>." *Nelson's Illustrated Bible Dictionary*, PC Study Bible (Nashville: Nelson, 1998).

8　"KE'NITES (ke'nits; 'pertaining to copper-smiths'). A group of metalsmiths who traveled throughout the mineral-bearing region in the Wadi Arabah. They are first mentioned in <Gen. 15:19> as one of the nations to be 'given' to Israel. They descended from the Midianites and developed extraordinary skill in metalwork. They settled down early along the SW shore of the Dead Sea, SE of Hebron <Judg. 1:16>. Hobab, the son of Reuel, was a Kenite and acted as a guide to Israel in the wilderness <1:16; 4:11>. Their nomadism is suggested in the OT by numerous individual Kenites described as living in various places. Besides their residence SE of Hebron, they were found in the Wadi Arabah <Num. 24:21>, in Naphtali <Judg. 4:11> and in the Davidic-Solomonic era they are mentioned in southern Judah <1 Sam. 15:6; 27:10>. Heber, mentioned in <Judg. 4:11> and <5:24>, was a Kenite, and the ascetic Rechabites mentioned in <1 Chron. 2:55> were also of Kenite extraction (m.f.u.)." *New Unger's Bible Dictionary* (Chicago: Moody Press, 1988), 626.

9　"HO'BAB (ho'bab; 'beloved'). The son of Reuel the Midianite <Num. 10:29; Judg. 4:11>, 1440 B.C. He has usually been identified with Jethro <Ex. 18:5,27; cf. Num. 10:29>; but it is rather his father,

Reuel, to whom the title 'Moses' father-in-law' is intended to apply in <10:29>. That Jethro and Reuel were names of the same person seems evident from <Ex. 2:18,21; 3:1>. Hobab would, therefore, be the brother-in-law of Moses. When Jethro returned to his home <18:27>, Moses prevailed upon Hobab to remain (as seems implied by the absence of any refusal to his second request in <Num. 10:29-32>) and act as guide through the desert. We find his descendants among the Israelites <Judg. 4:11>." *New Unger's Bible Dictionary* (Chicago: Moody Press, 1988), 494.

10 "[And pitched . . . unto the plain of Zaanaim.] It was a sort of debatable land (Stanley, 'Sinai and Palestine,' p. 332), this powerful nomadic chief having secured the quiet enjoyment of the pastures there by the adoption of a neutral position. (In addition to what is said in the passage referred to, see an account of the Yehud Chebr, the Arab descendants of Heber the Kenite, in Schwarz's 'Descriptive Geography and Brief Historical Sketch of Palestine,' 1850). It is not unusual, even in the present day, for pastoral tribes to feed their flocks on the extensive commons that lie in the heart of inhabited countries in the East (see the note at <Judg. 1:16>). 'The plain of Zaanaim,' or Zaanannim (see the note at <Josh. 19:11>) ['ad (heb 5704) 'eelown (heb 436), at the oak or terebinth of Zaanaim; Septuagint, heoos druos pleonektountoon, as far as the oak of the overreaching; Stanley, 'the oaks of the wanderers']. The site of the encampment was under a grove of oaks or terebinths in the upland valley of Kedesh." *Jamieson, Fausset, and Brown Commentary*, PC Study Bible, (Nashville: Nelson, 1998).

11 "An ancient Canaanite fortress city in northern Palestine, situated about 16 kilometers (10 miles) northwest of the Sea of Galilee (see Map 3, C-1). When Joshua and the Israelites invaded Palestine, Hazor was one of the most important fortresses in the land <Josh. 11:10>. This was due to its enormous size, its large population, and its strategic location on the main road between Egypt and Mesopotamia."*Nelson's Illustrated Bible Dictionary*, PC Study Bible (Nashville: Nelson, 1998).

12 "Harosheth (identified by Conder with El Harathlyeh, see <Judg. 4:6>) is marked by the addition of the Gentiles, as in Galilee of the nations <Gen. 14:1; Isa. 9:1>. The name Harosheth signifies workmanship, cutting and carving, whether in stone or wood <Ex. 31:5>, and hence, might be applied to the place where such works are carried on. It has been conjectured that this being a great timber district, rich in cedars and fir-trees, and near Great Zidon <Josh. 11:8>, Jabin kept a large number of oppressed Israelites at work in hewing wood, and preparing it at Harosheth for transport to Zidon; and that these woodcutters, armed with axes and hatchets, formed the soldiers of Barak's army." F. C. Cook, ed., *Barnes' Notes, The Bible Commentary* (Grand Rapids: Baker, 1996), 423.

13 "'Very well,' Deborah said, 'I will go with you. But because of the way you are going about this, the honor will not be yours, for the Lord will hand Sisera over to a woman.' So Deborah went with Barak to Kedesh"(Judges 4:9).

14 Dave Bodine, *PNWP Ministries*, December 10, 2001, <http://www.pnwp.net> (December 10, 2001), Northwest Revival News.

Choices
of
Surrender

Trials in Transition

*". . . Esther also was taken to the king's palace and entrusted to Hegai, who
had charge of the harem. The girl pleased him and won his favor.
Immediately he provided her with her beauty treatments and special food.
He assigned to her seven maids selected from the king's palace and moved
her and her maids into the best place in the harem . . . . Before a girl's turn
came to go in to King Xerxes, she had to complete twelve months of beauty treatments prescribed for the women, six months with oil of myrrh, and
six with perfumes and cosmetics" (Esther 2:8-9, 12).*

Esther had accepted the fact that the Lord had planted her in the palace
of the king of Persia, but she wondered if she would ever really make the
transition in her heart from Mordecai's house to Xerxes' palace. So far,
there had never been a year of her life that did not hold some unique
opportunities for change and growth. She wondered what trials might
await her in this next year, before the "parade" to the king even began. For
the moment, she was grateful for the Persian custom of purification
through beauty treatments and special diet for twelve months. At least it
would delay the dreaded day when she would have to go before the king.

    "Then again," she wondered as she looked out onto the courtyard of
the servants and concubines from her apartment window, *"will the treatments really delay the dreaded day, or will they hasten it?"* Her mind raced,

"Hasn't Mordecai told me many times that my steps are ordered by the Lord and that my times are in His hands?[1] *Could it be that my steps are now being ordered by chamberlains and eunuchs and that my times are in the hands of a heathen king? Could it be that this apartment in the palace of a heathen king was ordered of the Lord for me?*[2] *Could it be that these seven maids, one for every day of the week, represent Jehovah's perfect love to me in some way?*[3] *And what of this special diet and these luxurious beauty treatments, could they add anything to God's handiwork? Besides, hasn't Mordecai always taught me that true beauty comes from within?"*

The questions continued to pour from her mind faster than her mouth could speak them, *"Who is this chamberlain, this master Hegai?*[4] *He may be a master to me, but is he not a mere servant to the king? Is he worthy of my submission? Then again, should I even be considering his worthiness?"* She knew she could submit to him outwardly, but would she be able to surrender to his tutelage from within? Would he be found to be worthy of her trust?

This eunuch, Hegai, who had charge of the king's harem, did seem especially kind to Esther. He allowed her to linger in her chambers in the early morning hours with fresh fruit and tea, while the other pageant contestants had to eat together. According to her maidens, Hegai had provided the very best apartment for her. She knew he favored her in this way because he sensed her need for a place of solace before the daily schedule began. This allowed her time to spend in prayer and meditation. She was truly grateful to him for this luxury.

For Esther, this did seem to be a season of continual prayer and meditation before a holy God. When she, along with several of the other "candidates," were in the hot baths each day, and the others were busy talking about one another's flaws, Esther's mind was continually focused on the beauty of the Lord. She was continually amazed by His incredible goodness to her in the midst of this trying circumstance. While clarity of purpose seemed far from her understanding, she had a sense that the Lord's mercy and goodness was following her. Even though challenges confronted her daily, she was aware of the nearness of His presence.

Esther was young, at the dawn of her young adulthood and newly separated from the only family she had. Once she entered the king's harem, she was not allowed to have contact with any men other than the king's chamberlains who were in charge of the harem. She could confer with no one other than her handmaidens and her new instructor, Hegai. She knew what the proposed, long-range goal for this venture was to be, but the personal cost of getting there was still obscure.

Mordecai had told her to be careful not to reveal her ethnicity and to refrain from speaking freely of everything that came to her mind. She knew it was important to obey his advice. For although she was no longer allowed to go outside the king's courtyard, she could feel an ominous dark cloud, even within the palace walls. She could feel it in the spirit realm. This was not only a season of trial and transition for Esther, it was a season for her spiritual hearing to be sharpened, as well. So indeed, the lingering quiet moments in the mornings and the petitions of her heart in the hot baths were edifying to her soul.

Perhaps the prayers of Mordecai had gone before her and the Lord was watching out for her. *"Though my heart yearns to be free,"* she thought to herself, *"if I submit to Hegai's mentoring as I did to Mordecai's tutelage, perhaps I will be instructed by the Lord through him."* She continued to wonder, *"Could it be possible that this eunuch of a heathen king could instruct me in matters that would open Jehovah's pathway before me and cause His light to shine brightly within my view once again?"*

With this in mind, Esther's knees went to the floor in her familiar posture of prayer and petition, and she cried out with the heart of a psalmist.

"O Lord, you have searched me and you know me. You know when I sit and when I rise; you perceive my thoughts from afar. You discern my going out and my lying down; you are familiar with all my ways. Before a word is on my tongue you know it completely, O Lord. You hem me in—behind and before; you have laid your hand upon me. Such knowledge is too wonderful for me, too lofty for me to attain. Where can I go from your Spirit? Where can I flee from your presence? If I go up to the heavens, you are there; if I make my bed in the depths, you are there. If I rise on the wings of the

dawn, if I settle on the far side of the sea, even there your hand will guide me, your right hand will hold me fast. If I say, 'Surely the darkness will hide me and the light become night around me,' even the darkness will not be dark to you; the night will shine like the day, for darkness is as light to you. For you created my inmost being; you knit me together in my mother's womb. I praise you because I am fearfully and wonderfully made; your works are wonderful, I know that full well. My frame was not hidden from you when I was made in the secret place. When I was woven together in the depths of the earth, your eyes saw my unformed body. All the days ordained for me were written in your book before one of them came to be, How precious to me are your thoughts, O God! How vast is the sum of them! Were I to count them, they would outnumber the grains of sand. When I awake, I am still with you. . . . Search me, O God, and know my heart; test me and know my anxious thoughts. See if there is any offensive way in me, and lead me in the way everlasting." [5]

HEADS HIGH AND HEARTS SURRENDERED

Like all the other maidens, Esther had to spend a year in purification through special beauty treatments and diet. While the outward treatments were doing their work, the Lord was at work from within. If she were to cleave successfully to the future that was set before her, she would have to die to herself, her hopes, and the expectations of yesterday. This yearlong preparation phase was as much a gift to Esther as it was a purification process. The "treatments" would not only be outward, but inward, as well. She would likely contend with struggles from within and trials from without, as she faced both the yearnings of her heart to return home and the rigid disciplines of her present circumstances that were to prepare her for her future. As she surrendered to the Father's will, He would be very present with her in this transition season and would enable her to leave the past and cleave to the future.

Just as every new husband looks into the eyes of his bride to see if she is looking to him rather than to her father, so too would Xerxes look for that kind of desire in the eyes of his next queen. It was essential that Esther confronted every trial that crossed her pathway with her head held high and her heart surrendered.

Psalm 144:12 says, *". . . our daughters will be like pillars carved to adorn a palace."* As this verse describes, this was Esther's season of carving, for there was a palace to be adorned, not with natural beauty, but with the beauty of the Lord.

A young friend of mine, Sara Paulson Brummett, was crowned Miss Oregon in 1992. Today, Sara is a successful Christian vocal artist. Prior to this current season of success in her life, she lived a surrendered life under the tutelage of her parents, high school teachers, and Bible college professors. During these years of development, training, and preparation for what the Lord had for her in the future, her submission to these trusted mentors served as preparation for future advisers who would open the doorway to statewide and national exposure.

Her preparation for the Miss Oregon pageant, though contemporary, must have been somewhat similar to Esther's. In a portion of her personal testimony, Sara writes:

> *The preparation that I went through wasn't pleasant, but I love a challenge and competition has always inspired me to work hard like nothing else. The training process was definitely for the purpose of winning the crown, but I knew it was also a training ground for future ministry and growth in my own life. Mock judges were set up as a panel to interview me every week, on everything from personal opinions and beliefs to current events and politics. Speech coaches worked with me, critiquing every expression and inflection. The committee members worked with me for onstage poise, criticizing every inch of my body and*

telling me how to improve it (hours at the gym!). Trainers worked with me at an athletic club to learn weightlifting and cardiovascular training. Professional hairdressers and makeup artists worked with me to train me to do my own hair and "stage" makeup. The pageant director and I traveled to California to shop for gowns and clothes to be worn for interviews—a full "pageant wardrobe," with sub-sequent fittings.[6]

ISSUES IN TRANSITION

I'm sure there were many varied emotions that ran through both Esther and Sara's hearts during their year of processing. Perhaps loneliness and fear were among them. Loneliness, coupled with fear of the unknown, seems to invariably be experienced in the midst of transition.

Even though loneliness and apprehension may have met Esther at every turn, in those early days of transition, her only hope was to cleave to the Lord and to His presence. While she was very much alone, neither loneliness nor fear were destined to be her sole companions, for a daughter of the Lord is never truly alone. The challenge of this truth is just as David wrote, *"Is not the Lord your God with you? . . . Now devote your heart and soul to seeking the Lord your God . . ."* (1 Chronicles 22:18).

Even in the midst of transition, she did not allow loneliness, fear, or ambivalence to overcome her. She chose to cling to her God and listen for His voice. While the beauty treatments were massaged into her skin, she devoted her heart to seeking the Lord and allowing His Spirit to be the great masseuse of her soul. Even though she was enclosed in palace walls, she was free in her spirit.

> *"The beauty of the Lord will not shine brightly through us if we cling to the arms of loneliness and fear, rather than the arms of God."*

As it was with Esther, so it should be with us, as well. The beauty of the Lord will not shine brightly through us if we cling to the arms of loneliness and fear, rather than the arms of God. His light cannot shine through a self-defeating, ambivalent mindset, but it can break through any wall built by the enemy of our souls.

JUST AS I AM

An incredible contemporary example of one who overcame feelings of ambivalence and loneliness is Charlotte Elliot. She was born in 1789 and, as a young woman, was well on her way to becoming a recognized artist. However, by the age of thirty she was a bedridden invalid, and loneliness and fear of the future were her constant companions. She felt useless and was to the point of utter despair, when Jesus Christ came into her life as her personal Savior.

Christ exchanged her despair for His freedom. Her heart sang out with David's words, *"We have escaped like a bird out of the fowler's snare; the snare has been broken, and we have escaped. Our help is in the name of the Lord, the Maker of heaven and earth"* (Psalm 124:7-8).

From this salvation experience, she had a desire to help spread the Gospel in the best way she knew, by helping to raise money for her brother who was a financially poor pastor. She wrote the hymn "Just as I Am, Without One Plea," hoping to give to her brother's ministry any money that it made.

It was originally published in *The Invalid's Hymnbook*. Of course, today this well-known hymn of the church has been published in hymnbooks around the world many times over. It has been sung in multiple crusades for Christ, as many a lonely and desperate person has found his or her way to a personal relationship with Jesus Christ. Let the words of the first three verses of her song capture your heart once again, noting the third verse especially:

> *Just as I am, without one plea,*
> *But that thy blood was shed for me,*

And that thou bidst me come to thee,
O Lamb of God, I come, I come!

Just as I am, and waiting not
To rid my soul of one dark blot,
To thee whose blood can cleanse each spot,
O Lamb of God, I come, I come!

Just as I am, though tossed about
With many a conflict, many a doubt,
Fightings and fears within, without,
O Lamb of God, I come, I come![7]

Charlotte Elliot had, like Esther, discovered a way to transform her loneliness, fear of the future, and entrapment into a focused message that would bring hope to many throughout the generations. The message of her song reveals that her only hope, regardless of her circumstances, was to be found in her Savior.

Ambivalence may very well have been a struggle for Esther in this season of transition. Just as Charlotte was trapped in a physical body that would not obey her commands, Esther may have felt trapped by her circumstances, by her heritage, and by the culture in which she lived. Yes, she was in a palace, but was it a "green pasture" for her, as the psalmist says? This Persian culture and its past monarchs had already taken from her a national homeland and added to her a Babylonian name. Mordecai had required of her not to reveal her ancestry and to watch her words. She must have pondered daily in this year of transition, *"Am I to be trapped forever in this Persian maze and never be allowed to truly be who I am?"*

> *"In dying to ourselves, we cross the threshold into destiny."*

Just as it was with Esther, so it is with us today. In dying to ourselves, we cross the threshold into destiny. Esther had to die to herself and to her own desires and expectations during this season. She could not change her circumstances, but she could adjust her perspective in the midst of the circumstances. She could not tear down natural walls of stone or timber, but she could dismantle the walls within her heart.

In cocooning herself in with God and tuning her ear to His voice, rather than the voices of her circumstances, she could hear the voice that rose above the circumstances. The courage that would be required of her in the future was encased in her ability to respond to God, rather than her visible circumstances in this season. She would one day be the beautiful queen who would move a king's heart, but it was in dying to her own desires "today" that she would embrace the courage to die for others "tomorrow."

LOOKING THROUGH CIRCUMSTANCES AND SEEING GOD.

Like Esther, you too must look through your circumstances and see God. If you can't see Him today, then you must continue to stand in faith and trust, for He alone sees the end from the beginning and is leading and guiding your steps. These opportunities come in a variety of ways.

For me, one of these opportunities came when I turned thirty years of age. I thought I was in the best season of my life. I had my health, a loving husband, adoring and fun-loving children, and a ministry that I found to be fulfilling. Then, just as suddenly as my birthday had come and gone, my emotions began to turn upside-down and inside-out.

I didn't know what was happening to me. The steadiness of my nature seemed volatile and unpredictable. Scenes that had once brought laughter and amusement to my heart irritated and grated against my nerves. I cried if someone said hello, and I cried if she didn't. My legs felt like lead when I walked up stairs, and my energy came and went with my mood swings. The even-tempered and joyful person I had been had become emotionally unpredictable at least two weeks out of the month, sometimes three. At times, I feared I was losing my mind.

This was a season when premenstrual stress was hardly discussed or written about, much less acknowledged by many doctors. However, I began to chart my symptoms and discovered a pattern. There seemed to be a "rhythm" to these symptoms, and I was determined to discover the reason.

The more I charted and the more I read and studied, the more I realized I was not losing my mind, but I was losing my season of predictable hormonal surges. Though the knowledge I gained was freeing, I still felt trapped by these conflicting hormones. I needed to adjust and to make some changes in my personal exercise program and eating habits. When I did this, my hormones began to adjust, as well.

In the midst of the transition, I had to require my spirit, not my emotional surges, to be in control. Like Esther, as I continued to trust the Lord, I aligned my will to His and applied the practical disciplines that were required. By doing so, in time I was able to walk out of those plaguing symptoms.

Psalm 23:3 says of the Good Shepherd, *"He restores my soul."* In the natural setting of a sheepfold, if a sheep wanders from the flock and goes off to graze alone, he can put himself in grave danger. He not only may encounter wolves and steep mountain cliffs, but he also may overindulge and lay down to rest without the watchful oversight of the shepherd.

If he eats too much and accidentally rolls over on his back, he becomes "cast," or "cast down." When a sheep becomes cast, he will kick his legs vigorously in an attempt to roll himself back over. If he is unable to do so, he could die within hours.

When the shepherd finds a sheep that is cast down, he comes to his side and rubs his legs to get the blood circulation flowing again. He then gently rolls him back over onto his feet to a restored position.

The next time you find yourself in a season of transition or a place of feeling hemmed in or lost, let the Good Shepherd come and massage your spirit and get His life-blood flowing in you again. Let Him touch your perspective and restore you to even pathways in which to walk. Perhaps your humble surrender to the Lord will lead to the rescue of other lives around you.

TRANSITION—THE ONE CONSTANT IN LIFE

There are many transitions and periods of adjustment in a woman's life. It often seems that just as we finish one period of transition and get settled comfortably into the next season, another transition begins. Seasons and transitions come and go, but Jesus is always the one constant we can depend on.

Think about it. Just when you have gotten out of diapers, are solidly on your feet, and are running with confidence, you transition from the carefully scrutinized baby years into the not-so-closely-watched formative years. Here, you discover what it is like to cut your own bangs and sleep with bubblegum tangled in your hair. Just when you figure out how to brush your own hair, so your Mom won't braid it so tightly that you look like a Boston Bull Terrier, you run into the teen years and bump into acne, cramps, and boys. Then when you've adjusted to the hormones and emotions of the teen years and have noticed the opposite sex, you are hurled into your young adult years. Parents are insistent upon career goals and a college education, while grandparents, aunts, and uncles come wondering when you're going to find "prince charming." Just when you've gotten everyone to leave you alone about your education and your future husband, you are out of college with nowhere to go, and the "prince," who you suspect is a "frog" incognito, comes knocking on your door. Then, just when you say "I do" to the most charming "prince" who comes a-knockin', your "bliss" turns into "blisters," and you find yourself working harder than the trash compactor or the washing machine combined. Just when you've adjusted your schedule to your husband, your career, and your home, parenthood doesn't even knock—it comes barging through the door, demanding food, clean laundry, and focused attention. And just as you've finally adjusted to sleepless nights and embarrassing cracker crumbs on restaurant floors, your adoring toddler becomes a teen, daring you to tell her not to leave the house "dressed like that." Then, when your teen has settled into a phase when you can allow her to leave the house without fear of being embarrassed by what she may wear or say, she steps into young adulthood and asks, "Whatever happened to your wardrobe, Mom? You're not going out in that are you?" When you've finally molded and shaped your "little lambs" into model adults, they have the audacity to leave you and take your heartstrings with them.

Of course, these transitions only scratch the surface of many women's lives. Single or married, there are also the constant adjustments to your changing body and hormonal fluctuations. Just when childhood departs, your hormones take charge, with mood swings and a bloated abdomen. And just when you've finally adjusted to this monthly "blessing," gravity begins to take over and your body needs not only a bend and a stretch, but a total lift. When you finally adjust to the cruel mirror in front of you, menopause, with its endearing "mental-pause," begins to settle in, as well, and this little couplet becomes your theme song:

I can live with my arthritis, and my dentures fit me fine.
I can see with my bifocals, but I sure do miss my mind.[8]

> "When all is said and done, transitions and seasons come and go, but Jesus remains forever."

When all is said and done, transitions and seasons come and go, but Jesus remains forever. Christian speaker Tony Campalo says this: *"You may be at 'Crucifixion Friday' now, but I want to tell you that 'Resurrection Sunday' is coming!"*

Change lives continually at your doorstep, so you might as well put yourself in neutral and let God do the driving. The curves of life are coming, and you can "take 'em easy" or "take 'em hard," but you are going to have to take them. The way you do so is dependent upon you and your surrender to the Owner of the "car" and the Creator of your soul.

Paul the apostle says in 1 Thessalonians 5:8, *"But since we belong to the day, let us be self-controlled, putting on faith and love as a breastplate, and the hope of salvation as a helmet."* Truly, these must have been the garments that Esther learned to put on during this year of transition, and they must be ours, as well.

If Esther had given in to any of the negative emotions that longed to capture her heart, all the beauty treatments would have been of little use. Inner stress almost always expresses itself outwardly, as we are one in body, soul, and spirit. She had to maintain her peace and her trust to maintain her beauty. It was the gift within the gift that set her apart from the others.

It is the gift within the gift, within you, that will do the same in your life. Paul writes in Colossians 1:26, *"To them God has chosen to make known among the Gentiles the glorious riches of this mystery, which is Christ in you, the hope of glory."*

May we, like Esther, surrender to the Father's will and glean all that He has for us in our seasons of transition. May we be purified inwardly and adorned outwardly in such a way that those who do not know Him will yearn for His touch upon their lives.

Seasons of Processing

GEN. 1:14 *"And God said, 'Let there be lights in the expanse of the sky to separate the day from the night, and let them serve as signs to mark seasons and days and years.'"*

DEUT. 11:13-15 *"So if you faithfully obey the commands I am giving you today—to love the Lord your God and to serve him with all your heart and with all your soul—then I will send rain on your land in its season, both autumn and spring rains, so that you may gather in your grain, new wine and oil. I will provide grass in the fields for your cattle, and you will eat and be satisfied."*

DEUT. 28:12-14 *"The Lord will open the heavens, the storehouse of his bounty, to send rain on your land in season and to bless all the work of your hands. You will lend to many nations but will borrow from none. The Lord will make you the head, not the tail. If you pay attention to the commands of the Lord your God that I give you this day and carefully follow them, you will always be at the top, never at the bottom. Do not turn aside from any of the commands I give you today, to the right or to the left, following other gods and serving them."*

PS. 1:3 *"He is like a tree planted by streams of water, which yields its fruit in season and whose leaf does not wither. Whatever he does prospers."*

ECCL. 3:1 *"There is a time for everything, and a season for every activity under heaven:"*

SONG 2:12 *"Flowers appear on the earth; the season of singing has come, the cooing of doves is heard in our land."*

JER. 8:7 *"Even the stork in the sky knows her appointed season, and the dove, the swift and the thrush observe the time of their migration. But my people do not know the requirements of the Lord."*

EZEK. 34:26 *"I will bless them and the places surrounding my hill. I will send down showers in season; there will be showers of blessing."*

DAN. 2:21 *"He changes times and seasons; he sets up kings and deposes them. He gives wisdom to the wise and knowledge to the discerning."*

2 TIM. 4:2 *"Preach the Word; be prepared in season and out of season; correct, rebuke and encourage—with great patience and careful instruction."*

TITUS 1:3 *"And at his appointed season he brought his word to light through the preaching entrusted to me by the command of God our Savior."*

N O T E S

1 Psalm 37:23; 31:15

2 "The place appointed as a residence for the wives and concubines of the king was separated from the rest of the palace by a court. There were in it three sets of apartments: one set for the virgins who had not yet been sent for by the king, one for the concubines, and one for the queen and the other wives." James M. Freeman, *Manners and Customs of the Bible* (Plainfield, N.J.: Logos International, 1972), 204.

3 "[He (Hegai) speedily gave her things for purification, with such things as belonged to her] (cf. <Est. 2:12>). The seven maidens, one for every day of the week, were appointed to attend her in rotation. Their names are mentioned in the Chaldee paraphrase, as well as the day of waiting for each." *Jamieson, Fausset, and Brown Commentary*, PC Study Bible, (Nashville: Nelson, 1998).

4 "*Sarisim* is variously rendered 'chamberlains,' 'officers,' and 'eunuchs.' They were emasculated persons who had charge of the harems of Oriental monarchs, and who were also employed by them in various offices about the court. They often became the confidential advisers of the monarch, and were frequently men of great influence, and sometimes had high military office. . . . This was especially the case in Persia, where they acquired great political power, and filled positions of great prominence, and sometimes engaged in conspiracy against the life of the king . . ."James M. Freeman, *Manners and Customs of the Bible* (Plainfield, N.J.: Logos International, 1972), 203.

5 Psalm 139:1-18, 23-24

6 Quote from the personal testimony of Sara Paulson Brummett, used with permission, 1999; Sara Paulson Brummett, Williams & Associates, Inc. Spiritbound, P.O. Box 292785, Nashville, Tennessee 37229.

7 Charlotte Elliott, "Just as I Am, Without One Plea," Public Domain, *The Methodist Hymnal* (Nashville: Methodist, 1966), 119.

8 William McConnell, Couplet submitted to *Parables, etc.* (LaGrange, Ky.: Saratoga, 1982).

A Watchman on the Wall

"Esther had not revealed her nationality and family background, because Mordecai had forbidden her to do so. Every day he walked back and forth near the courtyard of the harem to find out how Esther was and what was happening to her" (Esther 2:10).

The question that had tormented Mordecai's thoughts day and night now bolted through his mind once again, *"How could I have allowed this to happen to my dear little Esther?"* The remorse he felt was like an undulating wave of grief that came from within the very depths of his being. His table was empty of her presence, and his heart was rent. There was no sunshine to greet him in the morning and no friendly banter to interrupt his studies. The atmosphere of the house was desolate, void of joy and laughter. Even the servants, who had mentored Esther in womanly chores and charms, walked about the house silently with mourning cloths neatly tucked in their belts to quickly catch their unstoppable tears.

Mordecai loved Esther like a daughter and felt personally responsible for her well-being. He wondered what her father, his deceased uncle Abihail, would think of his guardianship now that she was gone. He was plagued by doubt and wondered if he should have handled himself differently when the king's men had taken her. His waking hours were tortured and his nights were spent tossing and turning. Rest eluded him, in his emotional state, and his prayers reached out for solace and for answers.

He knew that he needed to continue to watch over her now, as any father would. He also knew that he needed to do it carefully, so as not to endanger her life further.[1] His care and caution needed to be intricately interwoven.

Mordecai appreciated his job as a doorkeeper at the main entrance to the palace now more than he ever had.[2] It allowed him reasonably free access to walk in front of the court of the women's house each day and casually ask a passing maiden or eunuch how the "maiden from Susa" was fairing.[3] One day, one of the eunuchs even offered this local maiden's name to him, so he could now ask about Esther by name without suspicion.

The Lord had been speaking to him in prayer concerning the looming threat to the Jewish people, as he discerned the impending darkness in Susa. *"Perhaps,"* he pondered, *"Jehovah Himself strategically planted my beloved Esther within Xerxes' palace walls. Could it be? Could my little Jewish disciple shine like a star and bring about the triumph and victory of our people, as her Babylonian and Jewish names imply? Was this her destiny?"* He longed to have more clarity. He knew the only answer would come in prayer, yet the quandary within his heart led him near the palace walls continually. He had always found that "watching while he prayed" and "praying while he watched" was helpful, and he would do so now in the midst of this perplexing situation.

This was a season of great personal stretching for Mordecai. He could feel his faith being tested as never before. He knew within himself that this was not only a time of personal sacrifice for him and Esther, but it was also the prelude to perilous days for the people of Susa. Mordecai realized that this was a season that required daily intercession and careful observation. There was a great need for a prayerful watchman to be on the wall, for a storm was brewing. As he pondered this need, his petitions rose up from within him, and his surrendered hands were raised to his loving God, *"Jehovah, my Lord and my King, my trust is in You and You alone. But my heart is heavy and burdened with many thoughts. I feel like Isaiah of old, when king Uzziah died and he cried out to you in his distress.*

"I too see You, Lord; yes, I also hear Your voice. I too cry out, 'Woe to me! I am ruined! For I am a man of unclean lips, and I live among a people of unclean lips, and my eyes have seen the King, the Lord Almighty.' [4]

"Oh Lord, You have touched my mouth and taken away my sin. I am forever grateful for Your atonement. I too, like Isaiah, hear Your voice asking, 'Whom shall I send? And who will go for us?' [5] *Oh God, here am I. Send me! Send me, Lord! Must my little Hadassah be in such a place of hedonism? Send me in her place!"*

A single tear ran down his cheek and nested softly in his beard, as Jehovah's Spirit gently ministered to his grieving heart. *"Yes, Lord, I do trust You. I trust that You have ordered Esther's steps just as You have ordered mine. Yes, I will do my part and trust You to watch over Esther. Together, we will watch. You will watch, and I will watch and pray. I am confident that 'there is a time for everything, and a season for every activity under heaven.'* [6] *Oh, increase my faith, Father."*

A PARENT'S ASSIGNMENT

This was, indeed, a season of personal stretching and trusting the Lord, not only for Esther, but for her beloved Mordecai, as well. The release of a child into the hands of God, when His hands are not apparent, is a challenge for any parent. When the Lord's hands are obvious, the release still tugs at the heartstrings, but when they are not

> *"The release of a child into the hands of God, when His hands are not apparent, is a challenge for any parent."*

within view, it takes great courage and faith to let the child go.

This was Mordecai's predestined assignment in this season. The mapped out lines of direction were indefinable from his natural perspective. It would take watching and praying to discern the Father's will and to restore peace in his heart. This would be his lot, to be a watchman from a distance and an intercessor on Esther's behalf daily.

This has been a parent's lot in life more than once in history. Many have had to release their children to spouses of whom they were unsure, or to vocations or geographic locations about which they felt hesitant. For twenty years, more or less, this child has been a part of the parent's every-day existence. Emotions, energy, and finances have all been focused and spent. There is a natural apprehension about separation that is momentary and recurring, at best, and indissoluble, at worst. This separation is necessary, but not necessarily painless.

When a child's life goes the direction that a parent planned, hoped for, and is proud of, the parent is still left with an empty table and emotions that betray him or her from time to time. Much to the surprise of many parents of adult children, these emotions erupt when least expected. Though the joy between a parent and child may be real and their love very much intact, the parent may still have momentary mental lapses into the pleasant memories of the past, creating emotional responses. This is neither good nor bad, it just is. This is neither emotional dependency nor a lack of appropriate separation skills, it is merely a grateful embracing of the sweetness of the past and should not be interpreted as anything more.

When a child's life goes a direction that is unplanned, the parent is often left with self-doubt, nagging questions, and perplexing assumptions. Depending on the gravity of the situation, he or she may also be left with anger, hurt, or shame, while being painfully reduced to watching from afar. The hopes and dreams he or she may have had for this child sadly dissipate, and the parent is left with little hope of any possible helpful intervention.

If the parent is only able to watch but not pray, because he or she does not have a personal relationship with a living God who hears and answers petitions, he or she is left in utter despair and hopelessness. This wounding and fruitless relationship leaves the parent wounded, full of pain, and lacking hope. If the parent does have a personal relationship with the living God, he or she knows that He hears and answers the petitions of the heart. Though wounded and disappointed, the parent's hope rests in the one who created the child; His eyes will see over walls too high for this child and be ever awake when the child's eyes slumber.

A PARENT'S PRAYER IN SEASONS OF WAR.

Many parents through the generations have had to bravely release their children during times of war, when the call to arms has captured the heart and mission of a nation. These releases can leave the parental heart suspended in a quagmire of emotion. In one minute pride soars high, in the next anxiety and fear reign. During war times, reassurance and answered prayer come only from the one true God.

> *"During war times, reassurance and answered prayer come only from the one true God."*

I have a friend, a missionary in Japan, whose father, like Mordecai, found the need to watch and pray as his daughter responded to the call of God on her life. Her name is Phyllis, and her childhood years were spent on a farm in Hay, a small town in eastern Washington. The latter part of her growing up years was spent in a larger town in the lower Yakima Valley, not far away.

When she was a teen, General Douglas MacArthur made a call to the nation for missionaries to go to Japan. Following World War II, the Japanese emperor renounced himself as god, and there was a spiritual vacuum left in the hearts of the Japanese people. It was a war-torn land full of broken and hungry hearts.

After spending two years in Bible college in Canada, Phyllis went to a school in Los Angeles, California, in 1951, to enroll in a three-month soul-winning course. During this course, the challenge of the needs of the Japanese people was continually put before the students.

In sharing her testimony about the call of God on her life, she said, *"In my growing up days I responded to many missionary altar calls: 'All who are willing to go to the mission field IF God should call you, please stand. . . .' It's easy to respond to that kind of altar call. However, in mid-October of 1951, during one of those challenges for Japan, I stood along with many others. God began digging deep into my heart, and I knew that just standing would get me nowhere. Therefore, in all sincerity I prayed in my heart, 'Lord, I'm going to Japan unless you close the door.' A great peace reigned in my heart."*

From this experience, at age nineteen, she went home and told her parents that she was going to Japan as a missionary, and she immediately began to raise the money to go. This was not an easy task, as there were not many people who were excited about investing their missions offerings in a young single girl who was "going alone." However, destiny and the will of God prevailed on behalf of this young, surrendered life, and financial provision was made. By the time Phyllis set sail for Japan, it was May of 1952, and she was twenty years old.

It wasn't until twenty-five years later that her father told her of his struggle to let her go. While both her parents were very dedicated to God and desired only God's will for their children, her father had battled in his heart day and night, often with tears flooding his eyes.

Questions had plagued his mind. *"Is going to Japan really God's will for Phyllis? Since she is single and so young, would it be right for me, as her father, to allow her to go?"* Numerous times he had decided to talk with her and tell her that he didn't think she should go, at least not until she was older and better prepared. Each time he made the decision to speak with her and discourage her from going, he envisioned his hand reaching out and taking his baby girl off the altar on which he had committed her to God for all of her days.

Even though he couldn't bring himself to speak with her about it, the battle raged in his heart. His constant meditations were, *"It's dangerous in Japan. The war has been over such a short time. The Korean conflict is on and could boil over into Japan. She isn't married. I am her father, and I must stop her."* However, he did not share his battle with anyone, not even his wife.

Then one night he had a dream. He dreamed that the family was saying farewell to Phyllis as she was about to leave for Japan. He picked up one of her suitcases and it appeared to be empty. He called her attention *to it, and she simply replied, "No, Daddy, I don't have anything to put in that one."* Then he noticed something written in small letters on the suitcase. Looking closely he saw the word "Sorrows." Her suitcase of "sorrows" was empty, only those with hope and joy were filled.

He immediately awakened from his dream. With tears and thanksgiving in his heart he prayed, *"Lord, you can have her. She can go to Japan even if I never see her face again. You have shown me it is your will."* His battle was over, and with peace in his heart he was able to say farewell to her as she embarked on her journey to Japan.

He planted his precious seed, not in a Persian palace, but in a land full of heathen temples and false gods, the needy land of Japan. Psalm 126:6 says, *"He who goes out weeping, carrying seed to sow, will return with songs of joy, carrying sheaves with him."* Through his seed, this beloved daddy would sing songs of joy and bear fruit in this distant land.

> *"He planted his precious seed, not in a Persian palace, but in a land full of heathen temples and false gods. . ."*

Phyllis went on to Japan and met a handsome, single young man from Arkansas, who was also there to fulfill the call of God on his life. He too desired to minister the love of Christ to the people of Japan. They married one year from the day that Phyllis had arrived.

When she returned home for the first time after her fond farewell, three and a half years had passed. The young, single girl her daddy had sent off to Japan *"even if I never see her face again,"* was now a happily married seasoned missionary with a bright-eyed baby boy in her arms. In the years to come, she would have six children altogether. Today all of these children are actively serving the Lord with their spouses and families. Two of them are presently pastors and leaders in Japan, and one more is preparing to go. The others are actively involved in churches in America.

In tribute to Phyllis's father on his ninetieth birthday, she wrote the poem, "With Pitcher in Hand":

It was a hot, sultry night in summertime Hay,
And upstairs the old house was doubly that way,
(sister) Zella was sleeping on her half the bed,
The middle was a line, we had both clearly said.

I drifted to sleep on that hot summer night,
No need for the lantern—it was still a bit light.
But sleep was not sound as I tumbled and tossed,
Careful even in my sleep, that the line was not crossed.
Much later I awoke, and my throat was so dry,
For Mama to help me, how I wanted to cry.
For it was Mama who brought to us water in the night,
And Mama who comforted us, no matter the plight.

Zella still sleeping in a comfortable heap,
And I drifted again into some kind of sleep.

Then there you were, Daddy, with pitcher in hand;
Close by my bedside, so tall you did stand.
The water you carried did sparkle and gleam;
And then I awoke—it was only a dream.

I've pondered that dream with the passing of time.
Its meaning to me is very sublime.
It was from you, dear Daddy, with pitcher in hand,
That we received water from God's Promised Land.
Crystal clear water that flows from the throne,
And all who partake do become God's own.

Thank you, dear Daddy, for standing so tall
With pitcher in hand, you have given to all.[7]

Yes, with this father's watchful eye, hearing ear, and willing hand, he gave his daughter to the Lord and to the land of Japan. After nearly fifty years of service, Phyllis and her husband are still ministering in Japan effectively. In giving his daughter, he has reaped a plentiful harvest in this distant land. His children and grandchildren are some of the most influential Christian Americans in the charismatic churches of Japan. They have been responsible for helping to birth several churches and raise up national leaders in this naturally prosperous, but spiritually needy nation.

In prediction of His own death on the cross, Jesus said in John 12:24, 26, *"I tell you the truth, unless a kernel of wheat falls to the ground and dies, it remains only a single seed. But if it dies, it produces many seeds. . . . Whoever serves me must follow me; and where I am, my servant also will be. My Father will honor the one who serves me."*

Mordecai never knew if he would ever see Esther again, but he watched over her in the best way that he could by releasing her, not into the hands of a heathen king, but into the very hands of God. In the same way, the father of young Phyllis will be forever linked in heart to Mordecai, as he too watched over and released into the hands of his Maker the most precious seed he had to offer. The fruit of these two fathers' dedicated offering is "many seeds," just as Jesus said it would be.

If you are a biological, adopted, or surrogate parent today, offer your children afresh to the Creator and Maker of the Universe, our Lord Jesus Christ. Allow Him to plant them where He wills and multiply His seed through yours. Pour them out as an offering to Him. As the young missionary to Japan says of her faithful "Mordecai," *"With pitcher in hand, you have given to all."*

Watching & Waiting

PS. 130:6 *"My soul waiteth for the Lord more than they that watch for the morning: I say, more than they that watch for the morning." (KJV)*

PS. 141:3 *"Set a watch, O LORD, before my mouth; keep the door of my lips." (KJV)*

HAB. 2:1 *"I will stand upon my watch, and set me upon the tower, and will watch to see what he will say unto me, and what I shall answer when I am reproved." (KJV)*

MATT. 25:13 *"Watch therefore, for ye know neither the day nor the hour wherein the Son of man cometh." (KJV)*

MARK 14:38 *"Watch ye and pray, lest ye enter into temptation. The spirit truly is ready, but the flesh is weak." (KJV)*

1 COR. 16:13 *"Watch ye, stand fast in the faith, quit you like men, be strong." (KJV)*

COL. 4:2 *"Continue in prayer, and watch in the same with thanks giving;" (KJV)*

1THESS. 5:6 *"Therefore let us not sleep, as do others; but let us watch and be sober." (KJV)*

2 TIM. 4:5 *"But watch thou in all things, endure afflictions, do the work of an evangelist, make full proof of thy ministry." (KJV)*

HEB. 13:17 *"Obey them that have the rule over you, and submit yourselves: for they watch for your souls, as they that must give account, that they may do it with joy, and not with grief: for that is unprofitable for you." (KJV)*

1 PET. 4:7 *"But the end of all things is at hand: be ye therefore sober, and watch unto prayer." (KJV)*

PS. 27:14 *"Wait on the LORD: be of good courage, and he shall strengthen thine heart: wait, I say, on the LORD." (KJV)*

PS. 37:7 *"Rest in the LORD, and wait patiently for him: fret not thyself because of him who prospereth in his way, because of the man who bringeth wicked devices to pass." (KJV)*

PS. 37:34 *"Wait on the LORD, and keep his way, and he shall exalt thee to inherit the land: when the wicked are cut off, thou shalt see it." (KJV)*

PS. 39:7 *"And now, Lord, what wait I for? My hope is in thee." (KJV)*

PS. 123:2 *"Behold, as the eyes of servants look unto the hand of their masters, and as the eyes of a maiden unto the hand of her mistress; so our eyes wait upon the LORD our God, until that he have mercy upon us." (KJV)*

PS. 130:5 *"I wait for the LORD, my soul doth wait, and in his word do I hope." (KJV)*

PROV. 20:22 *"Say not thou, I will recompense evil; but wait on the LORD, and he shall save thee." (KJV)*

ISA. 30:18   *"And therefore will the LORD wait, that he may be gracious unto you, and therefore will he be exalted, that he may have mercy upon you: for the LORD is a God of judgment: blessed are all they that wait for him." (KJV)*

ISA. 40:31   *"But they that wait upon the LORD shall renew their strength; they shall mount up with wings as eagles; they shall run, and not be weary; and they shall walk, and not faint." (KJV)*

LAM. 3:25-26   *"The LORD is good unto them that wait for him, to the soul that seeketh him. It is good that a man should both hope and quietly wait for the salvation of the LORD." (KJV)*

HOS. 12:6   *"Therefore turn thou to thy God: keep mercy and judgment, and wait on thy God continually." (KJV)*

MIC. 7:7   *"Therefore I will look unto the LORD; I will wait for the God of my salvation: my God will hear me." (KJV)*

HAB. 2:3   *"For the vision is yet for an appointed time, but at the end it shall speak, and not lie: though it tarry, wait for it; because it will surely come, it will not tarry." (KJV)*

ZEPH. 3:8   *"Therefore wait ye upon me, saith the LORD, until the day that I rise up to the prey: for my determination is to gather the nations, that I may assemble the kingdoms, to pour upon them mine indignation, even all my fierce anger: for all the earth shall be devoured with the fire of my jealousy." (KJV)*

ROM. 8:25   *"But if we hope for that we see not, then do we with patience wait for it." (KJV)*

NOTES

1   "Why Mordecai charged her to keep her nationality secret is not easy to determine. Perhaps he feared for her safety. Or possibly he was granted by the Lord a special premonition of coming trouble for Israel and the part Esther might play in delivering her people." *Wycliffe Commentary*, PC Study Bible, (Nashville: Nelson, 1998).

2   "Mordecai occupied, apparently, a humble place in the royal household. He was probably one of the porters or doorkeepers at the main entrance to the palace." F.C. Cook, ed., *Barnes Notes The Bible Commentary* (Grand Rapids: Baker, 1996), 493.

3   "The harem is an inviolable sanctuary, and what is transacted within its walls is as much a secret to these without as if they were thousands of miles away; but hints were given him through the eunuchs." *Jamieson, Fausset, and Brown Commentary*, PC Study Bible, (Nashville: Nelson, 1998).

4   Isaiah 6:5

5   Isaiah 6:8

6   Ecclesiastes 3:1

7   Used with permission from Phyllis Kaylor, 1326-5 Minami Masunaga, Arao City, Kumamoto Ken, JAPAN 864-0032

Submitted Selections

"And this is how she would go to the king: Anything she wanted was given her to take with her from the harem to the king's palace. In the evening she would go there and in the morning return to another part of the harem to the care of Shaashgaz, the king's eunuch who was in charge of the concubines. She would not return to the king unless he was pleased with her and summoned her by name. When the turn came for Esther (the girl Mordecai had adopted, the daughter of his uncle Abihail) to go to the king, she asked for nothing other than what Hegai, the king's eunuch who was in charge of the harem, suggested. And Esther won the favor of everyone who saw her" (Esther 2:13-15).

The year of beauty treatments was coming to an end, and Esther could feel the tension building among the girls in the harem. She could see it in their eyes when they passed, going to and from the hot baths. Her maidens had told her there were fights breaking out between some of the competitors. In some cases, it had been so bad that hair-pulling and biting had occurred. Thanks to Hegai, she and her maidens had been moved from where the majority of competitors lived into what were considered to be the king's best apartments. Even though she may have been gossiped about for such a move, she didn't fear any bodily harm.[1]

Though she and her maidens had been somewhat distanced from

the other "competitors" in recent months, they still heard rumors that several maidens had already been summoned and returned to the harem of concubines in the care of Shaashgaz. They heard that this had brought great sorrow to those who were rejected, but hope to those who remained. [2]

As for Esther, she was at peace and confident that Jehovah's will would be done. Whether His will was for her to be one among many of the king's concubines or to be his chosen queen, she was at peace in her heart. Her confidence did not rest in the selection of an earthly king, but in that of a heavenly One.

In recent weeks, Hegai and Esther had combed through the various and sundry collection of jewelry, ornaments, and apparel from which she could select when it came time to go before the king. The variety of exquisite possibilities was overwhelming. Her senses were overloaded with the color, fabric, gold, silver, gems, and fragrances—every precious jewel and erotic scent known to mankind. Hegai had taught her so much, and yet she wondered which would be the wisest to choose. *"After a year of having little voice in any of my daily choices, this is my first real opportunity to show everyone in the palace that I have more than natural beauty to offer,"* she mused. *"I have a brain!"*

Those thoughts might have seemed brazen and brash a week ago, but now Esther was beginning to feel the pressure of making the most important wardrobe choice of her entire life. It wasn't even that she cared so much about the outcome of the king's decision, for she knew that whatever it was, her life rested in the hands of God. However, the pressure to be the best that God had made her to be and to represent His goodness and mercy meant everything to her. Besides that, she didn't want to misrepresent Hegai's best efforts, either.

While pondering these things, she became perplexed by the rise in her emotions. She didn't feel like a yearning psalmist or a frustrated prophet of antiquity; she felt like a stymied teen in need of enlightenment and release all at the same time. Feeling her emotions building, she immediately positioned herself in her favorite posture of petition and began to confess, *"Lord, things are getting a little out of sync around here. For months all I've heard from You and master Hegai is 'surrender.' Surrender, surrender, surrender. That's all I've heard month after month, either in word or by gesture, for almost a year now, and that's all I've done. I've even gotten used to it; in fact, I even enjoy it. I trust master Hegai now like I've always trusted Cousin Mordecai."*

Hegai, though devoted to the king and his every bidding, had now become her friend; she trusted him. He had been kind to her in numerous ways on many occasions. Though she knew that it would be to his advantage if the king selected her to be his next queen, she also believed that Hegai had her best interest in mind, as well. In recent weeks, he had even begun to exhibit some signs of fatherly care toward her. While he attempted not to show it, she knew that he had grown attached to her, as she had to him. She hoped that they would remain friends, regardless of the outcome of the king's selection.

She felt her frustration growing as she considered again the choice she would soon have to make, and her prayer became the honest confession of a young woman to her most trusted confidante. *"Now Hegai tells me that I need to start activating my brain again—at least for the purpose of one focused evening. What?! Reactivate my brain after a year—and reactivate it to choose something to wear before the king?! I can't! I won't! Oh, I have so many thoughts right now, Lord."* She groaned slightly as the tension within her became too much to contain. She was unaware of her tightly clenched fists and set jaw as she continued to vent her internal struggle to her Father God.

"How can I possibly choose something to wear that's fitting for a queen? Everything master Hegai has shown me is fitting for a queen, as far as I can see. I know I've been mentored well by You and by him in these months; but the bottom line is, as You well know, I am but a surrendered handmaiden in Your hand, Lord. It's there that I shall remain."

She sighed as her frustration began to give way and her faith began to build. She was relaxed and at ease now as her answer quietly made its way into her spirit. *"Thank you, Lord. That's it, isn't it! I shall remain under the shadow of Your wing and of that of master Hegai. I will defer to his wise tutelage once again. I will give the choice to him. The 'surrendered' will surrender once again. Lead on, Oh King Eternal, for in You I am secure."*

TRANSITIONS OF LIFE

Esther was so very wise to remain under the tutelage of her faithful mentor Hegai. As an American woman in this contemporary generation, it is difficult to imagine not making a decision of my own for an entire year. Then, having to make one about what to wear, knowing that my choice would affect the course of my destiny for the rest of my life, would surely short-circuit every cell in my brain.

As we all know, a year can go by quickly when we are surrendered to the Lord, allowing Him to work in our lives. Certainly this year of Esther's life must have moved slowly, at first, and then all-too-quickly toward the end, as most transitions do. It seems that all transitions in life have their panic moments and looming questions, and just when those are calmed and answered, the next transition greets us at the door.

I can still remember going to my first youth camp. The summer before, I couldn't wait to get there. In fact, I thought the following school year would never end. When I finally got there, with my bedroll under one arm, a Bible in one hand, and my suitcase in the other, all the bunks looked full. They were full! They were full of confident looking girls who were a year or two older than me; at least, they looked older and more experienced. Suddenly I felt like I had arrived before I was invited. Just as I turned around to leave, an older, experienced camper caught my eye and motioned to me to come over to a bunk next to hers. I plopped down on the bunk with gratefulness in my heart and *"What do I do now?"* on my lips.

The next transition season I remember was the first real date—the kind you go on without your parents driving the car. I took hours trying to figure out what to wear and how to fix my hair, and I spent an equal amount of time deciding whether I should answer the door when he arrived or let someone else in the family do it. He arrived, I went, and even though he was my friend, I suddenly couldn't formulate my words into an intelligible sentence, because this was "a date"—horror of horrors! When we both finally relaxed enough for the conversation to flow comfortably, the evening was over, and the dreaded "goodnight" at the door awaited us both. My heart was palpitating and questions raced through the maze in my mind. *"Do I invite him in? Do I shake his hand, kiss him goodnight, or turn and run without even a polite whisper of 'thank you for a nice evening'?"* All of this happened within a tortured moment while I pondered, *"I wonder what my older sister would do? Oh no, I don't have an older sister! I wonder what somebody's—anybody's—older sister would do right now!"*

With that question finally answered, behold, the next transition was waiting. It was cloaked in months of planning before the "big day"—the wedding day. When it finally arrived, I stood at the back of the church on my father's arm, waiting to walk down the aisle, and all I could think was, *"I'm just a few steps away from the rest of my life! Daddy, should I go?"*

It wasn't too many years after that transition before the next one showed up. If you have ever had a baby, you certainly know what it's like. It seemed as if the time would never arrive when I could hold that new life in my arms. Then the labor began, and as I cut the circulation off in my husband's hand by squeezing it so tightly, thoughts of *"I don't think I can do this"* began to fill my mind. When the delivery was made and emotions of joy and elation filled my heart, they placed that precious newborn into my arms. Suddenly, the realization of the overwhelming responsibility that I had for that new life hit me, and all I could think was, *"This is an eternal soul; what do I do now? Mom, where are you?!"*

Many other women have had similar transitions in their own lives. For most of us, these other kinds of transition are probably a tad more relatable than a nationwide beauty pageant.

> *"Whether changes are found in first dates, first babies, or first days at camp, they all have the common ground of panicked moments and imploring questions."*

Whether changes are found in first dates, first babies, or first days at camp, they all have the common ground of panicked moments and imploring questions.

A wise woman is one who not only looks for mentors, but who embraces them and invites them into her life. She doesn't balk at opportunities to learn from another, but she is grateful for the opportunity to put her strength together with another who is further along in the journey of life.

MENTORS WORTH FOLLOWING

One realization that I came to early in life was that I needed mentoring in my life; whether it was to come through a parent, a sibling, a friend or an instructor, I needed help. I am personally thankful for many wonderful mentors in my life.

One very special mentor to me is a woman by the name of Edie Iverson. She and her husband, Dick, pastored a church in Portland, Oregon, for over forty years. With the grace of God and their faithful leadership, the church grew from thirteen people to over three thousand people. Together they started a publishing company, a Christian school for children, a Bible college, a missions department, and a fellowship group for pastors around the world called "Ministers' Fellowship International."

Over the years, Edie set a disciple's feast before me continually, as she led the way in teaching, counseling, and administrating events for women. She led worship in the main church services, administrated the Sunday school program, and exhorted the congregation faithfully. She was also the Dean of Women of Portland Bible College for sixteen years. She gave herself faithfully and completely to the people in our local church for a major portion of her life.

Though she and her husband, Dick Iverson, have retired from the senior pastor position in the local church, Edie continues to be an example to me in the way that she ministers effectively and capably to pastors and leaders around the world. Through all these years, she has also been a faithful wife and mother. All of her children and grandchildren are serving the Lord today.

One of the main ways in which Edie mentored me was by her example of a woman who lived a surrendered life. I learned from her that living a submissive or surrendered life does not mean that you check your brain at the door. True submission comes from having something to submit, something to offer.

". . .living a submissive or surrendered life does not mean that you check your brain at the door."

Edie is an intelligent woman with perceptive insight. She has always been a discerning and knowledgeable leader within her own rite. I watched her choose to yield her insights to others many times over the years. Even if her perspective carried more wisdom than one being proffered, she wisely perceived that building a team was more important than pushing her own agenda. She purposely kept herself in a position of humility, and that in turn brought honor to her and helped build a faithful team. In the forty years that she and her husband pastored the church in Portland, it never once experienced a church split or a leadership team split. Both Edie and her husband were examples to the people they pastored of two lives surrendered to the will and purposes of God.

It wasn't just Edie's ability to administrate, teach, or counsel that trained me in working with people, but it was the way she did these things that truly mentored me. It was the grace in her speech, the kindness in her deeds, and the joy in her spirit that taught me more than any class she ever taught or any meeting she ever led. It was the love she gave freely, the time she gave willingly, and the faith in her God that she poured out in every step she took and in every word she spoke. It was these attributes that will forever remain engraved on my heart. These were the "beauty treatments" she massaged into my spirit, week by week and year by year. Today Edie travels extensively with her husband, but she continues to mentor me by being my friend.

Paul writes in 1 Corinthians 4:15, *"Even though you have ten thousand guardians in Christ, you do not have many fathers, for in Christ Jesus I became your father through the gospel."*

As Paul suggests, there are perhaps fewer mentors groomed as "spiritual mothers and fathers" in the truest sense than there are those willing to advise and offer instruction. However, when you find one of these gems, capture him or her with your hungry heart, surrender your predisposed mindset, and learn from him or her the true riches in Christ. Seek out spiritual mentors; I have found them to be everywhere, really. You just have to look through God's eyes to see them.

Don't expect the mentors that God has designed for you to look like someone else's mentor. Typically, first mentors are parents; Esther had a cousin instead. Typically, secondary mentors are teachers or mothers of friends; Esther had a fashion consultant and eunuch. Yours may come in the form of a coach, or a doctor, or a Sunday school teacher. I don't know what yours will look like, but I do know that you will likely need to lay down your preconceived ideas before you will recognize them.

"There is not one mentor who can teach it all or offer one method by which to learn it all."

There is not one mentor who can teach it all or offer one method by which to learn it all. Remember, Esther had Mordecai, and then she had Hegai. She listened and learned from them both, but God remained her primary mentor. He was the only one who could go wherever she went, the only one who could promise that He would always be by her side. It was Mordecai and Hegai's tutelage, combined with the whisperings of God's wisdom, as well as the attributes that He alone had given her, that gave her entrance to the king.

In the early 1900s, one young woman by the name of Evangeline Booth found in her father a true and trusted mentor. Her three sisters before her had all married with their father's blessing, and she wanted to marry a certain young man of her desire. He was a Christian and was actively involved in the Salvation Army alongside her family and friends, but her father did not feel that he could place his blessing on this marriage.

Evangeline submitted to her father, her "Hegai," and continued to serve the Lord joyfully and effectively in her gift of singleness for the remainder of her life. She was promoted to a general's position in the Salvation Army in 1904. Reports say that she *could hold large audiences spellbound for hours* with her speaking gift. She also launched her "World for God" campaigns during these years. These campaigns included travel, speaking, and initiating new centers for work throughout the world. One of her meetings in India drew a crowd of more than twenty thousand people.[3]

Evangeline Booth served the Salvation Army in America for thirty years. Through the power of her surrendered life, many poor, destitute, and homeless people were ministered to and rescued from lives of despair. Historians say that she had tens of thousands of loyal followers who revered her to the very end.

As challenging as it must have been for her to submit to her father's guidance when she so desired to be married, she obviously surrendered to the Lord and His will in this decision. As she yielded to the wisdom of the Lord and her father, she prospered perhaps in ways that she may have never been able to within the context of marriage. She refused to let this personal disappointment rob her of a fruitful destiny. Her heart reached across the generations and was knit together with Esther's, as she cleaved to her God and to her "Hegai" and effectively served the purposes of God in her generation.

MENTORING MOMENTS

Mentoring can be done in a moment or in a month. It can be done over a year or over a lifetime. It can be conveyed in words or in deeds of kindness. Mentoring is not limited to a set of rules or certain methods of

> *"The riches
> of mentoring are
> found when hearts
> connect. . ."*

development. The riches of mentoring are found when hearts connect and should not be measured in moments or hours spent.

I heard a story recently of a wealthy Christian woman in the city of Chicago. It was the Christmas season and was very cold and snowy outside. As her chauffeur drove her down one of the main streets of Chicago, she noticed a young child, who was obviously homeless, looking in one of the brilliantly displayed storefront windows.

She noticed his threadbare coat, ragged pants, and the bloodstained rags that wrapped his feet, cracked and swollen from worn shoes and severe cold. She also realized that he was not looking at the toys in the large display window. He was looking at some fleece-lined boots in the corner of the window.

She asked the chauffeur to stop the car. She then got out, offered her hand to the boy, and asked him if he would like to go into the store with her. She took him to buy some long thermal underwear first. Then she bought him a new flannel shirt and some new corduroy pants. In a near-by department, she bought him a new heavy coat with a thick fleece lining and a fleece-lined hat with earflaps and a chinstrap. She also bought him a pair of fur-lined mittens. Then she took him to the shoe department. She bought him a pair of heavy wool socks. As she reached for the fleece-lined boots, identical to the ones in the storefront window, it was as if the boy couldn't take the suspense any longer. He looked up at her and inquired, *"Lady, are you God's wife?!"*

She smiled and said, *"No, but I'm one of His daughters."*

He got the boots that he had wanted—the ones he had yearned for! For a few moments of surrender and following the lead, he got the boots. Hopefully, the new outfit helped to warm his heart as well as his body. He was mentored in the moment by the kindness of a generous-hearted woman and the compassion of a Savior.

Jesus Christ cares about every detail of your life. Whether you have an earnest need for some warm boots, an outfit to impress a king, or something in-between, Jesus cares. He cares enough to place mentors in your pathway to guide you along the way. Look through His eyes, and you will see them where you may least expect them. Whether you find a mentor in a parent, a pastor, or a kind passerby, look for the wisdom of Christ in people. When you find His wisdom, surrender; yield to the Master as He molds your heart and shapes your perspective. Through mentors, capture the lessons that are the true instructions to you from the Lord, for tomorrow you may be in the presence of a king.

> *"Whether you find a mentor in a parent, a pastor, or a kind passerby, look for the wisdom of Christ in people."*

Lives of Surrender

2 CHR. 30:8   *"Now be ye not stiffnecked, as your fathers were, but yield yourselves unto the LORD, and enter into his sanctuary, which he hath sanctified for ever: and serve the LORD your God, that the fierceness of his wrath may turn away from you." (KJV)*

ROM. 6:13   *"Neither yield ye your members as instruments of unrighteousness unto sin: but yield yourselves unto God, as those that are alive from the dead, and your members as instruments of righteousness unto God." (KJV)*

ROM. 6:16   *"Know ye not, that to whom ye yield yourselves servants to obey, his servants ye are to whom ye obey; whether of sin unto death, or of obedience unto righteousness?" (KJV)*

ROM. 6:19   *"I speak after the manner of men because of the infirmity of your flesh: for as ye have yielded your members servants to uncleanness and to iniquity unto iniquity; even so now yield your members servants to righteousness unto holiness." (KJV)*

EPH. 5:22   *"Wives, submit yourselves unto your own husbands, as unto the Lord." (KJV)*

COL. 3:18   *"Wives, submit yourselves unto your own husbands, as it is fit in the Lord." (KJV)*

HEB. 13:17   *"Obey them that have the rule over you, and submit yourselves: for they watch for your souls, as they that must give account, that they may do it with joy, and not with grief: for that is unprofitable for you." (KJV)*

JAMES 4:7 *"Submit yourselves therefore to God. Resist the devil, and he will flee from you." (KJV)*

1 PET. 2:13 *"Submit yourselves to every ordinance of man for the Lord's sake: whether it be to the king, as supreme;" (KJV)*

1 PET. 5:5 *"Likewise, ye younger, submit yourselves unto the elder. Yea, all of you be subject one to another, and be clothed with humility: for God resisteth the proud, and giveth grace to the humble." (KJV)*

NOTES

1   "... he changed her and her maids into the best of the house of the women, i.e., he took them out of the ordinary rooms and placed them in the best apartments, probably in the state-rooms, where those who were accustomed to be brought to the king used to dwell." Keil & Delitzsch, *Commentary on the Old Testament*, PC Study Bible, (Nashville: Nelson, 1998).

2   "After the king had once taken them to his bed, they were made recluses ever after, except the king pleased at any time to send for them; they were looked upon as secondary wives, were maintained by the king accordingly, and might not marry." *Matthew Henry's Commentary*, PC Study Bible, (Nashville: Nelson, 1998).

3   Ruth A. Tucker and Walter Liefeld, *Daughters of the Church, Women and Ministry from New Testament Times to the Present* (Grand Rapids: Zondervan, 1987), 373.

Partners of Provision

THE HIDDEN POWER OF A SURRENDERED LIFE

The Choosing of the Lord

"She was taken to King Xerxes in the royal residence in the tenth month, the month of Tebeth, in the seventh year of his reign. Now the king was attracted to Esther more than to any of the other women, and she won his favor and approval more than any of the other virgins. So he set a royal crown on her head and made her queen instead of Vashti. And the king gave a great banquet, Esther's banquet, for all his nobles and officials. He proclaimed a holiday throughout the provinces and distributed gifts with royal liberality" (Esther 2:16-18).

Stories among the servants flew from one apartment to another. The continual parade of queenly contestants to the king's quarters was weekly now, sometimes daily. The fighting and blatant verbal abuse among the contestants was intensifying and becoming more shocking than before. There were also rumors of devastated contestants who followed up their night with the king with self-inflicted beatings and attempted suicide.

Hegai sternly warned Esther's maidens not to upset her with some of the gruesome details that they had all heard. Aware that Esther was filled with genuine love and compassion for her "fellow contestants," the servants were all very selective in what they shared with her. Afraid that she would wear herself out fasting and praying through the night if she knew of such events, neither Hegai nor Esther's maidens wanted to ruin her chances of ascendancy to the throne, so they kept silent. There could be no choosing of a queen without comparisons being made; they all knew that. However, the realities of such a contest were abhorrent.

Esther could feel that Hegai and her maidens were being selective and cautious in what they said to her these days, but she was unsure why. She realized that none of her competitors had a personal relationship with Jehovah and would likely interpret the king's rejection as a judgment of their personal worth, and she was filled with compassion for them. She longed to minister to them the hope and life that lived within her. In months prior, when she had spent time with them in the hot baths, she could read the loneliness and fear in their determined and hard countenances. They feigned bravery, but their occasional tears and tightened voices betrayed their false display of self-assurance. They were as frightened as she had been initially, and her heart went out to them. She yearned for an opportunity to offer them more than what any earthly king could, a personal relationship with a living God, even if sharing her faith meant being sentenced to a concubine's destiny.

She realized that her day to be paraded before the king was very near. Hegai had made his final selection of her "queenly attire" several weeks ago; everything had been hemmed and tucked to perfection. They had decided upon the perfect hairstyle for such an occasion, not too stiff and untouchable nor overtly seductive, just soft and appealing. They had rehearsed her walk, her bow, and her stance repeatedly; her every movement flowed with a majestic look and just a touch of humble subservience. Hegai had considered carefully the king's possible questions and what her responses should be. He trained her in how to say just enough—not too much—as a noble queen would. If, perchance, the king should make overtures toward her, they had discussed thoroughly, in more detail than Esther had ever desired to know, the wifely art of bringing pleasure to a man, while revealing her virginal innocence.

The word had come that Esther's day to be presented before King Xerxes was to be within the week. As she pondered the nearness of her "day in court," her mind raced with many questions. *"Will I really be able to be calm and at peace in the presence of such an unruly despot, or will my emotions betray me and collide in a great whirlwind, causing me to tremble in his presence? Will I stumble as I enter his chambers, or will I glide across the floor like a swan on a lake at sunrise? Will I remember all that I have been taught, or will I falter in word and in deed? Will I find disdain and rejection in his presence or love and adoration? Will he be cruel or kind? Will he mock me or adore me?"*

Her thoughts continued like an unending marathon of sudden panic-filled ponderings. *"Am I to be as Abraham's Isaac, an unknowing lamb led to the slaughter? Will there be a ram in the thicket for me, like there was for him? Will I be a loveless concubine, a 'second wife' for the rest of my days, or will I find love in the arms of a king? Will I be married to a man who still longs for his previous wife, or will he have eyes only for me?"*

Mordecai was no longer in view, and Hegai's image was quickly fading. She was perplexed, as fear continued to edge its way into her heart. *"Who will be my partner, my kinsman, my mentor and guide in the future? Will I be alone as I enter the king's presence, or will the Lord go before me? Will the outcome of our meeting be determined by an earthly king and his personal attendants or by the one true God? What should I expect? What should I anticipate—the will of a king or the will of my God?"*

These questions continually replayed themselves through Esther's mind, in intermittent racing patterns as well as slow motion, in the days immediately leading up to her official encounter with King Xerxes. However, through the days of counsel with Hegai and precious moments with her King of Kings, she came to a resolve within her own spirit by the time the day of presentation arrived. The choosing would not be Xerxes'; it would be Jehovah's.

Though her heart had momentary palpitations, and uncertainty attempted to thwart the peace that surpassed even her own understanding, her petitions, on that early morning, were of utmost confidence in God.

Her prayer echoed the words of the psalmist of old and rang with praise to the God of her people. *"I will praise the Lord, who counsels me;*

even at night my heart instructs me. I have set the Lord always before me. Because he is at my right hand, I will not be shaken. Therefore my heart is glad and my tongue rejoices; my body also will rest secure, because you will not abandon me.[1] *Thank You, Jehovah, for Your comfort and Your counsel in recent days. How thankful I am that I have never had to walk alone in my journey. Man has not chosen my pathway, but You alone.*

"You are a shield around me, O Lord; you bestow glory on me and lift up my head. To the Lord I cry aloud, and He answers me from His holy hill.[2] *Thank You, for You are ever present, Lord. Your word is a lamp to my feet and a light for my path.*[3]

"Whisper in my ear and direct me in my pathway, God, for my day to go before the king has come. Once this day is over, my course will be set for the rest of my life—at least it looks that way to me from this apartment window. You have said in days of old that you 'watch over the way of the righteous.'[4] *Please watch over me this day, Lord. According to Your love remember me, for you are good, O Lord.*[5] *Yes, according to Your love remember me, for You alone are good."*

MONSTERS THAT STARE

Such a sacrifice of time and commitment to the process of learning, all for the sake of being chosen in one day, one moment of time, could arouse many varied emotions. Self-examination and comparison may have been monsters that stared Esther in the face, just as they have confronted many others throughout the centuries.

Because Esther had been placed in the best apartment and shown special favor from the head chamberlain, Hegai, she probably did have to face comparison by the other contestants. She may have also felt the spirit of competition within herself. One can only speculate on these things, of course, but it is not unrealistic to believe that this may have happened. Esther had to accept her own limitations and do the best with what assets she had been given, just as we all do.

President Harry Truman once said, *"Fame is a vapor, popularity an accident; riches sprout wings. The only thing that lasts is character."* Over-indulgence in self-examination and comparison with others would have neither helped nor resulted in a favorable decision on Esther's behalf. Her character and the steadfastness of her relationship with the Lord carried her through. That same formula works today.

If you have ever been a participant in statewide or national beauty pageants, Esther's story may stir in you kindred emotions. If so, you can probably identify with her emotional ups and downs. I'm sure you are extremely grateful that your marriage selection was not or will not be determined by such a short-lived, externally-based pageant, but you can probably identify with the very real issues of unwise comparison.

Even if you have not been in such a pageant, you can likely relate to some of Esther's emotions in regard to being chosen. Remember how it felt to play childhood neighborhood games, such as "Red Rover, Red Rover"? Can you recall your feelings during the selection process for the cheerleader squad or girls' volleyball team, high school homecoming queen, or beauty pageants within the local community? Maybe in your adult world, you have had to await the selection process for partnership in a firm, a promotion on the job, or advancement in your ministry position.

Some beauty pageant contestants say that the adrenaline rush is worth every tense moment. However, most contestants admit that, while they wouldn't trade the experience for any other, there are moments when they struggle with self-imposed, over-indulgent self-examination and comparison with others. This kind of comparison is easily observed in athletes, musicians, and artists, as well as other competitors during science fairs, spelling contests, agricultural fairs, chess contests, etc. Comparison also rears its ugly head in all forms of business life in the adult world. We all have moments of self-examination, when we compare our talents or skills with those of our peers. We all can relate to the desire to be chosen as the best candidate.

Even if your life is not set in an arena of competition, you must accept your own liabilities and assets. Mind-consuming self-examination and comparison with others, sadly, is a plague in the body of Christ that needs

> *"Mind-consuming self-examination and comparison with others. . . needs to be eradicated from the Christian community."*

to be eradicated from the Christian community. 2 Corinthians 10:12 says, *"We do not dare to classify or compare ourselves with some who commend themselves. When they measure themselves by themselves and compare themselves with themselves, they are not wise."*

Romans 12:3-6 says, *". . . Do not think of yourself more highly than you ought but rather think of yourself with sober judgment, in accordance with the measure of faith God has given you. Just as each of us has one body with many members, and these members do not all have the same function, so in Christ we who are many form one body, and each member belongs to all the others. We have different gifts, according to the grace given us . . ."*

May we follow the advice of this wise apostle and not live with competitive "pageants," comparing ourselves with each other. "Pageants" can come into our adult lives in the form of job promotions, ministry advancements, college scholarships, etc. They can ruin friendships and distort our perspectives of ourselves. Regardless of the apparent unfairness of life, we must move on into the future, embracing in friendship those with whom we come in contact, not wasting precious emotional energy comparing "apples with pears."

FOCUSING ON GOD

According to all historical accounts, it is obvious that God, in His love, did remember Esther on that day of choosing. Whether she was selected by Xerxes or not, she could not allow her focus to rest on that possibility alone on the day of her official presentation. Her focus had to remain on God's love and His will. Yearning after His will is what had carried her this far, and it alone would illumine her pathway at this juncture. Esther's focus speaks to us in our contemporary situations, also. When we stand before a scholarship board or an imposing boss, we too must remain focused on God's will.

Hegai had trained Esther in royal conversation and charm and dressed her like a queen, but the presentation of her queenly assets would be distinguished from all others only by the Lord's anointing. By anyone's estimation, her natural beauty was striking, but her wisdom and virtue were the assets that would set her apart from the other damsels. All were diamonds that sparkled, but only one was placed in settings of gold wrought by the Master's hand for this particular place of prominence. Just as our colleagues and fellow workers are equally capable, we too must rely on the Lord's anointing in our lives to set us apart for times of promotion. It is God who opens doors that no one can shut, and He does so in accordance with His will and His timing.

> *"It is God who opens doors that no one can shut, and He does so in accordance with His will and His timing."*

Esther had pondered Hannah's song of declaration when yielding to the planting of the Lord, and what a comfort it must have been to her at this time of choosing, as well. *"He raises the poor from the dust and lifts the needy from the ash heap; He seats them with princes and has them inherit a throne of honor. For the foundations of the earth are the Lord's; upon them He has set the world"* (1 Samuel 2:8).

Who would have thought that a Jewess hidden away in a Persian palace, a captive in a land far from home, and an orphan with only one relative who cared, would be chosen to be the queen of such a great empire? Only God. When God does the choosing, no man can dispute it. *"What, then, shall we say in response to this? If God is for us, who can be against us?"* (Romans 8:31).

Just as Esther's personal pageant experience was an opportunity for the Lord to shine through her, my friend, Sara, writes thoughts of her experience in the Miss Oregon pageant:

I knew the Lord was with me, shining through me as I sang, walked on stage, and talked with the judges and pageant officials. My confidence definitely did not come from a feeling that I was the most talented, beautiful, poised, or intelligent, because there was an intense intimidation factor from the pressures of competition and comparison with the other contestants—some of whom had prepared for the Miss America pageant their entire lives. It came from His Spirit flowing through me that made me different from the rest. It was the fact that He had purposed me to be in this position and that for some reason, through something so shallow as a beauty pageant, He was showing me that I had been called "for such a time as this," to be in the secular spotlight making an impact for Him.

All this from a little girl with a dream to sing for the Lord. I had always thought I would have been happy just being a Christian singer within the church community, but the Lord has always taken me way out of my comfort zone and expanded my limited ideas of what His purpose for my life was. Even today, I'm given many media opportunities and invited places I would not have been without the secular platform of my former Miss Oregon title. The Lord knows what grabs the attention of the secular, depraved person and that is position, possessions, and popularity. In my case, it seems He used a "success" in their eyes to make an impression on the surface; then He revealed the deeper success of a life sold out to the Lord, not to the world and all its worthless, temporary values.[6]

Just as Sara was chosen by God and a panel of judges to be given the title of Miss Oregon, Esther was chosen by God and the king of Persia to be the queen of a great kingdom. From the moment King Xerxes met her, he did not see any of the other competitors from the awaiting harem. His mind was set, and his choice was made. The king loved Esther more than any of the other women who had come before him. It was time to party! He immediately made arrangements to place the royal crown upon Esther's head and pronounce her queen. This was done in the seventh year of his reign. Since he had divorced Vashti in the third year and had now been without a queen for four years, he made the coronation plans without hesitation.

In Esther's honor at her coronation, the king gave a great feast for all of his nobles and officials and called it "Esther's banquet." The assumption here is that, in compliance with the king, Esther made a public appearance, which Vashti had refused to do. This would have been done to bring honor to both her and the king. It would have reflected her obedience to him at a banquet where, in likeness, Vashti had rebelled against him.

He also proclaimed a holiday throughout the provinces and distributed gifts with great liberality. This holiday probably included a day off, as well as a remission of taxes.[7] Though proclaiming such a holiday was a common practice among Oriental kings, since there was not a coronation every day or every year, this holiday would have introduced Esther into the kingdom community with great favor. This was, indeed, a day to rejoice.

Granted, it had been a year of uprooting and transplanting, of solitude and invasion of privacy for Esther, but it had also been a time of unique closeness with the Master. It was a year that ended in the grandest celebration that she had ever experienced.

SOLITARY SEASONS THAT MOVE US ONWARD.

If we live surrendered lives, we should not be alarmed when similar experiences occur in our own lives. Uprooting and transplanting, solitary sea-

> *"We should neither be surprised by trials and tribulations, nor should we anticipate them at every turn in the road."*

sons, and times of invaded privacy come to all of us. Seasons of being overlooked and times of being mis-judged come to everyone. Whether we are in a positions of support or supervision, once the selection process has been completed, it is time to move on. We should neither be surprised by trials and tribulations, nor should we anticipate them at every turn in the road. The anticipation of negative experiences at every turn in life makes for a slow-moving journey of drudgery.

On the other hand, there will be many times to rejoice in God and party in His presence. Be careful not to ruin these moments by borrowing anticipated worries from the tomorrows; enjoy them. When you come out of a period of challenge, rejoice in the rains of refreshing; tomorrow's challenges will arrive soon enough. Most of the seasons in your life will have more bright spots than dark ones, if you look for them.

Sarah Hale was a woman who had faced seasons of confusion and darkness in her life and yet still had a heart to celebrate. She was born in 1788. By the time she was thirty-four years old, she was a widow with five children to support. During the first two years after her husband died, she attempted to start a millinery business but failed. She then decided to try writing and published her first novel, *Northwood*, in 1827.

Soon after the publication of her novel, she moved to Boston and became an editor for *Ladies Magazine* and later edited *Lady's Book*, another women's magazine. Lady's Book magazine became very popular among women in her day. Through her work as editor, Sarah dedicated herself and the magazine to "the progress of female improvement." She also continued to write during this time. Her most well-known work is the nursery rhyme, "Mary Had a Little Lamb."

Sarah accomplished much through her writing, editing, and administrative gifts and felt thankful to the Lord for the way in which He had orchestrated her life. She felt that she had much for which to rejoice.

She was so committed to gratefulness within her own spirit that she desired to see a national day designated to giving thanks to God. Her inspiration was to declare a thanksgiving holiday each year throughout the nation. Many statewide congressmen and senators rejected her idea on the basis of separation of church and state. One state governor even called her idea "theatrical claptrap."

With determination, Sarah lobbied congress year after year. By the year 1859, thirty states had declared Thanksgiving holidays on the last Thursday of November. From that point on, Sarah began to lobby Washington congressmen and made her focus a national holiday of Thanksgiving. On September 28, 1863, in the midst of the Civil War, she wrote to President Abraham Lincoln, requesting that he proclaim an annual day of thanksgiving. Due to recent Union victories at Gettysburg, Lincoln agreed to her request. On October 3, 1863, he officially designated the last Thursday of November in 1863 as a national day of thanksgiving.

It took Sarah Hale thirty-six years to accomplish her goal, but she hit the mark with her persistence. She was chosen by the Lord and her President to lead the way in a declaration of national gratefulness for God's goodness to America. Her proposal was the beginning of many days of focused thankfulness in American homes throughout the genera-tions to come. Sarah died on April 30, 1879, at ninety-one years of age. She wrote her last editorial at the age of ninety. A portion of it reads:

> *And now, having reached my ninetieth year, I must bid farewell to my countrywomen, with the hope that this work of half a century may be blessed to the furtherance of their happiness and usefulness in their Divinely appointed sphere. New avenues for higher culture and for good works are opening before them, which fifty years ago were unknown. That they may improve these opportunities, and be faithful to their high vocation, is my heartfelt prayer.*[8]

Though Sarah was never in a pageant and was never chosen by a king to be a queen, she, like Esther, was chosen by the Lord to do a great work. In the midst of contradiction and rejection, her persistence and surrender to the Lord's will in her life brought about a holiday in which Americans everywhere reflect upon gratefulness. Whether Americans grasp hands around a sumptuous dinner table, join in warmhearted banter around a football game, or pray together with tears of thankfulness in their eyes, they celebrate a day centered on gratefulness.

Esther's king understood nothing of the real celebration in his queen's heart, but Sarah Hale's president, being of kindred spirit, understood everything about the message in hers. "Esther's banquet," celebrated in naive elation, and Sarah's feast, celebrated in sincere faith, were both holidays that declared a message for all to hear—a message of gratefulness.

No matter what the trial or test, whether it is an adjustment to a new location, a tedious beauty treatment, or a moment of precarious choosing, the Lord never wastes anything for those who are surrendered to Him. He patiently takes the heartfelt confessions of trust and conscientiously weaves each strand together into an extraordinary tapestry that will amaze the eye of every beholder. He is always at work; He never slumbers nor sleeps.[9]

Esther's year in the palace and coronation banquet was merely a prerequisite to the trial and celebration that was yet to come for her and her people. She had been chosen "for such a time as this," and it was the time to rejoice. Though tests and trials come, when the Lord Most High makes His choice and blessings begin to fall, there is celebrating to be done. Rejoice, for the choosing of the Lord and the surrender of a fair maiden could bring about the rescue of a generation!

The Bible suggests nine ways to rejoice and worship God.[10]

SPEAK!

ROM. 15:6   *"With one voice glorify the God and Father of our Lord Jesus Christ."*

ACTS 4:24   *"And when they heard this, they lifted their voice to God with one accord, and said . . ."*

PS. 66:3   *"Say to God, 'How awesome are Thy works!'"*

"I would warn those who are cultured, quiet, self-possessed, poised and sophisticated, that if they are embarrassed in church when some happy Christian says "Amen!" they may actually be in need of some spiritual enlightenment. The worshipping saints of God in the body of Christ have often been a little bit noisy." (A.W. Tozer)

SING!

PS. 104:33   *"I will sing to the Lord as long as I live; I will sing praise to my God while I have my being."*

PS. 47:6   *"Sing praises to God, sing praises! Sing praises to our King, sing praises!"*

EPH. 5:19   *"Speaking to one another in psalms and hymns and spiritual songs, singing and making melody with your heart to the Lord."*

"Sing lustily, and with a good courage. Beware of singing as if you were half dead, or half asleep; but lift up your voice with strength. Be no more afraid of your voice now, nor more ashamed of its being heard, than when you sung the songs of Satan. . . . Above all, sing spiritually. Have an eye to God in

every word you sing. Aim at pleasing Him more than yourself, or any other creature. In order to do this, attend strictly to the sense of what you sing; and see that your heart is not carried away with the sound but offered to God continually; so shall your singing be such as the Lord will approve of here, and reward when he cometh in the clouds of heaven." (John Wesley)

SHOUT!

EZRA 3:13 *"The people shouted with a loud shout, and the sound was heard far away."*

PS. 32:11 *"Be glad in the Lord, and rejoice, ye righteous; and shout for joy, all ye that are upright in heart."*

PS. 35:27 *"Let them shout for joy, and be glad, that favour my righteous cause."*

"Israel's worship was distinctly vocal in character; it is to shout exultantly. It was normally accompanied with such instruments as produced a vigorous and loud noise. But the shout or cry of praise reinforced by loud instrumental noise is not an end in itself, nor is it merely expressive of strong religious emotion. The purpose of the praise cry (tehillah) or the ringing cry (rinnah) is to convey the life-soul of the worshipper to God." (A.S. Herbert)

LIFT HANDS!

LAM. 3:41 *"Let us lift up our heart with our hands unto God in the heavens."*

PS. 119:48 *"And I shall lift up my hands to Thy commandments, which I love; and I will meditate on Thy statutes."*

1 TIM. 2:8 *"Therefore I want the men in every place to pray, lifting up holy hands, without wrath and dissension."*

"In our case, not only do we raise our hands, we even spread them out, and, taking our model from the Lord's passion, even in prayer we confess to Christ." (Tertullian)

"Hands are the symbols of supplication. Outstretched hands stand for an appeal for help. It is the silent yet eloquent attitude of a helpless soul standing before God, appealing for mercy and grace." (E.M. Bounds)

PLAY INSTRUMENTS!

1 CHRON. 23:5 *"And 4,000 were praising the Lord with the instruments which David made for giving praise."*

PS. 150; 1 CHRON. 25; REV. 5:8; 14:2; 8:2; 9:14; 18:22

"Whatever may have been the exact description of the instruments of Bible times, enough information shows that they fell into the same basic categories as mentioned in Psalm 150. That is, stringed, wind, and percussion instruments." (Kevin Conner)

CLAP!

PS. 47:1 *"Clap your hands, all people! Shout to God with loud songs of joy!"*

ISA. 55:12 *"The trees of the field will clap their hands."*

PS. 98:8 *"Let the rivers clap their hands."*

"The name of Jesus has often made lame men leap as a hart, and has made sad men clap their hands for joy." (Charles Spurgeon)

STAND!

PS. 28:7   *"I praise him with my whole body."*

1 CHRON. 23:30   *"And (the Levites were) to stand every morning to thank and praise the Lord, and likewise at evening."*

PS. 135:2-3   *"Ye that stand in the house of the Lord, in the courts of the house of our God, Praise the Lord; for the Lord is good: sing praises unto his name; for it is pleasant."*

"According to Basil, in his 4th century treatise on the Holy Spirit, we stand up to pray on Sunday 'because that day is in some way the image of the future age.' Standing is an active posture. It is the posture of one who had been resurrected." (Marianne H. Micks)

BOW!

PS. 95:6   *"Come, let us worship and bow down; Let us kneel before the Lord our Maker."*

EPH. 3:14   *"I bow my knees unto the Father of our Lord Jesus Christ."*

PHIL. 2:10   *". . . every knee should (or must eventually) bow."*

"Kneeling is a way of saying, 'I fully understand who's Boss here. Far be it from me to try to manipulate you or play games with you. I'm well aware of my status in this relationship, and I deeply appreciate you taking time to interact with me.'" (Dean Merrill)

DANCE!

ECCL. 3:4   *"... and a time to dance."*

2 SAM. 6:14   *"Then David danced before the Lord with all his might ..."*

PS. 149:3   *"Let them praise His name with dancing."*

"Dancing is not a profane thing that one might introduce as if by force into the sanctuaries of our churches. It does not enter into the temples of prayer as a stranger, but rather as a daughter of God. Song is the joy of the voice; dancing is the joy of the body. Together, singing and dancing, both created by God, must, like all his other creatures, praise the Lord. . . . It is thus that God himself, in his word that manifests itself to us in Psalm 150, demands that we dance for his praise. Not as a concession made to the weakness of man does he ask for dancing, but as a valid means of praising him. Who dances for God, then, accomplishes his will." (Lucien Deiss & Gloria Weyman)

NOTES

1 Psalm 16:7-10

2 Psalm 3:3-4

3 Psalm 119:105

4 Psalm 1:6

5 Psalm 24:7

6 Quote from personal testimony of Sara Paulson Brummett, used with permission, 1999; Sara Paulson Brummett, Williams & Associates, Inc. Spiritbound, P.O. Box 292785, Nashville, Tennessee 37229.

7 "Of the honours the king put upon Esther. He graced the solemnity of her coronation with a royal feast (v. 18), at which perhaps Esther, in compliance with the king, made a public appearance, which Vashti had refused to do, that she might have the praise of obedience in the same instance in which the other incurred the blot of disobedience. He also granted a release to the provinces, either a remittance of the taxes in arrear or an act of grace for criminals; as Pilate, at the feast, released a prisoner. This was to add the joy." *Matthew Henry's Commentary*, PC Study Bible, (Nashville: Nelson, 1998).

8 Harold Ivan Smith, *A Singular Devotion* (Fleming H. Revell, 1990), 262.

9 Psalm 121:4

10 These "Nine Psalmic Worship Forms for Today's Church" are excerpts from Ernest Gentile, *Worship God!* (Portland, Ore.: City Bible [formerly Bible Temple], 1994), 146, 156, 160, 173, 181, 192, 198, 209.

Divine Partnering

"When the virgins were assembled a second time, Mordecai was sitting at the king's gate. But Esther had kept secret her family background and nationality just as Mordecai had told her to do, for she continued to follow Mordecai's instructions as she had done when he was bringing her up. During the time Mordecai was sitting at the king's gate, Bigthana and Teresh, two of the king's officers who guarded the doorway, became angry and conspired to assassinate King Xerxes. But Mordecai found out about the plot and told Queen Esther, who in turn reported it to the king, giving credit to Mordecai. And when the report was investigated and found to be true, the two officials were hanged on a gallows. All this was recorded in the book of the annals in the presence of the king" (Esther 2:19-23).

As the resident Queen of Persia, Esther was free to walk the halls and surrounding grounds of the palace. She loved to stroll along the beautiful palace walkways with her attending maidens and greet the various servants of the king as they went about their daily business. As she did so, she always looked forward to sauntering by the gate where Mordecai most often sat. The young palace guards were often a tempting distraction to her attendants, which made it easy for her to speak to him in passing without the suspicion of any onlooker.

Esther had continued to follow Mordecai's advice to keep her Jewish lineage a secret from the king and his associates. Though she was now a queen, she was still a "daughter" to Mordecai. She knew well that Jehovah's protection and blessing were woven within the fabric of her willingness to remain under the covering of this one who had been placed in her life in such a sovereign manner.

Through these sporadic and momentary exchanges, she was able to speak to him regularly, without anyone suspecting their hereditary connection. While they had to maintain somewhat aloof appearances, both of them had adequate opportunity to exchange knowing looks and simple congenialities.

To Esther and Mordecai, these brief encounters were blessings from the Father above and were not to be taken advantage of. These cherished moments made their separation bearable and their spiritual partnership more focused on discerning God's purposes for ordering Esther's steps in such a manner. She didn't come by every day. Neither she nor Mordecai wanted to give anyone reason to suspect their relationship.

Lately, she had found herself actually growing fond of and tender toward her husband, the king. It was as if God were putting a unique care and devotion in her heart toward him. She enjoyed her times with him more of late and felt a kindred desire from him, as well. She found herself wondering if her genuine care for him might translate into love one day; and if his care for her would do the same in him.

She mused, *"Could it be that Jehovah has partnered me, not only with Mordecai and Hegai, but now with the king, as well?"* How strange the ordering of her steps and the choosing of Lord had seemed to her at times. When she was a small girl, she never would have imagined that the intimate desires of her heart could turn toward the feared King Xerxes. She would have never anticipated such a unique partnering to be ordered by the Lord. Yet now, being in the king's presence on a regular basis, she could feel his vulnerabilities, as well as his strengths. She could feel the intermingling of their heartbeats. When his was weak, hers was strong; when hers was apprehensive and shy, his was bold and sure.

While on duty at the gate one day, Mordecai overheard two of the king's officers conspiring together to assassinate the king. He knew Bigthana and Teresh by rank and name, as he did all of the palace guards who worked the main palace doorway on their assigned days. He politely greeted them as he had every other day, and with barely a nod, they distractedly responded in return.

Due to the regularity of his station and his insignificance in their eyes, he had become like an invisible doorpost to them. They vented their anger toward the king to one another in hushed tones, yet with enough volume that Mordecai could easily hear them. His ears were sharp, and their voices rose with intensity. They were filled with anger toward the king for sacrificing so many of their friends and brothers to the battlefields of Greece. They were determined to do away with him before the empire collapsed and before they too were sent to the Grecian killing fields. They were indignant and bent on getting their revenge, boasting to one another that they would surely be honored as heroes and rise in rank quickly after their deed was done.

Realizing that the success of Teresh and Bigthana's plan would not only end the rule of King Xerxes, but would put Esther in harm's way as well, Mordecai determined to report this to his cousin, the queen. Though his hearing was sharp and his spirit watchful, he now needed an avenue for immediate communication. He had hoped to see the queen today, as he frequently did, but the sun was now high in the afternoon sky, and she usually strolled by in the mid-morning, rather than in the heat of the day. The urgency to see her was building within him as he turned from the palace walls and began to intercede.

"Father, I know that there have always been those who would desire to do away with the king. There were perhaps even days when I would have desired it to be so myself. But let it not be so, Father. Not today.

"What would become of my little Esther if the king were destroyed? Most certainly her light would be extinguished. Surely this untimely demise could not be in your master plan for her life.

"Father, for the sake of my Esther, as well my king, let her come by my

gate this day. Speak with her Lord and direct her to walk by this way today. Allow Your faithful servant a gateway to the queen, and to her a doorway to the king. Let knowledge of this evil plan preserve the king and Your purposes for Your people in the days that lie ahead. Oh Father, send Esther by before it is too late."

Just as he finished his heartfelt prayer and turned back toward the palace gate, Esther strolled by slowly, as if she were inspecting the lilies in the fountain near the gate. At the same time, her maidens giggled and flirted with Bigthana and Teresh, drawing their attention away from the queen. She looked stunning in her gold-trimmed gown of purple silk. Her eyes sparkled with a clear but subtle excitement to see her beloved Mordecai nearby.

He drew near the gate and motioned for her to come closer. Her maidens were still engrossed in their flirtations, and the guards were deceitfully boasting of their exploits as faithful servants of the king. Esther drew nearer the gate, feigning interest in some flowering ivy on the bars of the gates. In a whisper, Mordecai revealed to her the plot of Bigthana and Teresh and told her to speak to the king about their scheme as soon as possible.

Esther felt momentarily terrified but grateful at the same time. She discretely returned to the fountain and called for her maidens to return to her at once. They immediately responded and followed her back into the palace. She then prepared herself for her usual afternoon tea with the king and an evening of intimate sharing. Only this time, she had more to talk about than the frivolous events of her day or inquiries about affairs of state.

THE UNSEEN WEAVER

Esther did give her report of Teresh and Bigthana's plot to the king that evening. She did not take any undeserved credit for knowledge of this plot but carefully gave the appropriate credit to the humble gate porter named Mordecai.

That evening and the following day, the report was investigated and found to be true. The two scheming culprits were put to death, and Mordecai's report was duly noted in the king's records. When all was said and done, trust was increased between the king and his queen, and Mordecai's name was underscored in the king's carefully kept annals.

Unbeknownst to the king, Esther's unseen God was working at the shuttle of his heart with providential intent. Through current events, an unlikely team was being prepared and woven together for the future. Mordecai's action was intertwined with honor for the king and heart devotion for the queen. The three were an unlikely team that would soon take its place in the pages of Jewish history.

"UNLIKELY TEAMS"

Other unlikely and unique teams had saved the lives of Mordecai's ancestors in prior generations, as well. The stories of Rahab, Jonathan, and the men of Jabesh Gilead were recorded with heroic detail and preserved that Israel might remember its rich and blessed heritage. Mordecai thought of them now, as he wondered how this chain of events would play out for him and Esther and King Xerxes.

When the nation of Israel first entered the Promised Land, Canaan, Joshua's spies came to search out the city of Jericho for its vulnerabilities. Rahab, a prostitute in the city, gave them hospitality, and when the king of her city demanded that she hand them over, she hid them in her home. Before the spies left, she implored them, *"Now then, please swear to me by the Lord that you will show kindness to my family, because I have shown kindness to you. Give me a sure sign that you will spare the lives of my father and mother, my brothers and sisters, and all who belong to them, and that you will save us from death"* (Joshua 2:12-13).

They responded, *"Our lives for your lives! . . . If you don't tell what we are doing, we will treat you kindly and faithfully when the Lord gives us the land"* (Joshua 2:14). The alliance of this prostitute and these spies was unlikely but strategic.

Another "unlikely" team included another one of Mordecai's favorite heroes of old, King David, the son of a shepherd who later became king by God's sovereign plan. When he was still a young man, he was invited into King Saul's castle. Jonathan was Saul's son, a prince-in-waiting. Saul ousted David and determined to kill him for fear that he would take his throne, but alas, it was too late. The weaving of hearts and souls in friendship had taken place between the two possible heirs to the throne. With the understanding of God's will in his heart, Jonathan had but one request of David before his departure from the capital city. *"But show me unfailing kindness like that of the Lord as long as I live, so that I may not be killed, and do not ever cut off your kindness from my family—not even when the Lord has cut off every one of David's enemies from the face of the earth"* (1 Samuel 20:14-15).

David's response came later, after many battles and many victories, when he asked, *"Is there anyone still left of the house of Saul to whom I can show kindness for Jonathan's sake?"* (2 Samuel 9:1). When Jonathan's son, Mephibosheth, who was crippled in both feet, was brought to David, he said to him, *"Don't be afraid . . . for I will surely show you kindness for the sake of your father Jonathan. I will restore to you all the land that belonged to your grandfather Saul, and you will always eat at my table"* (2 Samuel 9:7).

Were the shepherd boy, David, and Prince Jonathan an unlikely kingdom match? Perhaps they were, but their friendship and commitment to one another ushered in the next generation. Jonathan's family lived on in safety and David's line was established forever. Nathan the prophet spoke this promise to David and his household from the Lord, *". . . I declare to you that the Lord will build a house for you: When your days are over and you go to be with your fathers, I will raise up your offspring to succeed you, one of your own sons, and I will establish his kingdom. He is the one who will build a house for me, and I will establish his throne forever. I will be his father, and he will be my son. I will never take my love away from him, as I took it away from your predecessor. I will set him over my house and my kingdom forever; his throne and will be established forever"* (1 Chronicles 17:10-14).

As Mordecai pondered the future ramifications of his bold choice in getting such a message to the king through Esther, the story of David's promise to the men of Jabesh Gilead crossed his mind. Historically, when the people of Jabesh Gilead heard that the Philistines had killed Saul, all of their valiant men journeyed through the night to where Saul and Jonathan's dead bodies were. They then carried the bodies back to Jabesh, gave them an appropriate burial, and fasted for seven days in honor of their lives.

These courageous men of Jabesh Gilead found and buried David's king, Saul. When David discovered the brave deed of kindness these men had done for his beloved king, he sent this message to them, *"The Lord bless you for showing this kindness to Saul your master by burying him. May the Lord now show you kindness and faithfulness, and I too will show you the same favor because you have done this"* (2 Samuel 2:5-6).

As Mordecai meditated on this historical account, he couldn't help but wonder if it also prophetically revealed great future rewards for his present acts of kindness. Yes, the record was clear—the pathway to a future of hope was not only obvious, it was right. Mordecai had made his move and revealed to Esther the plot of the two scheming officers of the king.

Was this "team" also an unlikely match for any long-term profit? Yes, perhaps. But the reels of history kept playing in Mordecai's mind. Though the integrity and behavior of one of Jehovah's servants was outlined clearly in His Holy Word, only time would tell what this unseen God really had in mind.

PLAYING YOUR POSITION

Teamwork, interlaced with compassion and activated by the wisdom of God, can be your greatest reward and your greatest sacrifice. It can simultaneously be a crown of joy and a challenge to the heart. This story, entitled

"Teamwork, interlaced with compassion and activated by the wisdom of God, can be your greatest reward and your greatest sacrifice."

"Linked Together," was sent to me in 1998. The author is unknown, but the message clearly parallels Mordecai's story, and perhaps yours and mine, as well.

> *A few years ago at the Seattle Special Olympics, nine contestants, all physically or mentally disabled, assembled at the starting line for the 100-yard dash. At the gun, they all started out, not exactly in a dash, but with a relish to run the race to the finish and win.*
>
> *All, that is, except one boy who stumbled on the asphalt, tumbled over a couple of times and began to cry.*
>
> *The other eight heard the boy cry. They slowed down and looked back. They all turned around and went back, every one of them. One girl with Down's syndrome bent down and kissed him and said, "This will make it better." All nine linked arms and walked across the finish line together.*
>
> *Everyone in the stadium stood, and the cheering went on for several minutes. People who were there are still telling the story. Why? Because deep down we know this one thing: What matters in this life is more than winning for ourselves. What truly matters in this life is helping others win, even if it means slowing down and changing our course.*

Pastor Dick Iverson of Ministers' Fellowship International in Portland, Oregon, says this: *"What I am a part of is more important than the part I play."*

> *"What I am a part of is more important than the part I play."*

This must have been Mordecai's realization. It must have also been the understanding that Joseph adopted when he became second in command to Pharaoh in Egypt, rather than the leader of his family tribe in Canaan. This same revelation must have come to Daniel in Babylon as he found himself serving Nebuchadnezzar. In fact, I wonder if Jesus may have had a similar thought as He left heaven and came to earth in submission to the Father. The interweaving of such teamwork is both rewarding and impacting, but it requires personal self-lessness on the part of the team members.

You may find yourself in a similar circumstance at this time. Perhaps life has not turned out exactly as you had planned, and you are not where you had hoped to be at this time in life. You, like Mordecai, may be stand-ing by a gate, waiting for someone you have mentored to pass by. You may have the heart, vision, and capabilities to spearhead a project, church, or corporation, but you find yourself at the gate, attempting to cover for a supervisor, pastor, or boss who may never know about or rec-ognize your sacrifice. You may have the skills and capabilities to lead and administrate a team, but you find yourself second-in-command, cover-ing and protecting a leader who barely acknowledges your existence.

Should you continue to stand by the gate and guard someone who is hardly aware of your presence? What happened to the potential that so many spoke to you of when you were young? To whom did you yield that potential? Has your life remained surrendered to the one who gave you life, or has it been swallowed up in a position-conscious mentality? Is "what you are a part of" more important than "the part you play"?

In the Christian world, being part of the whole must take precedence over one's personal position. If not, Christianity will cease to exist. For truly this attitude of service is the very heart of Christ: *"Who, being in very nature God, did not consider equality with God something to be grasped, but made himself nothing, taking the very nature of a servant, being made in human like-ness. And being found in appearance as a man, he humbled himself and became obedient to death—even death on a cross!"* (Philippians 2:6-8).

> *"In the Christian world, being part of the whole must take precedence over one's personal position."*

Strange companions—the Son of God and mankind. And yet, His surrender to the Father set an example for us, that we might also surrender to the Father's will and lay down our lives for the sake of others.

As it was with Esther and Mordecai, so may it be with you. You too are uniquely woven together in a tapestry that is singular to your own personal destiny and the destiny of a generation. To accomplish your destiny, a continual selfless willingness to serve a greater cause is needed.

Mordecai may have felt that he had lost his personal life focus forever, as well as a close relationship with his "little Hadassah." Esther may have felt that she had been engulfed in the palace-world around her. You may feel that you have been swallowed up by family agendas and daily needs, and you may long to break out on your own, not caring about the needs of other's any more. But it is the unseen weaving of the Master at the shuttle of your heart that continues to intertwine you with those around you as well as your future destiny. If this description fits you, reach out in selflessness once again and watch your destiny and the destiny of a generation unfold before you.

Today, whether you are like Mordecai sitting by the gate, Esther strolling the halls of a palace, or the king in need of a word, remember, *"What you are a part of is more important than the part you play."* Be bold, be kind, and be discerning. Step up and take your place. Walk through the door that has been opened to you with honor and with zeal. For the Master weaver is at the shuttle of destiny once again. Though often overlooked from a natural perspective, He is weaving relationships together unmistakably for His kingdom purposes in the earth.

Partnering Together

"Together"

PS. 34:3   *"Glorify the Lord with me; let us exalt his Name together."*

PS. 33:1   *"How good and pleasant it is when brothers live together in unity."*

JER. 31:12-13   *"Therefore they shall come and sing in the height of Zion, and shall flow together to the goodness of the LORD, for wheat, and for wine, and for oil, and for the young of the flock and of the herd: and their soul shall be as a watered garden; and they shall not sorrow any more at all. Then shall the virgin rejoice in the dance, both young men and old together: for I will turn their mourning into joy, and will comfort them, and make them rejoice from their sorrow." (KJV)*

AMOS 3:3   *"Do two walk together unless they have agreed to do so?"*

LUKE 9:1-2   *"When Jesus had called the Twelve together, He gave them power and authority to drive out all demons and to cure diseases, and He sent them out to preach the kingdom of God and to heal the sick."*

ACTS 1:4   *"And, being assembled together with them, commanded them that they should not depart from Jerusalem, but wait for the promise of the Father, which, saith he, ye have heard of me." (KJV)*

ACTS 20:7   *"On the first day of the week we came together to break bread...."*

ROM. 8:17   *"And if children, then heirs; heirs of God, and joint-heirs with Christ; if so be that we suffer with him, that we may be also glorified together." (KJV)*

EPH. 2:5-6   *"Even when we were dead in sins, hath quickened us together with Christ, (by grace ye are saved;) And hath raised us up together, and made us sit together in heavenly places in Christ Jesus:" (KJV)*

EPH. 2:21-22   *"In Him the whole building is joined together and rises to become a holy temple in the Lord. And in Him you too are being built together to become a dwelling in which God lives by His Spirit."*

EPH. 4:16   *"From Him the whole body, joined and held together by every supporting ligament, grows and builds itself up in love, as each part does its work."*

COL. 2:2-3   *That their hearts might be comforted, being knit together in love, and unto all riches of the full assurance of understanding, to the acknowledgement of the mystery of God, and of the Father, and of Christ; in whom are hid all the treasures of wisdom and knowledge." (KJV)*

1THESS. 4:17   *"After that, we who are still alive and are left will be caught up together with them in the clouds to meet the Lord in the air. And so we will be with the Lord forever."*

1 THESS. 5:10-11   *"He died for us so that, whether we are awake or asleep, we may live together with Him. Therefore encourage one another and build each other up, just as in fact you are doing."*

"One Another"

JOHN 13:34	*Love one another*
1 THESS. 4:18	*Comfort one another*
HEB. 10:24	*Consider one another*
HEB. 3:13	*Exhort one another*
ROM. 14:19	*Edify one another*
ROM. 15:14	*Admonish one another*
1 PETER 4:10	*Minister to one another*
COL. 3:13	*Forbear one another*
EPH. 5:21	*Submit to one another*
EPH. 4:32	*Forgive one another*
COL. 3:16	*Teach one another*
ROM. 12:10	*Prefer one another*
JAMES 5:16	*Pray for one another*
1 PETER 4:9	*Be hospitable to one another*
1 PETER 5:14	*Greet one another*
1 JOHN 1:7	*Fellowship with one another*
ACTS 2:46	*Eat with one another*
PHIL. 2:2	*Think with one another*
ACTS 2:45	*Share material possessions*
1 COR. 12:26	*Rejoice with one another*
1 COR. 16:20	*Embrace one another*
GAL. 6:1	*Restore one another*
GAL. 6:2	*Bear one another's burdens*
COL. 4:11	*Work with one another*
HEB. 10:25	*Worship with one another*

Dark Plots

". . . King Xerxes honored Haman, son of Hammedatha, the Agagite . . . All the royal officials at the king's gate knelt down and paid honor to Haman, for the king had commanded this concerning him. But Mordecai would not kneel down or pay him honor. . . . When Haman saw that Mordecai would not kneel down or pay him honor, he was enraged . . . Haman looked for a way to destroy all Mordecai's people, the Jews, throughout the whole kingdom . . ." (Esther 3:1-2, 5-6).

They were merely the descendants of adversarial forefathers, players in a conflict that had begun a thousand years prior to their existence. Haman was an Amalakite, a proud descendant of the once great King Agag. Mordecai was a Benjaminite, a descendant of the chosen but rejected King Saul. These two were participants in an ancient dispute, perhaps unknown to each other initially, but quickly realized in the halls of destiny. Even though the origin of their dispute had not begun with them, they were now bitter enemies facing off in the courtyard of a heathen king.

Haman's descendants, the Amalekites, were the first to attack the Israelites after their journey out of Egypt, and Moses had prophesied to the generations to come, *". . . The Lord will be at war against the Amalekites from generation to generation."* [1]

True to God's Word, generations later the prophet Samuel said to

Saul, *"This is what the Lord Almighty says: 'I will punish the Amalekites for what they did to Israel when they waylaid them as they came up from Egypt. Now go, attack the Amalekites and totally destroy everything that belongs to them. Do not spare them; put to death men and women, children and infants, cattle and sheep, camels and donkeys.'"*[2] Saul did attack the Amalekites and tasted victory; however, he disobeyed the Lord and did not completely destroy them.[3] The Lord spoke to Samuel the prophet of His grief over Saul's disobedience, and Samuel went to Saul with a rebuke for him and a sword for the spared leader, Agag. The prophet brought death to Agag, but a remnant of his people lived on, due to Saul's disobedience. That day the kingdom was torn from Saul's hands and was eventually given to David.

Ironically, it was an Amalekite warrior of Agag's who brought death to Saul and then boasted to David of his "good deed." David had the young warrior killed immediately after he confessed to killing Saul, *"the Lord's anointed."*[4] Sadly, the ramifications of Saul's disobedience would continue to be written on the pages of Israel's history for generations to come.

Little did Mordecai, the Benjaminite, realize that generations after the disobedience of his ancestor, Saul, he would be the one to meet with the descendant of the archenemy of his people at the gates of this Persian city. Not only would he be a thorn in the side of this Amalekite, but he would also one day bring about his demise and break through generational bondages.

Little did Haman, the proud son of Hammedatha, the Agagite, realize that there was unfinished business between the unseen God of the Jews and his ancestors. He was incapable of fully assessing what the unfolding of his destiny would really mean. For now, he was the king's honored noble. Xerxes had given him a seat of honor higher than all the other nobles. All of the royal officials at the king's gate knelt down and paid homage to him as if he himself were the king. Everyone bowed in his presence and hastened to acquiesce to his every whim. He loved the adulation; it stirred within him a desire for more.

"Though I have found favor in the eyes of the king," Haman pondered,

"will I find favor in the eyes of Xerxes' queen, as well? On the other hand, while it is true that Esther has a position of authority as the royal queen, I have reason to doubt that she has any genuine influence over the king these days. It seems to me that I have more influence over the king than anyone else, even the queen." A subtle but fiendish smile came across his face as he contemplated this thought.

Though Esther had been chosen and placed as the king's queen, Xerxes' lust for sensual attention currently preoccupied his time. This vain preoccupation had, in itself, contributed to Haman's increasing authority. In recent months, the king had a continual entourage of beautiful women presented before him for his personal viewing. More paraded before him now than before the official pageantry had begun. Some had just completed their year of beauty treatments, and others, who had already been before him, had contested for a "second look" by the king. All were hopeful of unseating Esther. Xerxes' attention had definitely been diverted away from his queen, as well as kingdom issues. *"This lustful weakness of the king's is all the better for me,"* Haman mused.[5]

Xerxes relied on Haman to function in his stead in numerous matters these days. Haman felt truly deserving of the all the honor being bestowed on him. He relished all the bowing, the lauding, the recognition of his significance. Every royal subject bowed as he came within view—except one. Haman fumed within himself as his thoughts turned from narcissism to burning frustration; he began to pace and spew curses toward an invisible presence in the room.

"Yes, I've noticed that non-bowing, dishonoring old man as I ride through the gate each day. Now reports of him are coming to me from my own royal officials; they have noticed his arrogance, too. They tell me that he's a Jew; I should have guessed as much. How dare this Jewish peon refuse to bow to me! He's an irritating little fly in my ointment. I must deal with him immediately or other Jewish pests may have the audacity to follow in his footsteps.

"These 'one-God' Jews have annoyed me long enough! In fact, this miniscule people group has not only been a nuisance, it has been a hin-

drance to the prosperity of my people for generations. They have gained wealth in abundance while my fellow Persians have been distracted by frivolity. After all, what have any of these Jews really offered Susa, and how have they contributed to my plans for the future?!"

Haman paced back and forth even more rapidly in front of the fireplace in his office. As he turned, the breeze caught the corner of his cloak, and the fire nearly lapped it up. He moved so quickly that the flames could not catch him, but a silent guard near the door watched over him closely, as this curious demonstration of angry rambling continued. It was obvious, as Haman rhythmically banged one fist into the other and continued pacing, that the fire burning in his heart was hotter than the one in the fireplace.

"What kind of fool does this Mordecai presume me to be?!" he barked to his unseen provoker. *"Does he think I am ignorant of the historical conflict between our people? Does he think he can get away with some kind of religious exemption in my kingdom?! Does he think I will be deprived of the prestige and respect that is due me? No! He must show honor to whom honor is due—and that would be me! He must bow!"*

A devilish scheme began to formulate in his mind. Still agitated, he continued his diatribe. He stopped abruptly in front of his terrace window overlooking the entrance to the palace. *"What am I thinking? That stubborn old Jew will never bow; they never do. I will devise a plan that will ring throughout the entire kingdom and send a message far and near. I'll deal with Mordecai and the whole lot of those Jews once and for all. When I am finished, every knee will bow and every tongue will confess that Haman is the noblest in the land!"*

<hr />

Both Haman and Mordecai were participants in a battle that had begun long before their time. Each man had an enemy to confront and a battle plan to construct. Would Mordecai bow low to this Agagite and compromise as his forefather Saul had? Or would he bow only to the one true God and risk a fresh confrontation with this generational nemesis? Where would destiny lead? Was this the time when Jehovah would *"punish the Amalekites for what they did to Israel,"*[6] or would the fulfillment of this prophecy be left for another time? Perhaps the demise of this enemy would require not only the mettle of a man, but also the courage of a queen.

THE ONGOING WAR

The ongoing saga of war between those who are followers of Christ and those who are self-proclaimed gods, or the followers of other gods, is still taking place today. In fact, unknown to most Americans today, the real battle is just heating up around the world. Sadly, blood is still being shed for the acknowledgement of the one true God. The dark plots of Satan are still scheming against God's people today, just as they were in Haman and Mordecai's day. In the closing decade of the twentieth century, Christians in many nations were persecuted for their faith.

> In China, "*. . . five Protestants from Shaanxi were detained and severely tortured . . . 'without a word of explanation.' They were singled out because the authorities suspected them of contact with foreigners. . . .*"[7]

> In Sudan, "*. . . the village of Wud Arul* [a Christian village], *about two kilometers north of Sokobat, was attacked. Raiders came at dawn, storming through the whole area, looting and burning homes to ashes; kidnapping women and children (even babies); killing old men and women. . . .*"[8]

> In Saudi Arabia, "*Oswaldo Magdangal pastored a small Christian group in Riyadh, Saudi Arabia . . . he was arrested for involvement in an 'illegal fellowship,' he was informed by the Metowah, the Saudi Religious Police, that he was the country's most notorious 'public enemy.'*"[9]

In Pakistan, *"The Frontier Post reports, '. . . This year there have been incidents of raids on Christian villages by communally-incited armed hordes who plundered their houses and dishonored their women. Kidnapping of young girls and their forcible conversion to Islam is another aspect.'"* [10]

In Egypt, *"A British human-rights group investigating complaints of conversion under duress says there is disturbing evidence that some Islamic extremists are using rape to force Christian girls to convert. 'Conversion offers marriage to a member of the Islamic group and security for the victim . . . Returning to the family after the rape would result in potentially fatal consequences, as the victim is no longer a virgin. Alarmingly, there are reports that this practice is becoming more widespread.'"* [11]

In Indonesia, *"'I am a soldier of Christ' and 'Jesus' were the final words of Roy Pontoh, age 15. Though threatened by a mob, Roy, who had just attended a Bible camp on Ambon Island in January, refused to renounce Christ. An attacker swung a sword at him, missed and ripped his Bible. The next swing sliced open Roy's abdomen. His body was thrown into a ditch and recovered by his family four days later. Earlier the mob had stabbed to death pastor Mecky Sainyakit and another adult from the camp."* [12]

These reports are unnerving to the human soul. Without faith and the understanding of God's ultimate purposes, such accounts have the potential of robbing Christian believers around the world of their peace in their stance with Christ. The enemy is cunning; he is the father of deception. He is at work in the earth, stirring hearts to rebel against the knowledge and will of God. He relishes in creating a fog of confusion and a fire of evil desire in the minds of those who lack understanding of the one true God.

The cloud of deception that covers the mind of a persecutor is much more than a covering fog; it is a demonically-inspired, saturating presence. Following the terrorist attack against America on September 11, 2001, prime-suspect Osama bin Laden released videotape for Americans to view on December 11, 2001, the three-month anniversary of the attack. In the report he stated, *"Our terrorism against the United States is blessed, aimed at repelling the oppressor so that America stops its support for Israel."* For one to feel that the murder of thousands of innocent lives is "blessed," reveals the depths of deception. This kind of statement exposes the deception that Satan himself had when he thought that nailing Jesus to a cross could do more than "bruise His heel."

Just as deceived minds and hate-filled schemes of the enemy were not new in Mordecai's day, neither are they new in our day. Satan is a defeated foe and his ill-equipped underlings lack the wisdom required to overcome the servants of the Lord. The power of a truly surrendered life is one that thwarts the intentions of the enemy and vanquishes his dark plots.

No matter how evil or wicked are the plans of those inspired by the enemy of our souls, our God will rescue us in times of trouble. He will help us and deliver us. Whether His deliverance comes from the vantage-point of heaven or earth, it will come.

> *"No matter how evil or wicked are the plans of those inspired by the enemy of our souls, our God will rescue us in times of trouble."*

Hebrews 11: 32-40 (Message) says, *". . . Gideon, Barak, Samson, Jephthah, David, Samuel, the prophets . . . Through acts of faith, they toppled kingdoms, made justice work, took the promises for themselves. They were protected from lions, fires, and sword thrusts, turned disadvantage to advantage, won battles, routed alien armies. Women received their loved ones back from the dead. There were those who, under torture, refused to give in and go free, preferring some-*

thing better: resurrection. Others braved abuse and whips, and yes, chains and dungeons. We have stories of those who were stoned, sawed in two, murdered in cold blood; stories of vagrants wandering the earth in animal skins, homeless, friendless, powerless—the world didn't deserve them!— making their way as best they could on the cruel edges of the world. Not one of these people, even though their lives of faith were exemplary, got their hands on what was promised. **God had a better plan for us: that their faith and our faith would come together to make one completed whole, their lives of faith not complete apart from ours."**

Little does the enemy know that, though he is cunning, the power of a surrendered life to Christ can dispel and triumph over any darkness. Our lives cannot be defeated by his schemes of enmity, for our lives are not only interwoven with the examples of those who have gone on before us, but with the very life of our Lord Jesus Christ, who rules and reigns throughout eternity.

> *"Little does the enemy know that, though he is cunning, the power of a surrendered life to Christ can dispel and triumph over any darkness."*

When we are destined for a place of influence in the kingdom of God, as Mordecai and Esther were, we must always keep an "ear to the ground" and discern the intent of "wolves" that may be cloaked in "sheep's clothing."' Jesus warned his followers, *"Woe to you when all men speak well of you, for that is how their fathers treated the false prophets"* (Luke 6:26). We must adhere to trusted confidantes and resist the temptation to naively cozy up to those with flattery on their lips and evil intentions in their hearts. Prayer and discernment are essential to those in positions of influence, whether that position is in the local neighborhood, a place of employment, or a political arena.

We should, along with Clement of Rome, entreat the Lord, as he did at the turn of the second century.[13]

Almighty God, Father of our Lord Jesus Christ,
> *grant, we pray, that we might be grounded*
> *and settled in your truth by the coming of*
> *your Holy Spirit into our hearts.*

What we do not know,
> *reveal to us;*

What is lacking within us,
> *make complete;*

That which we do know,
> *confirm in us;*

And keep us blameless in your service,
> *through Jesus Christ our Lord.*[14]

Wisdom cries out to us today, as it did to those at the turn of the second century, to be alert to the ways of the enemy and intercede to the Father on behalf of our generation. For it is through alertness and intercession that discernment comes, and it is in discernment that we will stand when the enemy says to bow, and bow when the commanding presence of the Lord is near.

The Dark Plots of the Enemy

PS. 37:12-17, 32-40 *"The wicked plot against the righteous and gnash their teeth at them ... The wicked draw the sword and bend the bow to bring down the poor and needy, to slay those whose ways are upright. But their swords will pierce their own hearts, and their bows will be broken. Better the little that the righteous have than the wealth of many wicked; for the power of the wicked will be broken, but the Lord upholds the righteous. . . . The wicked lie in wait for the righteous, seeking their very lives; but the Lord will not leave them in their power or let them be condemned when brought to trial. Wait for the Lord and keep his way. He will exalt you to inherit the land; when the wicked are cut off, you will see it. I have seen a wicked and ruthless man flourishing like a green tree in its native soil, but he soon passed away and was no more; though I looked for him, he could not be found. Consider the blameless, observe the upright; there is a future for the man of peace. But all sinners will be destroyed; the future of the wicked will be cut off. The salvation of the righteous comes from the Lord; He is their stronghold in time of trouble. The Lord helps them and delivers them; he delivers them from the wicked and saves them, because they take refuge in Him."*

PS. 2:1-2 *"Why do the nations conspire and the peoples plot in vain? The kings of the earth take their stand and the rulers gather together against the Lord and against his Anointed One."*

PS. 42:9 *". . . Why must I go about mourning, oppressed by the enemy?"*

PS. 55:2-3   *". . . My thoughts trouble me and I am distraught at the voice of the enemy, at the stares of the wicked; for they bring down suffering upon me and revile me in their anger."*

PROV. 27:6   *"Wounds from a friend can be trusted, but an enemy multiplies kisses."*

PS. 119:95   *"The wicked are waiting to destroy me, but I will ponder your statutes."*

ISA. 32:6-7   *"For the fool speaks folly, his mind is busy with evil: He practices ungodliness and spreads error concerning the Lord; the hungry he leaves empty and from the thirsty he withholds water. The scoundrel's methods are wicked, he makes up evil schemes to destroy the poor with lies, even when the plea of the needy is just."*

The Responsive Deeds of the Lord

PS. 8:2   *"From the lips of children and infants you have ordained praise because of your enemies, to silence the foe and the avenger."*

PS. 18:17-19   *"He rescued me from my powerful enemy, from my foes, who were too strong for me. They confronted me in the day of my disaster, but the Lord was my support. He brought me out into a spacious place; he rescued me because he delighted in me."*

PS. 41:11-12 *"I know that you are pleased with me, for my enemy does not triumph over me. In my integrity you uphold me and set me in your presence forever."*

PS. 55:22 *"Cast your cares on the Lord and he will sustain you; he will never let the righteous fall."*

PS. 56:9 *"Then my enemies will turn back when I call for help. By this I will know that God is for me."*

PS. 61:3 *"For thou hast been a shelter for me, and a strong tower from the enemy." (KJV)*

PS. 89:21-23 *"My hand will sustain him; surely my arm will strengthen him. No enemy will subject him to tribute; no wicked man will oppress him. I will crush his foes before him and strike down his adversaries."*

PS. 106:10 *"He saved them from the hand of the foe; from the hand of the enemy he redeemed them."*

ISA. 59:19 *"So shall they fear the name of the LORD from the west, and his glory from the rising of the sun. When the enemy shall come in like a flood, the Spirit of the LORD shall lift up a standard against him." (KJV)*

LUKE 10:19 *"I have given you authority to trample on snakes and scorpions and to overcome all the power of the enemy; nothing will harm you."*

The Intercessions of the Encompassed Believer

PS. 64:1 *"Hear my voice, O God, as I voice my complaint; protect my life from the threat of the enemy. Hide me from the conspiracy of the wicked, from that noisy crowd of evildoers."*

PS. 74:21-23 *"Do not let the oppressed retreat in disgrace; may the poor and needy praise your name. Rise up, O God, and defend your cause; remember how fools mock you all day long. Do not ignore the clamor of your adversaries, the uproar of your enemies, which rises continually."*

PS. 107:1-2 *"Give thanks to the Lord, for he is good; his love endures forever. Let the redeemed of the Lord say this—those he redeemed from the hand of the foe."*

PS. 17:1-2 *"Hear, O Lord, my righteous plea; listen to my cry. Give ear to my prayer—it does not rise from deceitful lips. May my vindication come from you; may your eyes see what is right."*

PS. 27:7 *"Hear my voice when I call, O Lord, be merciful to me and answer me."*

PS. 28:2 *"Hear my cry for mercy as I call to you for help, as I lift up my hands toward your Most Holy Place."*

PS. 61:1 *"Hear my cry, O God; listen to my prayer."*

N O T E S

1 Exodus 17:15

2 Samuel 15:1-3

3 *"But Saul and the army spared Agag and the best of the sheep and cattle, the fat calves and lambs— everything that was good. These they were unwilling to destroy completely, but everything that was despised and weak they totally destroyed"* (1 Samuel 15:9).

4 2 Samuel 1:16

5 *"When the virgins were assembled a second time . . ."* (Esther 2:19). Even though Esther had been chosen and placed as the king's queen, the inference here is that the king was enjoying a regular entourage of beautiful women being presented before him. This passage may refer to a group of girls who had just finished their season of preparation, or may have been, as some scholars suggest, an earlier group of contestants who were being given a second "look." Who these "virgins" are is not really a matter of concern here. The point is that the king's attention was diverted from Esther, his queen, as well as more serious matters of his kingdom. Haman was obviously functioning in the king's stead in numerous matters.

6 I Samuel 15:2

7 Taken from Paul Marshall with Lela Gilbert, *Their Blood Cries Out* (Nashville: Word, 1997), 13. Used by permission. All rights reserved.

8 Ibid.

9 Ibid., 28.

10 Ibid., 33, citing *Frontier Post* (April 21, 1994).

11 Ibid., 35, citing *The Observer* (June 5, 1994).

12 *World Christian* (June 1999), 17.

13 "Clement of Rome is believed to have been the third bishop of that city after the apostle Peter. He is thought to have been martyred at about the turn of the second century." Duane W.H. Arnold, trans., *Prayers of the Martyrs* (Grand Rapids: Zondervan, 1991), 116.

14 Ibid., 30.

Preliminary Actions

First Reactions

"When Mordecai learned of all that had been done, he tore his clothes, put on sackcloth and ashes, and went out into the city, wailing loudly and bitterly . . . In every province to which the edict and order of the king came, there was great mourning among the Jews, with fasting, weeping and wailing. . . . 'All the king's officials and the people of the royal provinces know that for any man or woman who approaches the king in the inner court without being summoned the king has but one law: that he be put to death. The only exception to this is for the king to extend the gold scepter to him and spare his life. But thirty days have passed since I was called to go to the king'" (Esther 4:1, 3, 11).

For Haman it was a time to rejoice. With a fiendish gleam in his eye, he sat leaning on one arm on his cushioned chaise lounge, which had recently been placed near the window in his palace office. As he glanced over to the gate of the king's palace, he relished the pandemonium that "his news" was beginning to create. With an arrogant upturn of his head, he breathed in deeply the new tension in the air that he alone had created beyond the palace walls. He could feel the apprehension in the city, and his wicked heart began to beat with satisfaction.

The dispatches had been sent throughout all the king's provinces. The message was clear: *"all Jews—young and old, women and little chil-*

dren—on a single day" were to be killed. The people would be annihilated, and their hard-earned goods would be plundered.[1] In one fell swoop, he would teach Mordecai and these "one-God" Jews a lesson. He would cut out the heart of this unbowing Mordecai by dealing ruthlessly with him and his people. He would show them, once and for all, who was in charge!

With a fiendish smirk on his face, he chuckled menacingly at how easy it had been to persuade King Xerxes. He had merely informed the distracted king that a "certain" race of people, who were scattered throughout his entire kingdom, did not obey his laws and that it would be in his best interest not to tolerate them any further.[2] The king was so distracted by his own unquenchable lust that Haman didn't even have to mention which ethnic group or specific laws to which he was referring. Had he admitted that it was only one law concerning bowing down to nobles and only one Jew who refused, the king might have told him to deal with it personally on his own time and not to bother him with such a frivolous matter. However, due to the king's own gluttonous frivolity, all Haman had to do was make an inference that smacked of Vashti's past disloyalties, and the signet ring was on his hand. He could do as he pleased; life and death now rested in the power of his command.

While the king and the wicked Prince Haman were drinking their wine and mulling over minor issues of government, the entire city of Susa was in a state of confusion. Since Susa was the capital of the Persian Empire, it was the main residence for many wealthy Persians of high rank. Being religious people themselves, devout to many gods, they were generally sympathetic toward other religions. When this edict went throughout the streets of the entire empire, many were baffled by its hostile message and disturbed by its intimidating threats to a religious people.[3]

———•:•◦:•———

Though many Persians were perplexed when the edict was announced in each province, the Jews were horrified and cried out in utter desperation to the one true God. Terror penetrated the hearts of the people, and mourning and confusion reigned in the provinces of Xerxes.

For Mordecai, this was a time to mourn deeply. He exchanged his courtly attire for garments of mourning and walked the streets, wailing loudly and bitterly. He threw dust into the air, and the dirt settled over him, covering his hair and garments. He then moved from the center of the city and planted himself in the city square, in front of the king's gate, to demonstrate his great remorse even further. He tore his garments and wailed louder still. He bemoaned the dispatches being sent throughout the kingdom, and he vehemently petitioned God on behalf of his people. His wailing and weeping could not be silenced.

For Esther, it was a time of confusion. When her attendants came to her with word of the gatekeeper Mordecai's lament, she was distressed and perplexed. Her emotions ran rampant. The sound of mourning was not to be heard near or within the palace walls. Only sounds of peace and joy were to be heard in and around the palace. His voice was obviously making palace news. She feared for Mordecai's life.

With the news of Mordecai's wailing also came the message that he was throwing dirt all over himself, a Jewish demonstration of utter despair. The Persians valued cleanliness, and they associated a lack of cleanliness with the devil and disease. They measured out harsh punishment to those who they thought might spread disease by their uncleanness.

Esther's maids and attending eunuchs knew, by now, that she had a fond affection for the "dear old gatekeeper," so she immediately sent Hathach, her most faithful eunuch, to deliver fresh clothing to Mordecai. She included orders for him to cease his mourning so near the king's gate. Mordecai returned the clothing with a message that penetrated her heart, threatened the lifestyle she presently knew, and opened the way for the next step of her destiny. He sent her a copy of Haman's edict and urged her to go into the king's presence to beg for mercy and plead with him for her people.

She was horrified at the message Hathach returned to her but fought to mask her emotions, lest the eunuch become suspicious of the true closeness she had with this "dear old gatekeeper." He had, however, willingly and discretely carried the message, *"Beg for mercy and plead with him for YOUR people,"* directly to her. She trusted Hathach; he had always been loyal to her. Besides, she had things other than herself to think of at the moment. She calmly dismissed Hathach and her maidens and asked them to leave her alone for a while. As soon as they departed, she fell to her knees and urgently cried out to the Lord.

"What am I to do with such news? The copy of this edict for the annihilation of the Jewish people is horrifying. How devastated my dear cousin Mordecai must be. To identify with his people in such an overt demonstration is no small matter in the open streets of Susa. . . . 'His people.' Did I really just say that, Lord? Have I been away from the old neighborhood so long that I have forgotten that they are my people, as well?"

She bowed herself lower to the floor and began to weep, as waves of sorrow and mourning swept over her soul. Tears of compassionate agony on behalf of her people dropped from her eyes, forming pools of despair on the marble floor. Then suddenly something new began to take form from within her. A righteous indignation began to fill her spirit, and she spoke with deliberateness. *"I knew Prince Haman was a wicked man. I have always had a sickeningly strange feeling in my spirit when I observed him approaching or leaving the king's presence. Now I know why. He is a wicked man who desires to oppress my people, just as so many have before him."*

Then she sought the Lord again, pleading, *"What am I to do with these facts that Mordecai has sent to me? He wants me to go into the presence of the great Xerxes and plead for mercy for our people; surely he has forgotten what danger that could bring to me.[4] It has been thirty days since the king has even called for me; he's obviously busy with the affairs of state. Perhaps he has even found another young maiden from his never-ending parade who is more to his liking than myself. Doesn't Mordecai realize that while I am a queen, I am also a mere subject in the hand of the king?! Hear me, Lord, I pray; I have need of Your wisdom."*

Rising too quickly from her place of prayer, asking but not waiting for a response, Esther stood up and moved toward her writing table. She hastily called for Hathach and instructed him to go to Mordecai at once, bearing this message: *"All the king's officials and the people of the royal provinces know that for any man or woman who approaches the king in the inner court without being summoned, the king has but one law: that he be put to death. The only exception to this is for the king to extend the gold scepter to him and spare his life."*

"Tell him that thirty days have passed since I was called to go to the king," she instructed Hathach. *"Remind him that though I am Xerxes' queen, I am a mere subject in his hand. Tell him that his request places me in a very precarious and life-threatening situation. Wait for his response, and then return immediately to me."*

ENCOMPASSING SHOCK WAVES

Have you ever felt overwhelmed by the circumstances surrounding you? Have you ever been confused about which direction to go or which decision to make? Have mentors, whom you love and respect, ever pointed you in a direction, while your heart was unsure of the wisdom of their counsel?

Doubt and indecision must have been colliding like buses in a tornado in Esther's heart at this point in time. While you may not be the queen of a vast empire with the lives of your entire ethnic group at risk, you probably have been in situations that shocked your senses or caught you off guard. You may have been surprised at your own initial reactions. In those moments, lives may or may not have been at risk, but hearts probably were. Either way, the pressure was real and so were the shock waves.

One young mother describes her feelings at the miscarriage of her baby: *"I didn't want to wake up! I wanted the doctor to give me another dose of anesthetic to knock me out again. I didn't want to face reality. I wanted to crawl into my own little black hole and leave the world behind."* [5]

Another woman describes her emotions at the loss of her husband to death: *"The life of one very dear husband and father was snuffed out in a tragic accident. So alive one minute—gone the next. . . . it was the most traumatic experience of my life. It was a time of heartache, shock, fear, frustration, loneliness—and mistakes."* [6]

Another wife describes her emotions after the recent discovery of her husband's affair: *"I have times when I handle matters very rationally and am as calm as normal. But sometimes my emotions are sparked by just a look from my husband. I may get an empty aching inside or be tempted to charge toward him in a blind rage. I have no way of knowing which side of my personality will emerge."* [7]

> *"I was a Gretel without a Hansel lost in the woods. There was a wicked witch who would eat me if I would listen."*

Author Laurel Lee describes the emotions she felt during treatment for Hodgkin's disease, while her husband filed for divorce, leaving her with two young children and a newborn baby: *"I was in the wilderness of my life. I was a Gretel without a Hansel lost in the woods. There was a wicked witch who would eat me if I would listen. In my thoughts were my wars fought."* [8]

At the birth of a handicapped child, one mother says: *"My own world went out of order when Mike was born. I saw no way to make it right. . . . One day Mike cried with colic all day. By late afternoon my nerves were so frazzled they were ready to rip like silk at the slightest snag. Jimmy [her healthy two-year-old] came in from playing, happily dirty from head to bare foot. One look at him, and I began screaming . . . Suddenly I looked at him . . . here was this frightened, adorable child, wide-eyed, having not the least idea why his mother was screaming. I burst out crying and went down on my knees to hug him and tell him Mommy was sorry. . . ."* [9]

OVERWHELMED OR OVERCOMING

Startling news went around the world on September 11, 2001, as terrorists attacked the World Trade Centers in New York City and the Pentagon in Washington, D.C. By gaining control of passenger airplanes and hurtling them into the buildings, terrorists killed passengers and thousands of people in these buildings. They also hijacked one other plane, United Airlines flight 93. This flight did not reach its predetermined destination, due to the bravery of some passengers who attacked the hijackers and brought the plane down in a field, sixty-five miles southeast of Pittsburgh. The crash killed all forty-five on board, but no one else. The alleged target of flight 93 was either the Capitol building or the White House in Washington, D.C. The bravery of these men saved hundreds, perhaps thousands, of lives.

One of the "rescuers" on this flight was Jeremy Glick, a thirty-one-year-old husband, new father, and sales manager for the web site firm, Vividence, headquartered in San Mateo, California. Jeremy had a genuine love for life and enjoyed sports, such as helicopter skiing and scuba diving; he was a 6'1", 220-lb. former judo and wrestling champion. Jeremy and his wife, Lyzbeth, lived in upstate New York with his newest passion, their baby girl, Emerson, named after his favorite writer, Ralph Waldo Emerson. "Emmy" was born in July, almost three months prior to this event. Jeremy had not been originally scheduled to be on UA flight 93 but was unexpectedly able to catch the flight, as he anxiously headed for home to be with his wife and new baby girl.

With distinguishable intensity in his voice, Jeremy called Lyz on his cell phone from the plane. With a description of the skyjackers, he told her that his plane had been hijacked; he needed confirmation about the incidents at the Twin Towers, as other passengers were receiving that news from their cell phone calls to family members. Lyz confirmed what was happening, and Jeremy told her that he and a few other men on the plane planned to attack the hijackers and prevent this flight from a similar demise.

Lyz reported later, *"We said 'I love you' a thousand times. It helped us*

> *"We said 'I love you' a thousand times. It helped us pull it together."*

pull it together." [10] They continued their conversation for several minutes. Before their conversation ended, Jeremy told her, *"I want you to be happy in your life. I will be happy for you. You need to live your life."* [11]

Following the events of this day, Lyz thoughtfully contemplated, many times over, the lives of Jeremy and the other men with whom he had banded together to stop the presumed intentions of the terrorists on UA flight 93. As she considered the fact that Jeremy was not initially scheduled to be on the perilous flight that required the ultimate sacrifice, she said, *"Maybe God, or whatever, put them on there because He knew that they could stop some of the evil that was going on in the world. That's what I'd like to believe and tell our daughter."* [12]

DESPERATE TIMES

Each of these testimonies is an unexpected, life-changing experience that assaults the natural senses and challenges the spirit. Whether the loss is a child, husband, physical health, or emotional stability, unexpected experiences threaten our immediate sense of security and challenge our courage.

Following the September 11 terrorist attacks on America, Rev. Margaret A. Muncie of St. Michael's Episcopal Church in Manhattan is reported to have said, *"Sometimes, the grief, the sadness, the horror is overwhelming. All we can do is be silent unto God. And in the silence be touched."* [13] I am sure that Mordecai's mourning included waves of loud weeping and wailing, deep sorrowful groans, and quietness that beseeched God to reach down from heaven and touch the pain that was deep within his soul.

On September 14, 2001, at the National Day of Prayer and Remembrance service at Washington's National Cathedral, President

George W. Bush said, in honor of the victims of the September 11 attack:

> *God's signs are not always the ones we look for. We learn in tragedy that His purposes are not always our own, yet the prayers of private suffering, whether in our homes or in this great cathedral, are known and heard and understood.*
>
> *There are prayers that help us last through the day or endure the night. There are prayers of friends and strangers that give us strength for the journey, and there are prayers that yield our will to a will greater than our own.*
>
> *This world He created is of moral design. Grief and tragedy and hatred are only for a time. Goodness, remembrance, and love have no end, and the Lord of life holds all who die and all who mourn.*[14]

> "We learn in tragedy that His purposes are not always our own, yet the prayers of private suffering. . .are known and heard and understood."

You too may have been recently stunned by a turn of events in your own life. Don't be alarmed if your first reactions included protecting yourself or those close to you. In moments of crisis, it is very normal to cling to self-preservation and look for someone else to blame or defer to. It is natural to be shocked and numbed by an unplanned encounter or loss of hope.

For you, the unexpected may be the loss of a college scholarship, a job, a home, or something else. Whatever the shock, whatever the loss, one thing is usually true—these events initially stun the heart and disturb the soul. They usually require that you respond quickly and assuredly, just as Esther did. They also give you little time to think before they demand of you a response. Esther's first reaction was to protect and cover Mordecai and offer a logical reason for her own self-preservation. What will be your first reaction at the next unexpected incident in your life?

When all is said and done, do you think God will take that which the enemy means for your demise and use it for His good? What will you choose to see—the violence of the storm or the God who, in His sovereignty, has allowed the storm? That choice is up to you. Will your first reaction be your only response? As with Esther, this choice also will be up to you.

Psalm 60:3 says, *"You have shown your people desperate times."* Yes, God has allowed and will continue to allow us to experience desperate times, personally and nationally. But when difficult times come and we experience the horror that accompanies these tragedies, we also experience the incredible grace that He ministers to us through them. Our reactions to these hurdles and our responses to God in them, from beginning to end, can break us or mold us. The real struggles that come to us in life are not truly found in the difficulties themselves, but rather in what we lose if we choose to run from them.

> *"The real struggles that come to us in life are not truly found in the difficulties themselves, but rather in what we lose if we choose to run from them."*

Some first reactions, made in the spur of the moment, are better than the choices we may later make regarding the circumstances. Conversely, once time has allowed us to evaluate the situation, our initial reactions are sometimes mistakes we later regret. Though they may or may not help our understanding of the circumstances, all first reactions are allowed and received by the Father and are usually best resolved if they end in yielded prayer. Whatever first reactions you have to the challenges that are before you, remember, there is power in a surrendered life.

David on Distress

David's Petitions

1 CHRON. 21:13 *"... I am in deep distress. Let me fall into the hands of the LORD, for his mercy is very great; but do not let me fall into the hands of men."*

PS. 4:1 *"Answer me when I call to you, O my righteous God. Give me relief from my distress; be merciful to me and hear my prayer."*

PS. 25:18 *"Look upon my affliction and my distress and take away all my sins."*

PS. 31:9 *"Be merciful to me, O LORD, for I am in distress; my eyes grow weak with sorrow, my soul and my body with grief."*

PS. 35:26 *"May all who gloat over my distress be put to shame and confusion; may all who exalt themselves over me be clothed with shame and disgrace."*

PS. 69:29 *"I am in pain and distress; may your salvation, O God, protect me."*

PS 102:2 *"Do not hide your face from me when I am in distress. Turn your ear to me; when I call, answer me quickly."*

David's Proclamations

2 SAM. 22:7   *"In my distress I called to the LORD; I called out to my God. From his temple he heard my voice; my cry came to his ears."*

2 SAM. 24:14   *"...I am in deep distress. Let us fall into the hands of the LORD, for his mercy is great; but do not let me fall into the hands of men."*

2 CHRON. 15:4   *"But in their distress they turned to the LORD, the God of Israel, and sought him, and he was found by them."*

2 CHRON. 20:9   *"If calamity comes upon us, whether the sword of judgment, or plague or famine, we will stand in your presence before this temple that bears your Name and will cry out to you in our distress, and you will hear us and save us."*

PS. 55:17   *"Evening, morning and noon I cry out in distress, and he hears my voice."*

PS. 106:44-45   *"But he took note of their distress when he heard their cry; for their sake he remembered his covenant and out of his great love he relented."*

PS. 107:6   *"Then they cried out to the LORD in their trouble, and he delivered them from their distress."*

PS. 119:143   *"Trouble and distress have come upon me, but your commands are my delight."*

PS. 120:1   *"I call on the LORD in my distress, and he answers me."*

NOTES

1   *"Dispatches were sent by couriers to all the king's provinces with the order to destroy, kill and anni-hilate all the Jews—young and old, women and little children—on a single day, the thirteenth day of the twelfth month, the month of Adar, and to plunder their goods"*(Esther 3:13).

2   *"Then Haman said to King Xerxes, 'There is a certain people dispersed and scattered among the peo-ples in all the provinces of your kingdom whose customs are different from those of all other people and who do not obey the king's laws; it is not in the king's best interest to tolerate them'"* (Esther 3:8).

3   "Susa was now the capital of Persia, and the main residence of the Persians of high rank. These, being attached to the religion of Zoroaster, would naturally sympathize with the Jews, and be dis-turbed at their threatened destruction. Even apart from this bond of union, the decree was suffi-ciently strange and ominous to 'perplex' thoughtful citizens." F.C. Cook, ed., *Barnes' Notes, The Bible Commentary* (Grand Rapids: Baker, 1996), 496.

4   *"All the king's officials and the people of the royal provinces know that for any man or woman who approaches the king in the inner court without being summoned the king has but one law: that he be put to death. The only exception to this is for the king to extend the gold scepter to him and spare his life . . ."* (Esther 3:11).

5   Pam W. Vredevelt, *Empty Arms* (Portland, Ore.: Multnomah, 1984), 20-21.

6   Amy Ross Young, *By Death or Divorce . . . It Hurts to Lose* (Denver: Accent, 1976), 14.

7   Dr. Les Carter, *The Prodigal Spouse, How to Survive Infidelity* (Nashville: Nelson, 1990), 54.

8   Laurel Lee, *Walking Through the Fire* (New York: E.P. Dutton, 1977), 108-109.

9   Bette M. Ross, *Our Special Child, A Guide to Successful Parenting of Handicapped Children* (Old Tappan, N.J.: Fleming H. Revell, 1984), 38-39.

10 "Above and Beyond," *People Weekly*, Vol. 56, No. 14 (October 1, 2001), 54.

11 Ibid., 57.

12 Ibid., 57.

13 Ibid., 74.

14 MSNBC News E-mail (September 18, 2001).

Penetrating Truths

"When Esther's words were reported to Mordecai, he sent back this answer: 'Do not think that because you are in the king's house you alone of all the Jews will escape. For if you remain silent at this time, relief and deliverance for the Jews will arise from another place, but you and your father's family will perish. And who knows but that you have come to royal position for such a time as this?'" (Esther 4:12-14).

Esther waited anxiously in her chambers for Mordecai's response to her message. She couldn't sit. She paced, as was her customary behavior when she had acted prematurely before receiving guidance from her heavenly Father. She knew that she had sent her response to Mordecai before she really had her wits about her, and she wondered now what he was thinking. She hoped that the eunuch, Hathach, would represent her respectful demeanor to Mordecai, even though her message portrayed a shocked, pleading tone. Waiting seemed to be her lot in life; usually she did not mind, but today she was wrought with worry.

———•◦•———

Meanwhile, outside the palace Mordecai was surprised and saddened by the message he received through Hathach. The idea that his "daughter" and "disciple" seemed to care more for her own safety than the safety of their people made the depths of his grief deeper still. He took his time to evaluate the situation, as if Hathach were not even present and awaiting a response. *"Has Esther been behind the palace walls so long that she has lost sight of the people she is bound to in blood and in calling?"* Though the answer to this question was unclear, he knew that he had to boldly cross a line that mentors rarely did to see if there remained in Esther a surrendered heart.

The eunuch now stepped back from the "old gatekeeper" out of respect, seeing that Mordecai needed time to formulate his private thoughts. He waited patiently from a distance and was momentarily distracted by the ducks in the fountain pond nearby.

Mordecai knew well that all true mentors respected the line between influence and manipulation, and he feared that Esther might interpret his intrusion as a manipulative maneuver, rather than a heartfelt directive. It would never be his goal to require of her any type of reimbursement for his personal investment in her life; their years together had been as meaningful to him as he hoped they had been to her. But now, due to the strategy of an enemy and the destiny that the one true God had laid out for her, he had a request that would challenge the very fibers of their relationship. As he had unselfishly laid down his life for her, his last request was that she would, in turn, lay down her life for many.

In inner turmoil, he asked almost out loud, *"Esther, what are you thinking? To send me clothes from the king's palace at a time of such grieving in Susa was absurd enough, but now to send me this message, with concern for yourself alone, is utter blindness! Have you lived in the obscurity of palace life too long? Has it clouded your mind and darkened your discernment? How can you dare to weigh the impending bloodshed and certain annihilation of your people against your single sacrifice? Do you not know that your own family name will be obliterated from the pages of our Jewish history in this mass murder? Esther, how dare you weigh such a certainty against a mere possibility!"*

Mordecai realized that, in the midst of his anxious thoughts, he had begun to pace back and forth and slap his hands together. The polite eunuch was no longer distracted by the ducks in the pond and now looked his direction. It was time for Mordecai, the aged mentor, to boldly speak out, as he had in times past, with penetrating words and persuasive speech. This time his voice would have to cross the barrier of position and the realm of power. It would have to cut through fear and remain poignant, though it was a message born by a courier, rather than a heartfelt, personal confrontation. He wondered if there was still a genuine respect for his leadership in the heart of his young "disciple," Esther. Or had she grown beyond his grasp?

He knew that he must be strong in his confrontation but entreating in his message. He knew that the truth would penetrate her heart and dare to leave a devastating wound. He motioned for Hathach to draw near and said, *"Tell Queen Esther, 'Do not flatter yourself that you shall escape in the king's palace any more than all the other Jews. For if you keep silent at this time, relief and deliverance shall arise for the Jews from elsewhere, but you and your father's house will perish. And who knows but that you have come to the kingdom for such a time as this and for this very occasion?'* [1]

"Tell her that she has been destined to shine brightly in the midst of darkness from the foundations of the earth." By now, he and Hathach both had tears in their eyes, but he continued, *"Tell her to remember that she is called as a symbol of triumph for our people in their darkest hour. It is now time for her to glow like a star in the darkness of the night and to shine a light on the pathway of victory 'so that people may see and know, may consider and understand, that the hand of the Lord has done this.'"* [2]

Hathach bowed in respect to Mordecai and then quietly and quickly took the message to Queen Esther's quarters, knowing that she anxiously awaited him there.

Though functioning in the role of a mentor and father figure, Mordecai was risking his very head to send such a message to a Persian queen. He was also beseeching this dear disciple to put her life on the line on behalf of a people that had probably long since forgotten her. Besides the threat of bloodshed, he was risking losing the heart of the only "daughter" he had ever known. To lose a life was one thing, but to lose a relationship of love and friendship was a burden too heavy for his heart to bear. Should he risk this great loss and challenge her own adult ability to make decisions, or should he trust that God would "raise up another," knowing in his heart that the only "rescuer" for his people was his own dear "daughter"?

This was the time for him to speak penetrating truths to his Esther. If, after the investment of his love and mentoring, she could not receive the truth as it pierced her very soul, then so be it. He must take that risk for the sake of their people. After all, was there not a cause? Surely there was a need for a trumpet voice in the land, and it must be his, even if speaking out jeopardized his life and his years of faithful investment.

RISKY MENTORING MOMENTS

While you may be functioning fully in an adult capacity, there can come times when trusted advisors and mentors will step back onto the stage of your life with strong determinations and heartfelt requests. Those are risky times for both your mentor and you, the mentored. If the mentor is brash and not entreating, you may be offended and put off by the approach and, therefore, unable to hear the message. If you are unapproachable and unyielding, your mentor may be hurt by a loss of influence and well-earned respect. It is imperative that you both be considerate of one another and posture yourselves in surrender to the Father's will.

In these times, the mentor must boldly make the trumpet call, and then step back and trust that his or her past investment in your life will yield a good return. When faced with penetrating truths, you, as the disciple, must hear the heart of your mentor while discerning the will of your Master.

> *". . .you . . .must hear the heart of your mentor while discerning the will of your Master."*

Just as Esther needed to heed Mordecai's petition, she also needed to implore the Lord and hear from heaven. Many lives were at risk, and it was crucial that she consider, not only the petition of her mentor, but the will of her God, as well. So it is with us. As adults, we too must give due respect, not only to our mentors, but also to the voice of the Lord within our own ears. However, we must never lose sight of the fact that it is God who placed these mentors, parents, and guides in our lives, and they are voices to be esteemed, no matter what season of life we are in.

A MENTOR'S TRUMPET CALL

There have been many "Mordecais" who have bravely made the trumpet call to their "disciples" through the ages. The sixteenth president of the United States certainly was a "Mordecai" in his own rite, as he motivated an entire congress and stirred a nation to set its people free. In his address at Cooper Union, New York, on February 27, 1860, Abraham Lincoln stated, *"Let us have faith that right makes might, and in that faith let us to the end dare to do our duty as we understand it."* [3]

Later, at his first inaugural address on March 4, 1861, he declared: *"If by the mere force of numbers a majority should deprive a minority of any clearly written constitutional right, it might, in a moral point of view, justify revolution—certainly would if such a right were a vital one."* [4]

In Mr. Lincoln's second annual message to Congress, on December 1, 1862, he trumpeted:

> *Fellow citizens, we cannot escape history. We of this Congress and this administration will be remembered in spite of ourselves. No personal significance or insignificance can spare one or another of us. The fiery trial through which we pass will light us down in honor or dishonor to the last generation . . . In giving freedom to the slave, we assure freedom to the free—honorable alike in what we give and what we preserve. We shall nobly save or*

meanly lose the last, best hope of earth. Other means may succeed; this could not fail. The way is plain, peaceful, generous, just—a way which if followed the world will forever applaud and God must forever bless.[5]

Could it be that the heartstrings of the ancient Mordecai and the noble Mr. Lincoln have been interwoven in destiny on the pages of history? They were both spokesmen for the freedom of a generation that was about to go to war. Courage was required of them both, as it would be of others in the future.

More contemporary "Mordecais" cry out to each of us today to heed the needs of our own generation. This new millennial generation is experiencing more persecution than any other in Christian history. The statistics of rage and maliciousness are on the increase throughout the earth. Christians living in peaceful settings must not sit idly by while their brothers and sisters in Christ suffer at the hands of evil persecutors. The "Mordecai-cry" is clear and challenging; it provokes the senses and pierces the conscience.

> *"The "Mordecai-cry" is clear and challenging; it provokes the senses and pierces the conscience."*

Charles Colson, the chairman of Prison Fellowship Ministries, says, *"We must feel a sense of moral outrage that Christians, in this day and age, are being sold into slavery, and are being tortured for their faith."* [6]

Jack Hayford, former pastor of Church on the Way in Van Nuys, California, states, *"We need to shake awake those who are in power, to bring their attention to these injustices. And where we have a voice, speak out . . . Once you know, then you're accountable . . . Proverbs 3:23 and 24 says, 'Don't withhold to do good when it's in the power of your hand to do it. And don't say to your neighbor in need, "Come back tomorrow and I'll help."'"* [7]

Joseph M. Stowell, president of Moody Bible Institute, proclaims, *"It is imperative that we as a church marshal the power of prayer. We cannot sit* *by as if nothing is happening. Get on the phone, write letters, and let those in authority know what you believe. We have been confused, intimidated, and silent too long. We must stand and be counted." *[8]

Well-known speaker, Ravi Zacharias, the author of Deliver Us From Evil, states, *"The Bible is very clear about what we are asked to do for those who are victimized because of their faith. We are called upon to pray for them and lay claim to the civic privileges that God has given to us. It is our turn to speak up. The silence of many on behalf of the few ultimately diminishes and could destroy all of us."*[9]

Who should speak up about such injustices? Who is required to petition the Lord on behalf of those who are persecuted for righteousness' sake? Are the "Mordecais" of this generation the presidents of universities, the pastors of large churches, and the political lobbyists in Washington, D.C.? While these courageous believers are certainly valid and effective spokesmen, they are not the only ones with a causative voice today.

The majority of "Mordecais" in this world are common men and women who are risk-takers and dedicated mentors with keen perception and discerning vision. They are "proclaimers" of the truth. They are ordinary people who attempt extraordinary feats, often at the expense of their own comfort and under the scrutiny of colleagues or "disciples" who are looking on. They are the common ones among us who are willing to attempt the uncommon tasks and take the criticism that goes with it. They are the bold ones who are willing to bear the stripes, deflect the criticism, and influence this generation.

> *"The majority of "Mordecais" in this world are common men and women who are risk-takers. . .with keen perception and discerning vision."*

These "Mordecais" come in all shapes and sizes. Some of them are pastors and public speakers who, in one moment of time, will speak a word that will penetrate your heart and set your course for a lifetime. Some of them are mothers who will offer you a warm cookie in one hand

and a word from the Lord in the other. Some of them are grandfathers who have walked the walk of faith for decades and can draw you a map of both high and low points on the road of life. Some of them may be piano teachers or language tutors; others may be artists, songwriters, or athletic coaches. No matter how refined or abrupt they may be in manner, they all have one thing in common—they care. They care about you and the generation of which you are a part.

THE COST OF MENTORING

If you are the "Mordecai" in a young person's life, you must handle this responsibility with prayerful concern and tender consideration. However, if God has placed you in such a position of influence, and obvious disaster is on the horizon for your disciple, you must boldly speak the truth, even if you run the risk of severing your relationship. Part of Mordecai's calling was to bravely give his all, even if it meant sacrificing his personal comfort.

> *"Having influence will require of you personal comfort and perhaps even your life."*

If you desire to be influential beyond your own generation, you must settle this matter in your own heart once and for all. Having influence will require of you personal comfort and perhaps even your life. Influence yields great rewards, but it is costly. Knowing you have made a mark on a young person's life may warm you with sentiment on a cool, rainy evening, but having this kind of influence will also stretch you beyond measure when you least expect it.

Many athletic coaches are mentors and devoted "Mordecais" to their players. One such risk-taking "Mordecai" is a man by the name of Juan Elguezabal. He was the high school girls' basketball coach from Heppner, Oregon, during the AA high school tournament in the spring of 2000.

I was in attendance at this tournament with my husband, who is currently a coach of our Christian high school team. My husband's philosophy is that coaching basketball is a way to mentor young people concerning life. He calls basketball the "little game" that prepares us for the "big game" of life.

The team my husband helps coach came into this tournament with a forty-five-game winning streak. They were the defending state champions and the overwhelming favorites to repeat. Much to everyone's surprise, they lost their first game to a team no one thought would come close to them. This shocking disappointment left them stunned and bewildered. As my husband and the other coaches sought to pastor the girls through their agony, the next day's newspaper provided a life message that would help put things back into perspective. He brought the newspaper to the team meeting and read to the girls the front-page story about another attending team's coach, Juan Elguezabal.

What made Juan's coaching job special was not so much the fact that his team had made it to the state tournament, or that this would be his last season as a coach. What made it special to him was that his daughter, San Juanita, was on the team; they were a beloved father/daughter duo. While this held special significance for the two of them, a father coaching his daughter is not so uncommon at the ΛΛ level of high school basketball. It was neither his mentoring of his daughter nor the challenge of a state tournament that gave his story headlines in the local newspaper. Rather, it was the personal risk that he took in each game that enabled him to convey a message, not only to his daughter and his team, but to the tournament participants and local residents, as well.

When asked about his unique situation by the local newspaper, Juan reported,

> *A CAT scan and an MRI showed I have cancer all through my brain and lungs. They told me, "You could be dead in six months." That was just three weeks after they told me I had a clean bill of health. . . . The doctors told me to quit coaching, but I have to finish this year up. I think I owe*

that to them [his team]. . . . Every time I jump up [from the
bench], it takes just a little bit more protein from my body.
And the deficiency of protein takes away from muscle . . .
which makes me weaker.[10]

With life literally ebbing from his body with each game he coached, Juan remained steadfast to his commitment. To coach his daughter and his team through to the end would mean a victory for each of them, regardless of what the scoreboard read.

When interviewed, his daughter, San Juanita, said:

I wish I could be a little better in basketball so I could
show him I'm learning from him in the last sport he's
coaching. But I'm just happy he's my coach now. . . . Those
are the things I'll be able to look back on . . . the two rela-
tionships, as father and coach, that we've had. That's what
I love.[11]

Amy Papineau, the forward on his team, said:

I think we're all sad about what's going on. . . . He's a very
strong person and we [the team] admire his strength. Just
because something bad has happened to him, he's not
going to quit on life; we respect that.[12]

The story made the front page of the local newspaper, and the life message of a committed mentor penetrated the hearts of the entire community. *"The two relationships, as father and coach . . . that's what I love." "Just because something bad has happened to him, he's not going to quit on life; we respect that."* Those two statements from the hearts of these young players were rewards for this very brave and loving coach. Even though his team did not win the tournament and his natural life may have come to an end soon after, Juan's life message will live on in the hearts of these girls and all who read his story. His message was perhaps more subtle than the ancient Mordecai's, though no less impacting. For the tournament players, coaches, and newsreaders, it put every game into appropriate perspective.

Were there those on the sidelines wondering if Juan's sacrifice lacked in wisdom? Of course, there are always questioning sideliners. Did this role of coach and father cost him something? Yes, his very life-energy, in fact. Was it worth it? That question was never a consideration for him. For all those who mentor at great personal cost, purpose makes sacrifice reasonable.

President Abraham Lincoln was once quoted as saying, *"I do the very best I know how—the very best I can; and I mean to keep doing so until the end. If the end brings me out all right, what is said against me won't amount to anything. If the end brings me out wrong, ten angels swearing I was right would make no difference."* [13]

> *"If the end brings me out all right, what is said against me won't amount to anything. If the end brings me out wrong, ten angels swearing I was right would make no difference."*

Whether you have a message for a queen, like Mordecai, for a nation in turmoil, like Mr. Lincoln, or for a daughter, a basketball team, and so many more, like Juan Elguezabal, deliver it with boldness and assurance. Walk with your head held high and your faith solidly planted in the assurance of God's love. As President Lincoln said, if your perspective proves to be right, then what is said against you *"won't amount to anything,"* and if you happen to be wrong, *"ten angels swearing"* you were right *"would make no difference."*

The Power of Truth

PS. 25:5 *"Guide me in your truth and teach me, for you are God my Savior, and my hope is in you all day long."*

PS. 51:6 *"Surely you desire truth in the inner parts; you teach me wisdom in the inmost place."*

PS. 86:11 *"Teach me your way, O LORD, and I will walk in your truth; give me an undivided heart, that I may fear your name."*

PS. 119:30 *"I have chosen the way of truth; I have set my heart on your laws."*

PS. 145:18 *"The LORD is near to all who call on him, to all who call on him in truth."*

PROV. 16:13 *"Kings take pleasure in honest lips; they value a man who speaks the truth."*

ROM. 2:8 *"But for those who are self-seeking and who reject the truth and follow evil, there will be wrath and anger."*

1 COR. 13:6 *"Love does not delight in evil but rejoices with the truth."*

GAL. 4:16 *"Have I now become your enemy by telling you the truth?"*

GAL. 5:7 *"You were running a good race. Who cut in on you and kept you from obeying the truth?"*

EPH. 4:15 *"Instead, speaking the truth in love, we will in all things grow up into him who is the Head, that is, Christ."*

EPH. 5:8,9 *"For you were once darkness, but now you are light in the Lord. Live as children of light (for the fruit of the light consists in all goodness, righteousness and truth)."*

EPH. 6:14 *"Stand firm then, with the belt of truth buckled around your waist, with the breastplate of righteousness in place,"*

2 TIM. 2:25 *"Those who oppose him he must gently instruct, in the hope that God will grant them repentance leading them to a knowledge of the truth,"*

1 PET. 1:22 *"Now that you have purified yourselves by obeying the truth so that you have sincere love for your brothers, love one another deeply, from the heart."*

1 JOHN 1:6 *"If we claim to have fellowship with him yet walk in the darkness, we lie and do not live by the truth."*

1 JOHN 3:18 *"Dear children, let us not love with words or tongue but with actions and in truth."*

N O T E S

1   Esther 4:13-14 (Amplified)

2   Isaiah 41:20

3   John Bartlett, *Bartlett's Familiar Quotations*, Justin Kaplan, ed., 16th ed. (Boston, New York, London: Little, Brown and Co., 1992), 448.

4   Ibid., 449.

5   Ibid., 449.

6   Paul Marshall with Lela Gilbert, *Their Blood Cries Out* (Dallas: Word, 1997). Used by permission. All rights reserved.

7   Ibid.

8   Ibid.

9   Ibid.

10   Lance Ogden, "Quitting is not an Option – Heppner Coach Battling for his Life," *East Oregonian* (March 1, 2000), 1A, 5A.

11   Ibid.

12   Ibid.

13   John Bartlett, *Bartlett's Familiar Quotations*, Justin Kaplan, ed., 16th ed. (Boston, New York, London: Little, Brown and Co., 1992), 451.

CHAPTER TWELVE

Surrender that Opens the Door of Sacrifice

"Then Esther sent this reply to Mordecai: 'Go, gather together all the Jews who are in Susa, and fast for me. Do not eat or drink for three days, night or day. I and my maids will fast as you do. When this is done, I will go to the king, even though it is against the law. And if I perish, I perish.' So Mordecai went away and carried out all of Esther's instructions" (Esther 4:15-17).

Esther listened intently to every word that Mordecai had sent through her loyal eunuch, Hathach. The words penetrated her heart so deeply that she felt dizzy and weak and needed to sit. The message was fervent to the point of making her feel faint.

It was not that the words were sharp or harsh, for Hathach had done a remarkable job in his delivery of imparting the very heart of her beloved mentor, Mordecai. In fact, as strangely as it seemed, he had so closely imitated Mordecai's demeanor and tone that it was as if Mordecai himself had delivered the message. If anything, the eunuch's excellent delivery had made the words even more piercing. The message was penetrating, not because of its severity, but rather because it rang true in her spirit. But she still had to be sure. It wasn't that she didn't trust her cousin Mordecai; but if she were to risk death or banishment, she herself needed to hear from God.

As a child, she had known of the power of complete surrender to Jehovah through fasting and prayer. Without a doubt, she knew that this was where she should turn first. She also knew that there was power in the agreement of souls uniting in prayer. As she felt Jehovah leading her thoughts, she decided to call a fast for herself and her maidens and to also have Mordecai call the people of Susa to fasting and prayer. Though she felt anxious within herself, she also felt confident. Esther firmly believed, as they all set their hearts and ears toward Jehovah, that He would clearly lay out the strategy she should take and would also give her the courage to do what she must do.

She sent a reply back to Mordecai immediately. *"Go, gather together all the Jews who are in Susa, and fast for me. Do not eat or drink for three days, night or day. My maids and I will fast as you do. When this is done, I will go to the king, even though it is against the law. And if I perish, I perish."* Hathach summoned Esther's maids to her chambers and left immediately to deliver the message to Mordecai.

Esther spoke with her maidens of the edict to eradicate the Jews, and told them that if the king had not summoned her within three days, she planned to go into his presence on behalf of the Jews. In the meantime, she commanded that they all fast and pray with her to the God Jehovah and beseech His favor. The maids, knowing what approaching the king unannounced would mean for the life of their beloved queen, vowed quickly to fast and pray on her behalf. At Esther's request, the maidens left her quarters in quietness and contemplation.

In the solitude of her own room, Esther sat on the floor near her bed, but before she could utter a word of prayer, anxiety began to overtake her emotions. *"Where will I find the courage to do that which Mordecai is asking of me?"* she pondered within herself. *"If I find the courage, should I do it? And if so, how? Both Vashti and Mordecai displayed courage in the face of King Xerxes' commands with costly results. Vashti showed bravery by refusing to humiliate herself on Xerxes' drunken whim, and Mordecai did so by refusing to bow to the king's arrogant Prince Haman. Yes, both were brave, but both were also punished. Xerxes banished Vashti on the basis of violating protocol that was merely written in his heart. What will he do to me if I violate well-known protocol that has been inscribed clearly in his written laws?"*

Her thoughts waged war, one with the other. *"Mordecai's courage brought judgment, not only to himself, but now also to our people. Was Mordecai right in standing up to Haman, or was it a mistake? Could he not have outwardly bowed and inwardly stood?"* As the turmoil in her heart became yet more turbulent, she stood and asked aloud of the empty room, *"What about me?! I have to bow before the king every time I respond to his bidding. Everyone has to bow."* Pacing now, she gestured passionately as she continued, *"Yes, yes, it is a mere nod of the head and a polite bend at the waist, not a true bow prostrate before him; but nevertheless, it is a means of acknowledging his position of authority. Mordecai has never instructed me to do less, but then he has never instructed me to do more, either. Truth be told, my conscience has never been completely violated on this issue, as I have never really had to completely prostrate myself before Xerxes in acknowledgement of his godlikeness.*

"What then is this turmoil in my heart? How could I question Mordecai's sagely wisdom? Of course Mordecai could not bow to Prince Haman, giving divine homage to him. Haman is a mere mortal, and a wicked one at that! Of course he could not bow; but by not doing so, he is taking with him in punishment all the Jews of Persia, including me! Oh, how my heart churns! Am I destined forever to surrender my steps to others?"

This was the biggest decision of Esther's life. It would require her to surrender, not only to the perspective of a mentor, but to the Lord's word, as well. Realizing that her personal exile or punishment would bring no relief to her people, she was once again reminded that there was power in a surrendered life. Surrender had been her close ally before; it had always served her well. This, however, was not a matter of surrendering to Mordecai's petitions alone; this was a matter of hearing the voice of God and surrendering to His will. *"But to what,"* she wondered, *"am I to surrender?"* She knew "to whom" she was called to surrender, but "to what?" was the question that remained. *"Will it be death or banishment, victory or defeat?"* That question would only be answered in the presence of the one true God. She knew that she must seek His solution for the sake of her people.

Returning to her bedside and bowing on her knees, she buried her face in her goose-down pillow, set aside her own fruitless musings, and focused her questions and petitions toward the Lord. Beginning with humble repentance, she pleaded, *"Forgive me, Father, for being more concerned about my own personal demise than that of my people. My desire for self-preservation has led me down the pathway of vanity. Please forgive me, Jehovah, for I am Yours alone. Your mercies have been new to me everyday; please, let my focus be on Your intention, Your will, not my own.*

"I have faithfully surrendered to those You have placed as a covering over my life, and I have to admit that I have been blessed as a result. But today, I come to You alone, oh God. What would You require of me? I come to You on behalf of my people and with my people to seek Your face. Oh Lord Most High, it is You alone to whom I come. I come humbly with a sincere heart to hear Your voice. I come in earnest desire to know Your will."

As she stood, approaching her window and looking upwards toward the heavens, she cried out to her unseen but closely-felt God, *"Calamity is about to befall Your people. That wicked enemy, Haman, is out to destroy us all. Would You loose but one miracle from heaven on behalf of Your people? This is my earnest cry. Grant unto me favor in Your sight, and in the sight of the king, that Your people might be rescued from this malevolent death wish. Just as Your mercies are new to me everyday, oh God, let them be poured out on behalf of Your people this day."*

Kneeling once again, she humbly beseeched the Lord, *"Grant unto me wisdom and favor in the eyes of the king. Let Your strategy guide my thoughts and lead my steps. My life is Yours, great Jehovah. For me, to die is to be at peace in the bosom of Father Abraham; for me, to live is to walk in Your destiny. Both pathways are laden with Your beauty and unfolding purposes. Let it be to me according to Your will, oh God; I surrender all."*

———◆◆◆———

A YIELDED SACRIFICE

To tenderize the soul through prayer and fasting and to strengthen it through unity with others releases the human spirit into realms of great courage. It opens eyes, once blind, and ears, once deaf, to the needs of others and to the will and purposes of God. It exchanges courage for fear, strategy for confusion, and wisdom for lack of understanding. Through complete abandonment to the will and purposes

> *"Through complete abandonment to the will and purposes of God. . .boldness to do His bidding is released."*

of God—body, soul, and spirit—boldness to do His bidding is released.

Fasting was a means of earnestly humbling the soul for the clear purpose of seeking God's favor and grace. While prayer is not specifically mentioned here in Esther 4:15-16, it is obvious that the intent of the fasting was to seek the will and favor of God, which would, of course, include petitions and prayer on behalf of His people. Esther specifically petitioned God that He would enable her to do His will and that He would graciously preserve and deliver His people out of the hand of the enemy.

Her declaration, *"When this is done, I will go to the king, even though it is against the law. And if I perish, I perish,"* is not an expression of despair or hopelessness, but rather a statement of unblemished submission. It is a statement of resignation and ultimate surrender to the providence of God. It is a declaration of her confidence that, when she and her people had completed their time of waiting on God in humility and complete abandonment, she would have both the strategy and the faith to walk out His will. Regardless of what the outcome looked like on this side of eternity, she would have accomplished His purposes on the earth in her generation.

Many others throughout church history have also yielded themselves to God and His purposes to such an extent, even at the cost of their earthly lives. Two such women in the first century were Quinta and Appollonia.

> *[Quinta] was taken to the idol temple where they tried to force her to worship. When she turned away in disgust, "they bound her by the feet and dragged her through the whole city over the rough pavement, so that she was bruised by the big stones, beating her all the while." They stoned her to death and then attacked the homes of other believers.*
>
> *They then seized an elderly virgin, Appollonia. A fifteenth century artist's depiction of her includes a pair of pliers because her persecutors broke out all of her teeth. When they lighted a pyre to torture her, she jumped into the flames and ended her life a martyr.*[1]

Dietrich Bonhoeffer was another yielded beliver who became a voice in his generation, regardless of the personal cost. He was a German Lutheran pastor and theologian. During World War II, he was arrested and placed in a variety of prisons and concentration camps in Germany for preaching the Gospel of Jesus Christ and the truth of equality in Him regardless of race. On April 9, 1945, he was hanged in the Flossenburg concentration camp by the personal order of Heinrich Himmler. Before he died, he proclaimed, *"This is the end, but for me it is the beginning of life."* [2]

Yona Kanamuzeyi is another believer who laid down his life in perfect submission that the message of Christ on behalf of a people might live on. He was a prominent Christian pastor and supporter of a new republic in Rwanda. He was kidnapped and shot in 1964. Before he died, he prayed, *"O God, it was you who called me and sent me to this place. You know all about me—the days I have lived and the days that are left to me. If it is your will to call me home, I leave the decision to you."* [3]

In more current history, news reports of a school in Littleton, Colorado, in May of 1999, told of two teenage boys shooting, wounding, and killing several of their classmates and teachers. During the course of events, one of the questions the young captors asked their victims was *"Do you believe in God?"* If the answer was yes, they immediately shot the responder. Two months later on national television, one teenage girl testified about her bullet wounds for her testimony for Christ. Little did these captors realize that the one whose followers they were trying to kill was the only God who could set them free from the torment of their own minds.

Complete surrender may mean the loss of life on earth, but it may also involve living out your life in courage, as Esther did. Author Max Lucado presents this challenge to modern-day "Mordecais" and "Esthers": *"Have you been called to go out on a limb for God? You can bet it won't be easy. Limb-climbing has never been easy. . . . Ask Jesus. He knows better than anyone the cost of hanging on a tree."* [4]

> *"Complete surrender may mean the loss of life on earth, but it may also involve living out your life in courage. . ."*

Isn't that what we've all been called to do for Christ, in some way? Isn't "limb-climbing" part of our destiny? Isn't that the very thing that keeps us humbly dependent upon God, yet releases in us unexpected boldness, astounding even our own souls?

Rosa Parks is a contemporary American "Esther" who, as a young girl, was willing to do some "limb-climbing." She grew up in the state of Alabama during the twentieth century when slaves were free, but there still remained a great national dysfunction in regard to equality for African Americans. Blacks were expected to sit in the back of public buses, use separate toilets from whites, and were refused service in many restaurants. As President Clinton said at a Capitol Hill ceremony in Rosa's honor, *". . . for millions of Americans, our history was full of weary years, our sweet land of liberty bearing only bitter fruit and silent tears."* [5]

Rosa Parks was a seamstress who worked faithfully at her job in Montgomery, Alabama. On December 1, 1955, she was sitting in the segregated section at the back of the bus. It was the height of the Christmas shopping season, and, as the bus became more crowded, she and the other African Americans on board were expected to move further back in the bus. However, Rosa refused to give up her seat near the front of her section. She was tired of the discrimination and was determined to stay. Her determination was a brave step toward the integration of blacks, not only in Montgomery, Alabama, but also in all of American society. What may seem like a small statement in today's cultural setting was a huge step in 1955.

Rosa Parks received a standing ovation when President Clinton gave her the Congressional Gold Medal in June of 1999. Those present *"were politicians and activists, entertainers and admirers, who all knew they would not be as accomplished, as aware, or as free if Parks had not refused to give up her seat on a segregated Montgomery, Alabama, bus to a white man in 1955."* [6]

Just as Esther's ancestors had been brought to Persia as slaves, were freed, and were later discriminated against, so had Rosa Parks's ancestors been brought to America, set free, and then discriminated against. Just as Esther's people needed an activist, so did African Americans in the past century. Dealing with prejudice was a constant need in Esther's day, in Jesus' day, and it still is today. Christ proclaimed in Galatians 3:28-29, *"There is neither Jew nor Greek, slave nor free, male nor female, for you are all one in Christ Jesus. If you belong to Christ, then you are Abraham's seed, and heirs according to the promise."* This message rings true, throughout the generations, and is proclaimed on the lips of yielded vessels.

> *"Challenges for complete surrender to the will and purposes of God come to us each day. . ."*

Challenges for complete surrender to the will and purposes of God come to us each day in many ways and through various opportunities. They come to us, not only that we may be blessed, but also that others may be saved. The needs of those who are unable to speak for themselves are all around us. From children who need reading tutors to senior citizens who need transportation, from pregnant teens who know no other option but abortion to the abandoned child who needs a family—the list of people who have a great need for someone to stand up and speak on their behalf or to simply come alongside and meet their needs is endless. Some have practical needs, some have spiritual needs, and some have both. We, like Esther, need to seek God, hear from heaven, surrender to the Master's will, and then be bold enough to reach out on others' behalf.

What you are involved in today may be different from what you are designed to be involved in tomorrow. Seasons change, and so does the practical outworking of God's will in our lives. You may be in the very center of God's will for your life today, but if you stay in that place tomorrow, you may be left behind. In the wilderness in Old Testament days, God led His people by a cloud. When the cloud moved, they moved, or they were out from under His protection and blessing. We too must learn to "move with the cloud."

Judson Van de Venter was a man who knew how to "move with the cloud." He grew up in the mid-1800s on a farm near Dundee, Michigan. After graduating from Hillsdale College, he became an art teacher, and later, the supervisor of art for the public schools in Sharon, Pennsylvania. He had a great love for art and had hope of becoming a recognized artist one day.

He was also very active as a layman in his Methodist Episcopal church. Recognizing his spiritual gifts and talents in local evangelistic meetings, his friends encouraged him to drop his teaching career and pursue his calling as an evangelist. For Judson, this was a struggle, one for which he had to wait on God. He struggled with the decision for five years. He writes:

> I had struggled between developing my talents in the field of art and going into full-time evangelistic work. At last the pivotal hour of my life came, and I surrendered all. A new day was ushered into my life. I became an evangelist and discovered down deep in my soul a talent hitherto

unknown to me. God had hidden a song in my heart, and
touching a tender chord, He caused me to sing.

It was after this complete surrender to the Lord to full-time Christian service that he penned the words to the well-known hymn, "I Surrender All." As you read these words, whether for the first time or for the one-thousandth time, let them bring to you a moment of fresh commitment to God and His purposes for your life today.

All to Jesus I surrender, All to Him I freely give;
I will ever love and trust Him, In His presence daily live.

All to Jesus I surrender, Humbly at His feet I bow;
Worldly pleasures all forsaken, Take me, Jesus, take me now.

All to Jesus I surrender, Make me, Savior, wholly Thine;
Let me feel the Holy Spirit, Truly know that Thou art mine.

All to Jesus I surrender, Lord, I give myself to Thee;
Fill me with Thy love and power, Let Thy blessings fall on me.

Chorus:
I surrender all, I surrender all,
All to Thee, my blessed Savior, I surrender all.[8]

If you have not yet "surrendered all" to the Lord, join with Judson Van de Venter and Esther of old and yield to the Master's plans for your life today. After all, if you surrender and you perish, what can you truly lose if it is His will to have you on heaven's side? As the apostle Paul said, *"For to me, to live is Christ and to die is gain"*(Philippians 1:21). If you do not perish and you are yielded to God's purposes, surely your surrender will be but a more intimate molding into the image of Jesus Christ.

There is a common saying, "That which does not kill me, makes me a better person." Perhaps it is in the dying to ourselves that we become better and life is released to others. John the apostle says, *"This is how we know what love is: Jesus Christ laid down his life for us. And we ought to lay down our lives for our brothers"* (1 John 3:16).

Esther's faith statement, *"When this is done, I will go to the king . . . and if I perish, I perish,"* in contemporary vernacular declares, *"After I have humbled myself in unity with my people and bound myself to the will of my gracious and holy God, my perplexity will have been transformed into a positive certainty, and my questions into a strategy suitable for a king. I surrender all!"* In other words, her initial "Oh no!" was translated into a confident "I know!"

Through unity with others in prayer and fasting, we can walk out the will of God confidently and make a difference in our generation, whether it is in an idolatrous temple, a prison, a high school campus, or a city bus. When your "Oh no!" becomes a bold "I know!" your personal surrender has opened the door to sacrifice and you are ready to move with purpose and persuasion into the face of an enemy and the presence of a king.

Fasting and Prayer

Fasting

ISA. 58:6-9   *"Is not this the kind of fasting I have chosen: to loose the chains of injustice and untie the cords of the yoke, to set the oppressed free and break every yoke? Is it not to share your food with the hungry and to provide the poor wanderer with shelter—when you see the naked, to clothe him, and not to turn away from your own flesh and blood? Then your light will break forth like the dawn, and your healing will quickly appear; then your righteousness will go before you, and the glory of the Lord will be your rear guard. Then you will call, and the Lord will answer; you will cry for help, and he will say: Here am I ..."*

JOEL 1:14   *"Declare a holy fast; call a sacred assembly. Summon the elders and all who live in the land to the house of the LORD your God, and cry out to the LORD." (NIV)*

JOEL 2:15   *"Blow the trumpet in Zion, declare a holy fast, call a sacred assembly." (NIV)*

JONAH 3:5   *"The Ninevites believed God. They declared a fast, and all of them, from the greatest to the least, put on sackcloth." (NIV)*

MATT. 6:16   *"When you fast, do not look somber as the hypocrites do, for they disfigure their faces to show men they are fasting. I tell you the truth, they have received their reward in full." (NIV)*

MATT. 6:18   *"... so that it will not be obvious to men that you are fasting, but only to your Father, who is unseen; and your Father, who sees what is done in secret, will reward you." (NIV)*

Prayer

PS. 32:6   *"Therefore let everyone who is godly pray to you while you may be found ..." (NIV)*

PS. 55:17   *"Evening, and morning, and at noon, will I pray, and cry aloud: and he shall hear my voice." (KJV)*

JER. 29:12-14   *"Then you will call upon me and come and pray to me, and I will listen to you. You will seek me and find me when you seek me with all your heart. I will be found by you, declares the Lord, and will bring you back from captivity ... " (NIV)*

MATT. 5:44   *"But I tell you: Love your enemies and pray for those who persecute you." (NIV)*

MATT. 6:6-8   *"But when you pray, go into your room, close the door and pray to your Father, who is unseen. Then your Father, who sees what is done in secret, will reward you. And when you pray, do not keep on babbling like pagans, for they think they will be heard because of their many words. Do not be like them, for your Father knows what you need before you ask him."*

MATT. 9:38   *"Pray ye therefore the Lord of the harvest, that he will send forth labourers into his harvest." (KJV)*

MATT. 26:41 *"Watch and pray so that you will not fall into temptation. The spirit is willing, but the body is weak." (NIV)*

LUKE 18:1 *"Then Jesus told his disciples a parable to show them that they should always pray and not give up." (NIV)*

ROM. 8:26 *"In the same way, the Spirit helps us in our weakness. We do not know what we ought to pray for, but the Spirit himself intercedes for us with groans that words cannot express." (NIV)*

1 COR. 14:15 *"So what shall I do? I will pray with my spirit, but I will also pray with my mind; I will sing with my spirit, but I will also sing with my mind." (NIV)*

1THESS. 5:17 *"Pray continually." (NIV)*

1 TIM. 2:8 *"I want men everywhere to lift up holy hands in prayer, without anger or disputing." (NIV)*

JAMES 5:13-16 *"Is any one of you in trouble? He should pray. Is anyone happy? Let him sing songs of praise. Is any one of you sick? He should call the elders of the church to pray over him and anoint him with oil in the name of the Lord. And the prayer offered in faith will make the sick person well; the Lord will raise him up. If he has sinned, he will be forgiven. Therefore confess your sins to each other and pray for each other so that you may be healed. The prayer of a righteous man is powerful and effective." (NIV)*

NOTES

1   Ruth A. Tucker and Walter Liefeld, *Daughters of the Church* (Grand Rapids: Zondervan, 1987), 113.

2   Duane W.H. Arnold, trans., *Prayers of the Martyrs* (Grand Rapids: Zondervan, 1991), 102.

3   Ibid., 46.

4   Max Lucado, *God Came Near, Chronicles of the Christ* (Portland, Ore.: Multnomah, 1987), 42.

5   *The Oregonian* (June 16, 1999), 1.

6   Ibid.

7   Kenneth W. Osbeck, *101 More Hymn Stories* (Grand Rapids: Kregel, 1985), 136. Used by permission. All rights reserved.

8   Public Domain.

Blessed to be a Blessing

Abandonment to the Cause

"On the third day Esther put on her royal robes and stood in the inner court of the palace, in front of the king's hall. The king was sitting on his royal throne in the hall, facing the entrance. When he saw Queen Esther standing in the court, he was pleased with her and held out to her the gold scepter that was in his hand. So Esther approached and touched the tip of the scepter" (Esther 5:1-2).

It had been three days and nights since Esther had called her maids and all the Jews in Susa to fasting and prayer. The king had not called for her in that time, so this was the day when she had promised Mordecai that she would go into the king's presence and speak on behalf of the Jews, regardless of the outcome.

As she lay upon her bed, the sun peaked over the horizon in the early morning hour. In the beauty of that moment, she realized that if she allowed herself to lie there and ponder the magnitude of what she was about to do, she could easily let fear overtake her. Just the day before, her anxiety had been replaced by calm resolve, but in this moment her emotions were rising to the surface and weakly saying, *"Here I am Lord; okay, send me; but please, please go with me."*

She sat up too quickly and immediately felt lightheaded from fasting. Her momentary weakness made her pause at the edge of her bed, and she called one of her maidens to bring some weak tea and a small biscuit. She gingerly made her way over to her table and waited for the maid to return.

After she had taken two sips of tea and a small bite of her biscuit, intercession began to well up within her. She motioned for her maid to leave, as she pushed the tea back and bowed her head on the table. She reminded herself, *"It is because of the Lord's great love that I will not be consumed, for His compassions never fail. They are new every morning, and the faithfulness of Jehovah is great. I know that the Lord is good to those whose hope is in Him, and mine is in Him and Him alone. I know that the Lord is good to those who seek Him. I know it is also good for one to bear the yoke of the Lord while he or she is young."*[1]

Suddenly affected by her own confession, she felt strength come into her body and faith rise up within her heart. It was as if she had come up out of a grave and ascended to a new level. She began to proclaim, *"This is the day that You have made, Lord, and I will rejoice and be glad in it."*[2] In the past three days, she had felt like a lamb being led to the slaughter, but now, unexpectedly, she felt the roar of a lion rise up within her. Standing, she declared with new passion, *"Today is a day of destiny for me and my people. My soul glorifies You, Lord, and my spirit rejoices in God my Savior, for You have been mindful of the humble state of Your servant.*[3] *If this day marks the end of my time here on earth, then so be it. It will be with great joy that I join my forefathers on the other side in the bosom of Abraham. Whatever today's outcome may be, the generations to come will know that You have ordered my steps, and they will say that I was blessed, for the Mighty One has done great things for me—Holy is Your name."*

With continued boldness she announced to the Lord, *"I will go to the king's court, knowingly breaking his law, but honoring Your command. I will not be terrified or discouraged because I know that You are with me wherever I go. Oh Lord, I know that the king's heart is in Your hand and You direct it like a watercourse wherever You please. Oh Lord, direct his heart toward me."*

As the steam continued to rise from the teapot on the table, she knelt near the edge of her chair and confessed with a humble resolve, *"Even though one moment my faith is strong, the next my heart fails me; but I know that You have spoken, and I will obey. Yes, I go in faith, knowing that You have spoken and You will guide me and give me the tongue of an instructed disciple. My trust is in You, not in myself. Oh Most High, I am resolved to be an instrument in Your hand. I will obey Your voice. Here I am, Lord; send me now, lest my heart become faint again. Let the day begin!"*

Esther rose up from her time of prayer and summoned her maidens to come and prepare her to go before the king. Her concerns had been allayed, and her initial shock had now become a fixed resolved. Soon every hair was in place; with gold silk interwoven, her braids were piled loosely on her head so as to hold her crown in place in regal fashion. Then the maids used softened charcoal to line her beautiful brown eyes and brushed the colors of crushed flower petals on her eyelids and cheeks. Next they dressed her in the attire of a queen. The under-layer of her garment was a deep royal blue with a gold silk braid sewn along the floor-length hemline, and the over scarf was the purest white with striking alternating lapis and sapphire gemstones sewn along the edge and belted by a gold silk braid, tied and hung to one side, nearly to the floor. She cloaked herself in the royal garments of a queen, but more importantly, in the humility of a dedicated servant.

Just as she had specifically chosen to not marry an earthly king out of her own will, but rather the will of God, so too would she rather face the wrath of an earthly king than not adhere to the voice of Jehovah. As she approached the throne room, rescue would be her motivation, but the wisdom of a veteran warrior and the poise of a queen would be her means.

She would stand before her husband, the king, and before the awesome presence of the one true God. *"Will the king raise his scepter and extend to me his favor, or will he be offended by my unannounced appearance and have me slain or banished forever, as he did with Vashti?"* She pushed the unsettling question further from her mind with each step she took toward the king's hall, and her fears and the taunting of the enemy were left behind in the corridor. As the courage of the Lord entered her heart and she stepped within view of the king, everything within her said, *"Here I am."*

ADDING TO YOUR FAITH

It was on the third day, after Esther fasted, prayed, and totally surrendered to the will of God for the sake of others, that she rose up, put on her royal robes, and stepped into her greatest hour. Jesus Christ fulfilled his earthly purpose when He laid down His life at the cross that we might live in eternity with Him. Three days after He died and was buried, He rose again. Just as Jesus' day of destiny was found by abandoning His life and dying on a cross, so too did Esther discover her destiny through total abandonment to the cause. Such abandonment is necessary for us, as well. It is in complete surrender that destiny is fulfilled and generations are rescued.

> *"There is a time to pray, and there is a time to act."*

There is a time to pray, and there is a time to act. There is a time to proclaim *"Here I am, send me,"* and there is a time to go. Both are essential ingredients for people of influence. Prayer without action is void of fruitfulness, and action without prayer is vain. Once the Lord has given us His strategy and marching orders, we must take the cloak of His presence and, with courage, make that first step. Some blessings are simply His kindness to us, while others have destiny engraved upon them. Some come in the form of natural and spiritual provision, while others come through measures of His grace in places of influence. All are meant to be blessings with purpose. One truth is sure—we are blessed to be a blessing. To be the kind of blessing that penetrates hearts and affects history, we must walk with the Holy Spirit.

2 Peter 1:3-4 says, *"His divine power has given us everything we need for life and godliness through our knowledge of him who called us by his own glory and goodness. Through these he has given us his very great and precious promises, so that through them you may participate in the divine nature and escape the corruption in the world caused by evil desires."* Peter then goes on to say in the following verses, *"For this very reason, make every effort to ADD . . ."* At this point in the text, he instructs the believer to add to his or her faith qualities, such as goodness, knowledge, self-control, perseverance, godliness, brotherly kindness, and love.

The key word in this text is "add," from "epichorego" in the Greek language.

> *It is a vivid metaphor drawn from the Athenian drama festivals, in which a rich individual, called the "choregos," since he paid the expenses of the chorus, joined with the poet and the state in putting on the plays. This could be an expensive business, and yet "choregi" vied with one another in the generosity of their equipment and training of the choruses. Thus the word came to mean* **generous and costly co-operation.** *The Christian must engage in this sort of co-operation with God in the production of a Christian life which is a credit to him.*

Esther was about to engage in some very generous and costly cooperation with the Holy Spirit, trusting that He was leading and guiding her steps. Recognizing that her position of influence had been granted that she might be a participant in a great rescue mission and that she had, indeed, been blessed in order to be a blessing, she knew that her assignment was a grave one. She had fasted and prayed with one mind and one purpose in unity with her people. She had weighed the options and made her decision.

"HERE I AM!"

Is there a "king" whom God is asking you to approach on behalf of the cause of Christ? Would it be "inappropriate" by the standards of your company or organization to make this approach, as it was for Esther to approach the king? Is the hand of God still resting upon you and gently pushing you forward to do something for the sake of others? Has the enemy come with taunts and accusations in an attempt to persuade you otherwise? Is there not a cause? Are you willing to follow through with the prayer you prayed so long ago, *"Here I am Lord, send me"*?

The first three times in Scripture when God called man by name and man responded with *"Here I am"* produced unique and lasting fruit. The pattern is always the same. God called each person by name, waited for his or her willing response, gave His instructions, and then fulfilled a promise. Biblical hermeneutics tells us that all the "firsts" in the Bible are very significant and set patterns for important principals in the Word. This is known to Bible scholars as the "first mention principal." Therefore, we should take particular notice the first three times we read of man responding to God with *"Here I am."*

The first time in Scripture that God called a man by name and he responded with *"Here I am"* is found in Genesis 22:1. He called out to him, *"Abraham!"* and Abraham responded with a hearty, *"Hear I am."* If the Lord has ever tugged on your shirtsleeve to get your attention or whispered your name as you quietly meditated on His Word, you can probably identify with the feeling of this response in Abraham. It is so wonderful to hear God's voice and become aware that He knows us by name and desires a close relationship with us! There is nothing else quite like talking with the Master in personal conversation.

In Genesis 15, God had promised Abraham a son, an heir. The fulfillment of this promise did not come for many years. Only a decade or so after the promise was finally fulfilled, God's calling brought the test of the promise and of Abraham's trust in Him. Abraham was called upon by God to sacrifice on an altar his only son. He faithfully responded in obedience to God's command, and, as he walked out his own obedient response to the Master, God called him by name twice, *"Abraham! Abraham!"* Abraham responded without hesitation, *"Here I am,"* and God told him that He would provide the sacrifice in place of his son.

Has God ever promised you something through your personal time with Him or through a prophetic inclination and then seemingly taken His time in bringing it to pass? We tend to be very intent on having every promise fulfilled within our own time frame, according to our own desires. It is amazing to consider how God is not bogged down within an earthly time frame. We also seem intent on having every promise fulfilled on this side of heaven. I am not sure that God feels bound in this way.

God seems to have a different perspective on our wants, desires, and needs; He seems to do what He wants to do, when He wants to do it. It is amazing how He will bless us when we have no expectations and then keep us in a spiritual holding bay until circumstances are what He deems fit for the release of a miracle. He likes being God, I think. When you are in a relationship with Him and with other people, you learn quickly that patience truly is a virtue. Of course, He already knows, as He has been ordering our wayward steps for a long time, that some circumstances require patience of a divine sort.

> *". . .some circumstances require patience of a divine sort."*

Abraham and Sarah waited many years before the fulfillment of God's promise came knocking on their tent door. In fact, they were physically and biologically beyond their years when it came to having a natural baby. They had seemingly forgotten that God is not bound by the biology of our bodies. While He usually works within the timeframe that He created in us, He certainly is not bound by time when it comes to His desire to release the miraculous. When God's promise did come to Abraham and Sarah, it was exactly what He said it would be, and it brought great joy— not just joy, but great joy! The result of Abraham's obedient response to God was **the rescue of a promised son.**

The second time in Scripture when God called man by name and he responded with *"Here I am"* is in Genesis 31:11. Here He called out to Jacob in a dream, and Jacob responded quickly with *"Here I am."* It is so very important to respond quickly and obediently to the call of God. Just as a parent calls a child to come to his side and rejoices in hearing a quick and exuberant response, so too does God relish in our response to His voice. If it has been a while since you have responded to God's voice, do so today. Stop at this moment and yield yourself and your plans to Him. With this fresh surrender, the ability to move with purpose and persuasion will be restored to your steps. Often we cannot hear His voice because we have failed to respond to the last directive that He has spoken to us.

If you are longing to hear God's voice afresh, if it seems like an "eternity" since you have heard His gentle whisper within your spirit, humble yourself before Him and search your heart to see if there is any request to which you have neglected to respond in previous days. If there is, ask His forgiveness and, without hesitation, begin taking steps of response toward that which He has already asked of you. Then sit in His presence and be refreshed; enjoy His sweet, enveloping presence once again. Do not move from this place too quickly, for truly you are on "holy ground."

> *"To sit in the presence of the King of kings is a privileged position."*

To sit in the presence of the King of kings is a privileged position. Sit, meditate on His kindness, patience, gentleness, faithfulness, provision, sacrifice, and love, and then begin to read the letter that He wrote to you so long ago. Yes, pick up the Bible and begin to read; listen to the Master's voice once again, as He speaks to you through the written Word. Allow His Word to permeate your spirit, and you will be renewed with purpose, ready to step out and say once again, like Abraham and Jacob of old, *"Here I am."*

As with Abraham, God had also given Jacob a promise. As Jacob responded to God's call with that simple proclamation, "Here I am," God stepped onto the stage of his life and fulfilled the promise He had given so many years before. In Genesis 28, God had promised Jacob, through the blessing of his father, Isaac, that He would give him and his descendants the same blessing given to Abraham. He told Jacob that he would take possession of the land where he was living at the time, the land that God had given to Abraham. Then God sent him out.

Here in Genesis 31, when God called Jacob by name and he responded, God told him to leave the land he was in and return to his native land. Through his obedience to God's call, his reward was **the rescue of a promised family**.

The third time in Scripture when we see God calling someone by name and receiving a quick and obedient response is in Exodus 3:4. Because this call was based on the very covenant that God had made with Abraham, Isaac, and Jacob for His people, God called out to Moses with deep compassion, not once, but twice. Every time God called to a person twice in Scripture, something very special was about to happen. He called out, *"Moses! Moses!"* and Moses, a man who had not heard God's voice for a long time, responded with an initial, *"Here I am."* After the Lord told him who He was, Moses hid his face because he was afraid to look at Him.

Have you ever initially responded to a request from God with great faith and were later struck by fear as you reflected on the magnitude of the request? In my own life, I remember responding to parenthood in this way. Initially, I felt such confidence about being a parent and raising children to serve the Lord, and then, when my first child was born, I became overwhelmed at the realization that he was an eternal soul whom God had given to me, requiring good stewardship. God had placed him in my care, and that revelation was overwhelming. The stewardship of the task given to you by God, whether it will affect a single soul or a multitude of souls, is an awesome responsibility.

> *"The stewardship of the task given to you by God, whether it will affect a single soul or a multitude of souls, is an awesome responsibility."*

God longs to use us to bear good fruit and be fulfilled in the purpose for which He has created us, so He gently calls us by name at just the right time—after we have been in the desert for a while and are thirsty to hear His voice. He then waits to hear our eager response and is not at all put off by our insecurity about our own abilities; He knows that humble self-awareness will keep us utterly dependant upon His wisdom and guidance. He places within our hearts the courage to step out of hiding and back into the hearts of people yearning for the fulfillment of God's promises in their lives. He does not give us complete knowledge of the circumstances or every detail of the rescue at the outset; He simply requires us to trust and to listen. What a wise leader; He knows our frailties so well. As it was with Moses, when we acknowledge our own inadequacies to Him, He gently reminds us that He will be with us and that His presence will be sufficient for that which He is asking us to do.

> *"Moses left the desert one step at a time, knowing that the presence of God was with him. . ."*

Moses left the desert one step at a time, knowing that the presence of God was with him, and then God gave him the blueprint to handle each step of the journey. The fruit of his obedience to God's call was **the rescue of a promised nation**. As it was with Moses, so may it be with us. May we walk with His presence each day, read His blueprint carefully, listen to His voice, and be obedient to that which He has asked us to do.

The rescue of a promised son, a promised family, and a promised nation all came to pass because of the same response to God's call, *"Here I am."* If it has been a while since you have said those words to God, may you bravely take a step out of the desert and commit them to Him in prayer today. For it is through your individual heart response that the rescue of a generation can take place. If believers would step into rank, one by one, and march to the cadence of *"Here I am. Use me however you want, Lord,"* the song of victory would be heard in the land and a hell-bent generation would be rescued.

SECRETS FOR THE CAUSE

I have a friend who is an "Esther" in her own rite. She, like Esther, Abraham, Jacob, and Moses, said, *"Here I am. No matter what the cost, here I am to serve you, Lord."* She grew up in Northern Ireland, a land torn by civil war for many generations.

To better understand the atmosphere in which she lived, let us take a brief look at the history of Northern Ireland. The man known as St. Patrick came from Great Britain to bring Christianity to Ireland. The traditional connection between Great Britain and Ireland dates back to the twelfth century, through the arrival of the Anglo-Normans, and was strengthened through the arrival of Scottish and English settlers in the sixteenth and seventeenth centuries. In the nineteenth century, pressure for Ireland to have its own "Home Rule" was met with resistance by the Protestants in the northern counties. Two political parties rose up, the unionists and the nationalists, and in 1920, under the Government of Ireland Act, two "Home Rule" parliaments were established, one in Dublin in the South, and one in Belfast in the North. The Act was implemented in Northern Ireland but was ignored in the South, where the Irish Republican Army fought for complete independence from Great Britain. Today, Southern Ireland is a nation in its own rite, but Northern Ireland continues to struggle under the "Home Rule" Government of Ireland Act. Although the struggle is presented through the media as a war between Protestants and Catholics, it really is a political struggle between two groups in Northern Ireland, one that wants to stay under British rule, and one that wants to be independent of British rule. Presently, the North is under British rule, but the war has continued for many years. *". . . on 31 August 1994 the Provisional IRA announced that there would be 'a complete cessation of military operations.' This was followed on 13 October 1994 by an announcement by the combined Loyalist Military Command (CLMC), an umbrella group for some of the loyalist paramilitary groups, that it would 'universally cease all operational hostilities.'"*

Because the city streets have been a constant battleground for so many years, a number of British soldiers and Irish loyalists have been employed on the local police force. They and the Irish Republican Army have been in constant conflict at the expense of the people. The struggle has also resulted in many deaths, injuries, and a great lack of trust among neighbors, friends, and family members. Fear, bitterness, and hatred, along with an extreme lack of trust, runs in the veins of most Northern Irish people.

My friend, Ann, grew up in Northern Ireland in a Protestant home and came to know the Lord personally at a young age. As she stepped into her young adult years, she was offered a job with the local police department. For her to accept this job meant that she, like Esther, had to abandon herself to the cause and begin to live a life of secrecy. If she did not maintain the secret that she worked for the police department, her life and the lives of her friends and family would be in danger of potential assaults by the IRA.

Even though she loved her family and friends, most of them did not know when she accepted employment at the police department. Once she accepted this new position, she began to live a double life. She carried a card with her, identifying her as an employee of the agricultural department of the government rather than the police department. This was done as a precaution in case the army stopped her car at a roadblock for routine identity checks and vehicle inspections. If they could not easily recognize her as one of their own, she would not receive special treatment in any way and would thereby not become an obvious target. She was very much on her own, just as Esther had been so many years prior.

Ann had to constantly be on the alert to anyone who might be "on to her." She was trained to live defensively. There was a panic button by her bedside, linked to the police station, in case there was an attack on her home. She took different routes to work everyday, always being careful to alter her time of departure from home and her time of arrival at work. She carefully but nonchalantly checked under her car for bombs every morning and every time she parked in a parking lot. She never pulled up too closely behind someone at a stop sign or traffic light to prevent being easily boxed in and attacked. She also never talked about her job, not even to her most trusted friends.

Ann and a Catholic girl, with whom Ann had previously worked, had become quite close friends. When Ann changed jobs suddenly to work for the police department, many things went unspoken between the two of them, even though their friendship grew. In fact, when Ann's mother died, this friend offered her much-needed comfort and companionship, even though Ann was single and her friend was married and had children. Ann visited her friend's home regularly, played with the kids, had a "wee cup of tea," and talked to her about the Lord. She struggled with the constant dilemma of either lying to her friend about her work or breaking down and telling the truth. As a Christian, you can imagine her predicament as well as the quandary she would bring to her friend if she told her how "surrendered to the cause" she really was.

In Ann's own words, she describes the frustration of her situation:

> *The ethical line can become very blurred when you are in that type of job. Yes, there were times when I lied, but to have not done so could have borne tragic consequences. Sometimes I would become so overwhelmed with the weight of this that sleep was affected, emotions became frayed, and life became all too depressing. I constantly seemed to "hit the wall" between telling the truth and telling a lie to protect myself. I will admit that at first it was all so thrilling and it certainly got my adrenaline flowing, but soon that all disappeared and reality set in.*[8]

I am sure that there must have been times, at the loss of the tangible closeness to Mordecai, when Esther must have longed to "tell all" to those with whom she had become closest. The obstacles before her were enormous to the natural eye, and her discretion and timing had to be flawless for the mission to be accomplished. Every obstacle presented had its own life-threatening hurdle, but each would be taken in stride as the Lord guided her steps. The ramifications of her deeds were monumental to the entire kingdom; she had to remain steadfast. The obstacles were clear and had to be maneuvered around with great care.

The same was true with the task that the Lord had given to young Ann. For her to unveil her secret identity prematurely or to the wrong person could have cost, not only her own life, but also the lives of family members, friends, and co-workers. A lack of care on her part could literally have affected the already war-torn country. Her task was great, but her God was greater. She, like Esther, not only had to be careful about the details of her duty, but she had to remain "abandoned to the cause" in her heart.

> *"Her task was great, but her God was greater."*

Surely the example of Esther reached across the generations to Ann and instructed her in the way she should walk. Their pathways were interlocked forever, for the same God who had directed the steps of Esther had been faithful to tutor this young Irish girl in contemporary Northern Ireland, as well. With hearts interwoven, steps directed, and destinies mysteriously intertwined, these two were obedient to God in a day of difficulty in their nations, and they rose to the challenge. In their hearts and in their deeds rings the clear message of total surrender, *"Whatever the cost, here I am; send me."*

For Esther, Ann, Abraham, Jacob, and Moses to daily abandon themselves to the purposes of God for their generation, they needed to walk in generous and costly cooperation with the Holy Spirit as the apostle Peter in his second epistle instructs every Christian believer to do. This same challenge is presented to us on our doorsteps today. Will you, in generous and costly cooperation with the Holy Spirit, yield to the call of God and walk out your destiny with complete abandonment? Will you join with those who have already born the brunt and led the way, and say, *"Whatever the cost, here I am, Lord; send me"*?

"Here I am"

GEN. 22:1 *"Some time later God tested Abraham. He said to him, 'Abraham!' 'Here I am,' he replied."*

GEN. 22:11 *"But the angel of the LORD called out to him from heaven, 'Abraham! Abraham!' 'Here I am,' he replied."*

GEN. 27:1 *"When Isaac was old and his eyes were so weak that he could no longer see, he called for Esau his older son and said to him, 'My son.' 'Here I am,' he answered."*

GEN. 31:11 *"The angel of God said to me in the dream, 'Jacob.' I answered, 'Here I am.'"*

GEN. 46:2 *"And God spoke to Israel in a vision at night and said, 'Jacob! Jacob!' 'Here I am,' he replied."*

EX. 3:4 *"When the LORD saw that he had gone over to look, God called to him from within the bush, 'Moses! Moses!' And Moses said, 'Here I am.'"*

NUM. 11:21 *"But Moses said, 'Here I am among six hundred thousand men on foot, and you say, "I will give them meat to eat for a whole month!"'"*

JOSH. 14:10 *"Now then, just as the LORD promised, he has kept me alive for forty-five years since the time he said this to Moses, while Israel moved about in the desert. So here I am today, eighty-five years old!"*

1 SAM. 3:4   *"Then the LORD called Samuel. Samuel answered, 'Here I am.'"*

1 CHRON. 17:1   *"After David was settled in his palace, he said to Nathan the prophet, 'Here I am, living in a palace of cedar, while the ark of the covenant of the LORD is under a tent.'"*

PS. 40:7-8   *"Then I said, 'Here I am, I have come—it is written about me in the scroll. I desire to do your will, O my God; your law is within my heart.'"*

NOTES

1   Paraphrase of Lamentations 3:21-27

2   Psalm 118:24

3   Luke 2:47-48

4   Paraphrase of Isaiah 50:4

5   Michael Green, *Tyndale New Testament Commentaries, The 2nd Epistle General of Peter and The General Epistle of Jude*, Leon Morris, ed., 2d ed. (Grand Rapids: Eerdmans, 1987), 76.

6   *Brief History of Northern Ireland*, December 1999, <http://www2.nio.gov.uk/p_history.htm> (January 16, 2002).

7   This is a fictitious name due to the nature of the story.

8   This is a quote from an interview with Ann. Used with permission

Moving with Purpose and Persuasion

"On the third day Esther put on her royal robes and stood in the inner court. . . . Then the king asked, 'What is it, Queen Esther? What is your request? Even up to half the kingdom, it will be given you.' 'If it pleases the king,' replied Esther, 'let the king, together with Haman, come today to a banquet I have prepared for him.' . . . 'Then I will answer the king's question'" (Esther 5:1, 3-4, 7). (See also Esther 5-7.)

Only moments earlier, as Esther had stood in her apartment fully adorned and surrounded by her maids, she had felt so ready for this venture to the king's hall. Everything within her had said, *"Here I am Lord; send me. Here I am, King Xerxes; deal with me as you will."* She had imagined herself walking through the corridor to the king's grand hall with a regal confidence. Now the pounding beat of her heart and the weakness in her knees betrayed her. Beads of perspiration formed on her forehead, while her hands grew colder by the minute, as if life were draining from them. Her legs felt heavy, as though they were trudging up a stream against the current; her steps were delayed, as if her body could not interpret the instruction of her brain. It took everything within her to keep walking; but she did.

With single-minded perseverance, she continued to take the steps ordered by the Lord for her. She breathed in deeply the faith in which she had been fully immersed just minutes before, and she exhaled the fear that had begun to weigh her down. She could feel her steps lighten and her legs become free of the weights of the enemy. She felt blood flow into her extremities; her hands warmed, while her forehead cooled. As she came to the turn at the end of the corridor and passed into the inner court in front of the king's hall, she felt renewed confidence. She became quietly aware of the Lord's angels before, behind, and on each side of her. The sun was shining through the windowpanes and she could hear the symphony of finches singing and turtledoves cooing in the air; the blending of their peace and joy became hers in that instant. She stepped into the inner court and paused, waiting for the king to notice her.

King Xerxes sat on his royal throne in the grand hall, facing the entrance, as he addressed the usual business of the day. When he glanced up and saw Esther standing in the inner court, pleasure swept over him. She looked so beautiful that he was momentarily stunned by her exquisite grace, and he wondered why it had been so many days since he had called for her to come into his private chambers. The continual parade of maidens these past five years splashed across his mind momentarily, and he wondered why he had even bothered with them when he obviously had the most beautiful wife in the land at his beckoning call.

As baffling as it was to his eunuchs and officials nearby, without hesitation, he held out to her the gold scepter that was in his hand. As he did so, Esther realized that the "first-fruits" of Jehovah's unfolding blessings had just been made obvious.

She quickly prayed within herself to the Lord, *"Favor has been granted unto me by the king; let Your light, oh Lord, continue to shine upon me. As I cross the threshold into His presence and touch the tip of his scepter, let Your discretion guide me. Let my steps be taken with poise and my words be spoken with wisdom. It is in You, oh Lord, that I place my trust."* She then humbly approached the king and bowed as she touched the tip of his scepter. She touched it in homage, not to his greatness, but rather to the greatness of the one who was about to turn his heart like a mountain stream drawn toward the sea.

Next, came the king's entreating question with a promise attached, *"What is it, Queen Esther? What is your request? Even up to half the kingdom, it will be given you."* The warmth in his eyes was sincere, and it was apparent that he truly did want to please her. Just by coming to him as she did, she had stirred in him a renewed affection for her that had lain dormant of late. In his lascivious pursuit of other young women, he had forgotten his deep love for her, but seeing her now, his heart yearned to fulfill her every desire. He hoped that costly gifts would prove to her once again his devotion and somehow make up for his recent neglect and inattention.

———•◆•———

When Esther had been secure in her room in the presence of the Lord, the words she had planned to say sounded confident, strategic even; but now she faltered slightly. She could think of only one word—"dinner." She quickly regained her composure and offered her humble request, *"If it pleases the king, let the king, together with Haman, come today to a banquet I have prepared for him."* [1]

In the two seconds between Esther's request and the king's reply, Esther thought to herself, *"Now that the invitation to my naïve but powerful husband and the wicked but shrewd enemy has been made, will they respond favorably to my request, or will they deny me?"*

She had barely finished her thought, when the king ordered his servants to bring Haman to him at once so that they could go to Esther's banquet as she had requested. Xerxes wanted to spend time with her, and none of his governmental duties could keep him away from her now. He suddenly felt like a teenage boy in her presence; his heart flittered uncontrollably in his chest and he struggled to catch his breath. While he did wonder about the true nature of her request, he hoped, in his egotistical way, that she just wanted to be with him, that she had come because she missed him and longed for his attention. She had his attention now, and he would give her anything she asked.

⸻ ⸱•⸱ ⸻

Esther had gone to great lengths to prepare a delectable feast for the king and Haman. She had considered every detail, from the menu, the wine, and the table setting, to the lighting, the background music, and even the scent of the room. She had made sure that every aspect of this meal would please and satisfy her husband, the king.

As Xerxes reclined at her table, sipping the intoxicating, full-bodied wine she had selected and savoring the fine cuisine she had set before him, he again wanted to give her some kind of gift. She had gone to all this effort; surely she wanted something. He knew enough about feminine wiles to suspect that this pampering, this feasting, was meant to soften him up so he would grant her real desire. But he didn't mind; at this moment, in this luxurious setting beside his beautiful queen with his every need met, he wanted to grant her deepest desire. Xerxes inquired again, *"Now what is your petition? It will be given you. And what is your request? Even up to half the kingdom, it will be granted."* [2]

Hesitating momentarily, Esther thought, *"If I do not answer, will their curiosity turn to evil suspicion? Should I answer the king's question now or wait for the wicked enemy of my people to weave his web more tightly?"* She realized that timing was of the essence, but wisdom was essential. Her heart told her to wait. In the midst of her deliberation, the still small voice of God whispered to her spirit and guided her with reassurance. She was to wait. With confidence in her decision and the peace of her Father in her heart, she responded by requesting that they return the next day for another banquet and promised that she would answer the king's question then.

Xerxes was surprised, but pleased. He had enjoyed this meal so much that he would gladly return for another. He was impressed, not only by the food and wine, but by the grace, the dignity, the comely manner of his wife. Her very presence soothed him, and he would gladly interrupt his royal duties to dine with her again. However, his curiosity had been piqued, and he now wanted, more than ever, to find out what she desired and to grant her wish. While it would be hard to be patient until then, he would happily return to the banquet tomorrow, and when she asked, he would give her the world.

Haman left Esther's banquet that day a very happy man. He had been ordered, not asked, to attend, but he was flattered nonetheless. Previously, he had been unsure of his standing with the queen, but now he was assured of her favor. To attend a private banquet with the king and queen of Persia, not just once, but twice—this was the high point of his life! "Surely, I have arrived," thought Haman. *"I am the most powerful and influential man in all of Persia now. If these meals with the royal couple continue on a regular basis, my every whim will become law. I will be in a position to influence every aspect of government. The entire empire will be in my hands!"*

At that moment, he passed by the king's gate, and his egotistical thoughts were perforated as he saw the "unbowing Jew," Mordecai, standing in defiance. He instantly became enraged. *"This is the last time!"* he exploded, with his clenched fists waving in the air and his reddened face contorted in anger. He turned away from the sight of this hated Jew and stormed off toward home, muttering curses and plotting Mordecai's demise. Bystanders and onlookers watched him curiously as he grumbled and fumed and angrily made his way through the streets of Susa. His anger had subsided only slightly when he arrived at home.

Because of his position in the king's court, Haman was a popular man. Friends and neighbors would gather around him regularly to hear him tell of the goings on at the palace. Everyone wanted to be privy to some "inside" news or scandalous secret about the royal family. They all hoped that they would benefit in some way from knowing Haman and that he would keep them in mind as he "climbed the ladder" of success. This attention only served to inflate Haman's ego further. He loved to boast of his greatness and brag about his personal wealth, his sons, and all the ways that Xerxes had honored him above all the other nobles.

As he arrived home, he called Zeresh, his wife, and several of his friends together to eloquently relate his most recent news, that he alone had been invited, along with the king, to a banquet given by the queen and would return for another meal tomorrow. This news had the desired effect, and his audience was duly impressed that he had dined alone with the royal couple. But even the esteem of his peers did little to ease his frustration, and the fury continued to rage inside him over the impudence of one Jewish man. His face grew red, he slapped his hands on his hips and bellowed, *"But all this gives me no satisfaction as long as I see that Jew Mordecai sitting at the king's gate!"* [3]

Haman's wife and friends were stunned by this outburst. It was obvious that he would never be able to truly relish in his success until Mordecai was done away with once and for all. Everyone in the room realized the opportunity that this situation presented, and each of them secretly hoped that his or her own suggestion to Haman would be the ideal solution for his problem and would secure his favor. Perhaps he would reward one of them with a position in the royal court. His friends began brainstorming and presenting ideas, from the utterly morbid to the utterly ridiculous, until finally it was suggested that Haman build a seventy-five foot gallows this afternoon. In the morning he could ask Xerxes to have Mordecai hanged on it, and then he could go to Esther's banquet and have a *"completely wonderful day."*

As he listened to this plan, Haman's eyes narrowed and his mouth curled up on one side. This was the perfect solution to his problem! He quickly tightened his boots and rushed out the door without even acknowledging the help of his friends—he was on his way to build a gallows.

———•◦•———

Xerxes left Esther's banquet that day a very happy man, as well. But as the day wore on and he dealt with multiple decisions of state later in the afternoon, he became increasingly restless. He lay on his bed that evening, tossing and turning, unable to sleep or clear his mind of the political issues of his empire. Because there was nothing more tedious and dull than the monotonous recounting of past governmental decisions, he ordered that the book of the chronicles of his reign be read to him in an effort to bore himself to sleep. Rather than being lulled to sleep as the chronicle was read, he became aware that he had never officially honored the faithful gatekeeper, Mordecai, for revealing the plans of Bigthana and Teresh, the guards who had planned to assassinate him. He was disturbed by this oversight and planned to immediately remedy the situation first thing in the morning. Somehow this decision brought him peace, and while his eunuch droned on and on still reading from the chronicle, Xerxes rolled over and slipped quietly into a restful sleep.

———•◦•———

The next morning, when Haman entered the king's hall to speak with him about hanging Mordecai, Xerxes abruptly began the conversation with a question that piqued Haman's interest. Xerxes turned to him directly and asked, *"Haman, what should be done for the man the king delights to honor?"* [4]

Arrogantly assuming that the king was referring to him, Haman smiled coyly and responded, *"Have them bring a royal robe the king has worn and a horse the king has ridden, one with a royal crest placed on its head. Then let the robe and horse be entrusted to one of the king's most noble princes. Let them robe the man the king delights to honor, and lead him on the horse through the city streets, proclaiming before him, 'This is what is done for the man the king delights to honor!'"* [5]

The king loved the idea. *"Splendid! Because you truly know how to give honor to whom honor is due, I would like you, Haman, as the noblest of all my princes, to carry out this deed of honor for Mordecai, the gatekeeper."*

Haman was horrified. His mouth dropped open, and he stood speechless before the king. His head was swimming, and he thought he would faint. *"Honor Mordecai?"* he could hardly wrap his mind around the thought. *"I came here to have him hanged, and now I have to parade him around the city in the king's robe on the king's horse. How can I bring myself to do such a thing?"* he feebly thought. He knew that there would be no reversing the king's decision. Xerxes had given the command and expected it to be carried out without question. In fact, he had already turned his attention to other things. The matter was settled, and Haman had no choice. He left the king's presence immediately and obediently did as he was commanded in feigned respect, but with defeating humiliation deep within.

⋯•◦•⋯

Every block and every insincere proclamation from his own mouth was tortuous agony for Haman as he paraded Mordecai through the streets of Susa in royal array. People actually stopped and bowed in honor to Mordecai, while Haman, the prince, was reduced to a mere servant as he led the horse and cleared the way for Mordecai's procession. The humiliation was almost more than he could bear. *"Bowing to Mordecai,"* he thought bitterly, as he scanned the crowd with disdain. *"These ignorant people have no idea what they're doing—bowing to the man who refuses to bow!"* He turned his attention to Mordecai, who smiled in humility, embarrassed by the attention he was getting. *"I will see to it that you get what you deserve!"* he wanted to shout. *"Your punishment may have been delayed, Mordecai, but when it comes, it will be painful and severe—I will see to that! Enjoy the honor of today, for this is the last day that people will speak your name with respect. Tomorrow you will die as a criminal and your name will be forever shamed."* Haman paraded Mordecai through the streets, honoring him as he had been commanded, but tomorrow he would lead a parade of a different kind—he would parade him to the gallows and to his death. Today he led Mordecai upon the king's horse; tomorrow he would lead him by a rope around his neck. The pleasure of these thoughts gave Haman the fortitude to continue the procession, and the irony of what was in store brought him twisted satisfaction. He could be patient just one more day, for tomorrow he would have his enemy in a noose.

The king was happy. He had done a good deed, had probably increased his favor in the eyes of the city, and was now enjoying another wonderful dinner with his beautiful wife. Her beauty and demeanor were both appealing to him, and he was pleased to be with her. The dinner at the queen's table was once again divine; everyone was relaxed, including Haman after his ordeal.

Savoring his wine, Xerxes looked at her lovingly and once again repeated the question he had been patiently waiting to ask, *"Queen Esther, what is your petition? It will be given you. What is your request? Even up to half the kingdom, it will be granted."*[6] Even though this was the third time he had asked in three days, he had enjoyed every moment, from the minute he saw her in the inner court awaiting his acceptance until now. She was stunning in beauty and charming in manner; everything about her appealed to him. She was like an exquisite gemstone set in carvings of gold that needed careful guardianship.

Esther knew that this was her moment to speak and her appeal must be wise and concise. She humbly began, *"If I have found favor with you, oh king, and if it pleases your majesty . . ."* She paused momentarily for emphasis and then continued pointedly, *". . . grant me my life—this is my petition. And spare my people—this is my request. For I and my people have been sold for destruction and slaughter and annihilation. If we had merely been sold as male and female slaves, I would have kept quiet, because no such distress would justify disturbing the king."*[7]

Feeling stunned and wanting to protect his beloved wife from whomever threatened her life, Xerxes demanded, *"Who is he? Where is the man who has dared to do such a thing?"*[8]

Without a moment's hesitation, Esther pointed to Haman and declared, *"The adversary and enemy is this vile Haman."* [9]

Haman was immediately flushed with unmistakable guilt and terror. His plans were foiled, and he was doomed! The queen's accusations were accurate, but surprising nonetheless. If he had known such incriminations would be propelled in his direction, he would have eluded her invitations. His pride had been his downfall. He had been so "honored" by the invitation to the queen's quarters that he had failed to see the danger he was in.

Seeing the guilt on Haman's face, the king was in instant shock and turmoil. Enraged, he left his wine on the table and determinedly stepped out to the palace garden to think.

Realizing that Xerxes had already recognized his guilt and decided his fate, Haman remained in the presence of Queen Esther to beg for mercy. In desperation, Haman flung himself onto the couch where Esther was reclining to further beseech her forgiveness.

Just at that moment, the king stormed back into Esther's room. Horrified at what he saw, the king exclaimed, *"Will he even molest the queen while she is with me in the house?!"*

The infuriated King Xerxes grabbed Haman by his clothes, pulled him to his feet, and ripped the honored signet ring from his finger. Then Harbona, one of the eunuchs attending the king, suggested, *"A gallows seventy-five feet high stands by Haman's house. He had it made for Mordecai, who spoke up to help the king."*

"Hang him on it!"[10] said the king without a moment's hesitation.

The dream of palace life and promotion was over for Haman; the hand of fate and the God of the Jews had converged, and he had fallen short. Xerxes sent orders for Haman to be hanged on the gallows that he had built for Mordecai's death. Rather than the "non-bowing" Mordecai being suspended by the neck, now Haman, the "noblest prince of Persia," would hang there instead.

When dealing with naïve people in places of influence or a deathly wicked enemy, one must deal shrewdly. Patience is required and wisdom is essential. Knowing what to say and when to say it is very important. Listening to the Lord's voice and allowing Him to capture the spider in his own web, allows peace and victory to reign in the believer's heart and terror and destruction to ensnare the enemy.

Esther had several hurdles to jump before she could attain the prize. The king's decisions were easily swayed by his unreliable moods, and the enemy's tactics were cunning. She had to be "wiser than a serpent" to overcome the most obvious obstacles in her path.

THE SOURCE OF WISDOM

Do you ever lack wisdom in how to move with causative purpose and persuasion? Regardless of whether the obstacles in your pathway are similar to Esther's or not, you will need the wisdom of God to overcome whatever is before you and to succeed in that which God has asked you to do. Vashti was beautiful, but not wise; Esther was not only beautiful, but wise, as well.

Where does such wisdom come from?

- Wisdom is found in respect for the Lord.
  "The fear of the Lord teaches a man wisdom, and humility comes before honor"(Proverbs 15:33).

- Wisdom is found in sacrificial living.
  "Solomon . . . offered a thousand burnt offerings . . . 'Give me wisdom and knowledge, that I may lead this people.' . . . therefore wisdom and knowledge will be given you . . ." (2 Chronicles 1:6-12).

- Wisdom is found in life experiences.
  "Consider it pure joy, my brothers, whenever you face trials of many

kinds, because you know that the testing of your faith develops perseverance. Perseverance must finish its work so that you may be mature and complete, not lacking anything" (James 1:2-4).

♦ Wisdom is found by asking for it.

"If any of you lacks wisdom, he should ask God, who gives generously to all without finding fault, and it will be given to him" (James 1:5).

♦ Wisdom is found in reproofs.

"A wise son heeds his father's instruction, but a mocker does not listen to rebuke" (Proverbs 13:1).

♦ Wisdom is found in Christ.

"Jews demand miraculous signs and Greeks look for wisdom, but we preach Christ crucified: a stumbling block to Jews and foolishness to Gentiles, but to those whom God has called, both Jews and Greeks, Christ the power of God and the wisdom of God" (1 Corinthians 1:22-23).

WISDOM'S PROTOCOL

In Esther, we find a young woman who respected God and was willing to sacrifice everything to serve Him. She continually discovered His goodness through her own life experiences and responded to the reproofs and instruction of those whom God had placed as advisors in her life. We also find a young woman who, through all of these experiences, moved with purpose and persuasion, whether she was strolling along the palace walls or preparing a banquet feast for a naïve king and a wicked enemy. What was her pattern, and how can it apply to our lives today?

> *"If you are about to break protocol, you should know well the person whom you are about to offend by doing so."*

First, she knew and understood well the protocol of the day. If you are about to break protocol, you should know well the person whom you are about to offend by doing so. I would like to propose here the idea that Esther "knew her man." She knew, not only what he liked in a queen, but what he liked in the vision of a wife, as well. She knew how to best present herself to him, even in the midst of breaking a royal law.

What about you? Do you know the appropriate protocol and customs for what you are called to do? Do you really know the people before whom God has placed you to minister? Are you aware of their likes and dislikes? I think we should all "go to school" on those with whom we daily live and those to whom the Lord would have us minister in unique ways.

For example, if you want to minister to your boss effectively, you should be at work on time and work diligently while you are there. Do not take long breaks, and do not pilfer the company's goods. If you are in a nation that is not your own, learn the language. If you are in your own nation, extend yourself to a visitor. If you are in someone else's home, offer to help. If you are in your own home, serve others. If you want to influence a young person, be joyful, honest, and sincere. With a friend, be loyal; with a mate, be faithful; with a neighbor, take care of your yard; with a teacher, pay attention. With someone discouraged, share comfort food; with someone happy, rejoice; with someone in crisis, pray; with someone in love, listen; and with someone brokenhearted, care. The list of ways to minister effectively could go on and on. The point is that we need to know the appropriate protocol and customs of those whom we desire to effectively reach for the Lord.

After Esther humbly and endearingly extended her invitation to the king and Haman, she prepared for their arrival. I can imagine that she prepared a meal that was perfectly suitable to the king's tastes. Xerxes was so thrilled with her hospitality that he once again sought her petition and offered up to half of his kingdom. But Esther knew that the time was not quite right. Her patience was effective as she entreated the king because it allowed the Lord time to do a supernatural work in his heart.

We too need to be patient in the strategic moments of life. You may offer ice cream and home-baked cookies to the neighborhood children and relish watching them enjoy such special treats long before you ever petition them to consider the Lord Jesus. You might volley a volleyball many weekends with a frustrated young athlete long before you ever recommend that he or she change sports. You might type many a poorly-written term paper for a friend long before you ever suggest a remedial English class.

> "Jesus cared more about being who He was than preaching what He was about."

In today's fragmented culture, it takes so little to be above average. It takes so little to demonstrate true, genuine love and concern to people in need. We should be careful not to be so hasty in offering the Gospel to people that we miss being like Christ. We should care more about people than we do about getting another notch on our personal evangelism belts. When He walked the earth, Jesus cared more about being who He was than preaching what He was about. He loved to be with people, whether it was to share a story with them, laugh with them, cry with them—He simply loved to be with them. We should follow His example carefully.

We should care as much about the person we are attempting to influence as we do about the people we are attempting to rescue. For example, if, as a lobbyist, you can affect a politician's belief system, you will have changed his or her vote for life. If you hastily coerce a politician into a quick decision, you have only changed his or her vote for an issue and will have to return. In the Christian realm, sometimes we are so anxious to get people to make decisions for Christ, that we do not allow the Holy Spirit time to interact with their souls and bring them to a deep conviction and commitment that will change their lives forever. In our haste, we coerce them into a quick decision, and they struggle later because they made that decision for us rather than for Christ. Esther's example of patience, allowing the Lord time to work on the king, was a wise one.

While Esther was being patient, the Lord was at work. The enemy, Haman, was more irritated than ever by Mordecai's lack of honor and hastily ordered a gallows built on which to hang him. Meanwhile, the king was unable to sleep and ordered the record of his reign to be brought in and read to him. In it, he discovered that Mordecai had exposed two of his officers who had conspired to assassinate him, but had never been rewarded for his good deed. Little did either of them realize that the Holy Spirit was at work in the midst of their "orders," one for gallows and the other for chronicles, but both for posterity.

As Haman worked hard to bring honor to himself, the God who never slumbers or sleeps worked on behalf of Esther, Mordecai, and His people. Mordecai had been faithful to King Xerxes and his God through the avenues of loyalty and integrity. His day of honor had been long in coming, yet timely in the economy of God. Yes, patience and humility had done its work; honor would belong to Mordecai, and vengeance would be served on the platter of his impetuous and arrogant enemy.

Often, while the enemy is at work, devising schemes to bring ruin to God's faithful servants, the Lord is at work to bring about his demise. What the enemy despises, the Lord honors, and when one who is ruthless and wicked falls, God's servants are lifted up. God is always at work, whether it is behind the scenes or on center stage. He is always watching and waiting, ever so carefully,

> *"Often, while the enemy is at work, devising schemes to bring ruin to God's faithful servants, the Lord is at work to bring about his demise."*

marking boundaries and taking steps unseen by the natural eye but walked in by those surrendered to His will.

When the gallows was finished and Haman was unnerved by Xerxes' command to parade Mordecai through town in honor of his faithful service to the king, it was time for the second banquet. Esther's steps for a timely and proper appeal were simple:

♦ She prepared the atmosphere with another delectable meal. The king was relaxed in her presence and enjoyed her company.

♦ She patiently waited for the question, *"What is your request?"* and the offer, *". . . it will be granted."* Her patience was endearing as she entreated the king. Truly, this is evidence of the power of a surrendered life. Patience is a virtue that is nurtured in humble surrender.

♦ She spoke with concern for herself and for her people. The king adored her, not necessarily her people; so she spoke of herself first, as a way of weaving her people into the heart of the king. She crossed the threshold into destiny with wisdom and made her mark in history by laying down her life for the sake of her people.

♦ She spoke of consideration for him. She wisely included deliberate consideration of him as well as herself and her people. To be personally taken into account in the petition process surely struck a chord in the king's heart.

♦ She used concise language about the enemy: one noun, two pointed adjectives, and Haman's name. Out of an emotional need to be certain that the person with whom we are communicating gets "the whole picture," sometimes we short-circuit his or her attention span with too much detail. Esther's precise description makes the point and leaves the judgment to the king.

♦ She humbled herself and spoke with respect and regard for his opinion. She gave appropriate honor to him, not as a lesser person, but as a decision-maker in the hand of God. Unbelievers are not unintelligent; they are simply lost in their spiritual journey.

Regardless of the challenges that may confront you today, do as Esther did and prepare the atmosphere. Some of the simplest meals, such as pasta and meatballs, can taste like the finest Italian cuisine when served on china by candlelight. Some of the most stressful atmospheres in the office can be eased with a smile and an edifying conversation on a coffee break. Even if the wind and snow is blowing in blizzard-like conditions, some of the most relaxed times of fellowship can be enjoyed around a warm fireplace. Some of the hungriest tummies that come storming in the door can be soothed by the smell of vanilla warming on the stove, as long as cook-

> *"Regardless of the challenges that may confront you today, do as Esther did and prepare the atmosphere."*

ies come later, that is. Some of the rowdiest toddler nurseries can be calmed by lighthearted, happy music. Whatever the situation, whether it takes place at home, at work, or at church, learn from Esther and prepare the atmosphere.

These are two of the most common mistakes we humans make in our relationships: 1) we barge in with advice before a question has even been asked, and 2) we ask for a favor just before someone is about to offer one as a gift. Esther was patient and waited for the desired question to come. Whether it is with a child, a teen, a spouse, a boss, a friend or a pastor, be patient in conversation. Give others time to desire, to think, and to offer. Allow them time to deliberate and time to be active participants in the conversation.

When you engage in conversation that is of a sensitive nature, be sure to be sensitive to the main concerns of the other person, as Esther was with the king. You do not always need to hasten to your main point, but when you do get there, speak concisely. Certain personality types tend toward wordiness, using more adjectives and adverbs than anyone cares to hear and offering more "reasons why" than anyone needs to know. They always feel a need to paint the "bigger picture," when it may not really be needed. Again, learning from Esther's example would be wise. When it was time to reveal the people on whose behalf she made her request and the evildoer who had plotted against them, she was very succinct, and the king clearly got her point.

Esther's steps were precise and anointed with wisdom. She was willing to die for others because she had already died to herself through the preparation process. All of this preparation and total surrender must have worked into the very fabric of her being. We see the fruit of that preparation and abandonment empowering her as she moved elegantly but assuredly with purpose and persuasion. In doing so, she captured the heart of a king, brought demise to an enemy, and opened the door of hope to her people.

> *"Those who determinedly and carefully invest their lives in others are those who leave a lasting mark on the world."*

Those who determinedly and carefully invest their lives in others are those who leave a lasting mark on the world. They step into their destiny and fulfill it as they cross over the threshold of self-sacrifice and skillfully influence others with purpose and persuasion. You may not know when or where you will make your most significant mark in life, but, like Esther, the way you will make it is through purposed sacrifice saturated in the wisdom of God.

Wisdom

Where to Find Wisdom

IN CHRIST

COL. 1:2-3   *"My purpose is that they may be encouraged in heart and united in love, so that they may have the full riches of complete understanding, in order that they may know the mystery of God, namely, Christ, in whom are hidden all the treasures of wisdom and knowledge.*

1 COR. 2:6-8   *"We do, however, speak a message of wisdom among the mature, but not the wisdom of this age or of the rulers of this age, who are coming to nothing. No, we speak of God's secret wisdom a wisdom that has been hidden and that God destined for our glory before time began. None of the rulers of this age understood it, for if they had, they would not have crucified the Lord of glory.*

IN THE FEAR OF THE LORD

PS. 111:10   *"The fear of the Lord is the beginning of wisdom; all who follow his precepts have good understanding. To him belongs eternal praise."*

PROV. 2:6   *"For the Lord gives wisdom, and from his mouth come knowledge and understanding."*

IN SACRIFICE

2 CHRON. 1:6-12 *"And Solomon . . . .offered a thousand burnt offer-ings . . . wisdom and knowledge is granted unto thee; and I will give thee riches, and wealth, and honor. . . ."*

ROM. 12:1 *"Therefore, I urge you, brothers, in view of God's mercy, to offer your bodies as living sacrifices, holy and pleasing to God—this is your spiritual act of worship."*

IN ASKING

2 CHRON. 1:10 *"Give me wisdom and knowledge, that I may lead this people. . . ."*

PROV. 13:10 *"Pride only breeds quarrels, but wisdom is found in those who take advice."*

IN LIFE EXPERIENCES

JAMES 1:2-5 *"Consider it pure joy, my brothers, whenever you face trials of many kinds . . . If any of you lacks wisdom, he should ask God, who gives generously to all without finding fault, and it will be given to him."*

PROV. 14:16 *"A wise man fears the Lord and shuns evil, but a fool is hotheaded and reckless."*

IN REPROOF

PROV. 29:15 *"The rod of correction imparts wisdom, but a child left to himself disgraces his mother."*

PROV. 13:1 *"A wise son heeds his father's instruction, but a mocker does not listen to rebuke."*

The Fruit of Having Wisdom

DISCERNMENT

PROV. 2:2-5 *"Turning your ear to wisdom and applying your heart to understanding, and if you call out for insight and cry aloud for understanding, and if you look for it as for silver and search for it as for hidden treasure, then you will understand the fear of the Lord and find the knowledge of God."*

PROTECTION

PROV. 2:6-8 *"For the Lord gives wisdom, and from his mouth come knowledge and understanding. He holds victory in store for the upright, he is a shield to those whose walk is blameless, for he guards the course of the just and protects the way of his faithful ones."*

GUIDANCE

PROV. 2:9-10 *"Then you will understand what is right and just and fair—every good path. For wisdom will enter your heart, and knowledge will be pleasant to your soul."*

LONG LIFE, DURABLE RICHES & HONOR

PROV. 3:16 *"Long life is in her right hand; in her left hand are riches and honor."*

PEACEFUL PATHWAYS

PROV. 3:17 *"Her ways are pleasant ways, and all her paths are peace."*

HAPPINESS

PROV. 3:18 *"She is a tree of life to those who embrace her; those who lay hold of her will be blessed."*

AN INSTRUCTED TONGUE

PROV. 16:23 *"A wise man's heart guides his mouth, and his lips promote instruction."*

THE REJOICING OF OTHERS

Prov. 23:15-16 *"My son, if your heart is wise, then my heart will be glad; my inmost being will rejoice when your lips speak what is right."*

NOTES

1   Esther 5:4

2   Esther 5:6

3   Esther 5:13

4   Esther 6:6

5   Esther 6:8-9

6   Esther 7:2

7   Esther 7:3-4

8   Esther 7:5

9   Esther 7:6

10 Esther 7:8-9

The Rescue of a Generation

". . . If it pleases the king . . . if he regards me with favor and thinks it the right thing to do, and if he is pleased with me, let an order be written over-ruling the dispatches that Haman . . . devised and wrote to destroy the Jews in all the king's provinces . . . The king's edict granted the Jews in every city the right to assemble and protect themselves; to destroy, kill and annihilate any armed force of any nationality or province that might attack them . . . For the Jews it was a time of happiness and joy, gladness and honor . . . wherever the edict of the king went, there was joy and gladness among the Jews, with feasting and celebrating. . . . And all the nobles of the provinces, the satraps, the governors and the king's administrators helped the Jews, because fear of Mordecai had seized them. Mordecai was prominent in the palace; his reputation spread throughout the provinces, and he became more and more powerful . . . Mordecai the Jew was second in rank to King Xerxes, preeminent among the Jews, and held in high esteem by his many fellow Jews, because he worked for the good of his people and spoke up for the welfare of all the Jews"(Esther 8:5, 11, 16-17; 9:3-4; 10:3). (See also Esther 8-10.)

When King Xerxes realized that Haman had devised an evil plan of anni-hilation for the queen's people, he immediately commanded that Haman be hanged on his own gallows. Without delay, the king's servants covered Haman's head with the cloth of death, tied it tightly around his neck, and dragged him from the queen's quarters.

With angry righteous indignation, the king avowed through clenched teeth, so that only he and Esther could hear, *"How dare Haman act outside the confines of true nobility and misrepresent my pluralistic ideals. To think of my highest-ranking officer having the audacity to do so, especially within the capital city and within my very gates, is revolting! How dare he take advantage of his privileged position and come against the queen's people. After all, are not Esther's people my people? All of Persia's 'nations' are my people! Besides, isn't peace what kings usually offer a nation in exchange for a queen?*

"Enjoy hanging on your 'gallows of doom,' Prince Haman; may it be a message to all that such blatant and vile prejudice will not be tolerated in my kingdom. All nations shall benefit from the ethnic diversity under my reign, especially within my walls. So hang, duplicitous and vile Haman; hang until you are dead."

Even though Haman had become his closest confidante, the king had lost one queen through the advice of his council of "experts" and had suffered great sorrow as a result; he would not lose another. He had made this decision on his own. Oddly, even though there were no council members nearby to sanction this move, he felt secure in his decision, as if he had the support of many council members surrounding him. Even though he made it without a moment's hesitation, there was a strange peace about the judgment he had made within the chambers of his queen. For the first time in a long while, it seemed, his soul had found a unique resting place.

Noticing the unique calmness that had come over the king, contrasting the recent moments of high-pitched intensity, Esther knew that this was another crucial opportunity for her to make a revelation to her husband. She had already identified herself with the Jews; now she needed to openly identify herself with her beloved Mordecai. She wasn't sure why she felt this was a necessity, but having the obvious favor of the king, she revealed to him that Mordecai, the Jewish gatekeeper whom he had honored the previous day, was her dear cousin who had fathered her most of her days.

He listened intently as he turned the signet ring in his hand over and over again. He then placed the ring on his finger and requested that Esther accompany him to the grand hall. She immediately stepped in behind him as they quickly walked toward the throne room; each was in deep in thought, knowing that there were important decisions yet to be made.

Upon returning to his throne, where he was accustomed to making kingly decisions, Xerxes gave Esther the entire estate of Haman to do with as she wished. He then decisively picked up his gold scepter and called for his eunuchs to bring Mordecai to him at once.

Esther sat quietly and prayerfully on her throne, lower, but not far from Xerxes. She prayed earnestly within herself, *"Oh Lord, I have seen great things today. Please continue to lead my thoughts, words, and actions. May I stay in sync with your divine guidance and say and do that which You desire. I stand in awe of You and how You lead the thoughts of kings as well as Your own people. Lead on, oh King Eternal!"*

Before she could continue her heartfelt personal intercessions, Mordecai entered the grand hall, escorted by the king's eunuchs. Xerxes, now positioned on his throne in kingly fashion with his signet ring placed deliberately on his forefinger, acknowledged Mordecai's entrance and gestured for him to come forward. He commended Mordecai again for being a faithful servant at the palace gate and for saving his life in previous days. Then, much to Mordecai's surprise, he commended him for his fatherly role in Queen Esther's life. Mordecai, glancing at Esther, caught the concurring sparkle in her eye; he then bowed from the waist in acknowledgement of the king's compliments.

Much to the surprise of both Esther and Mordecai, Xerxes presented to Mordecai his trusted signet ring. Xerxes looked toward his queen with pleasure as he handed the ring over. She nodded to him in appreciation and appointed Mordecai to oversee the care of Haman's estate in her stead.

These gracious acts preserved Esther and Mordecai, but did nothing to preserve their people. Before the king could even dismiss Mordecai,

Esther once again fell at Xerxes' feet, weeping and pleading with him to right the wrong that Haman had committed against her people. She humbly beseeched him, *"If it pleases the king, and if he regard me with favor and thinks it the right thing to do, and if he is pleased with me, let an order be written overruling the dispatches that Haman son of Hammedatha, the Agagite, devised and wrote to destroy the Jews in all the king's provinces. For how can I bear to see disaster fall on my people? How can I bear to see the destruction of my family?"* [1]

In response, the king told Esther and Mordecai to write another decree on behalf of the Jews and seal it in his name with his signet ring. The new edict granted the Jews in every city in the kingdom the right *"to assemble and protect themselves; to destroy, kill and annihilate any armed force of any nationality or province that might attack them."* [2]

Tears of rejoicing instantly formed in Esther and Mordecai's eyes simultaneously. Their smiles could not be restrained; Esther clapped her hands like a child who had just received a surprise pony on a warm spring day. Xerxes smiled in approval as Esther recovered her composure; she then prostrated herself before him in thankfulness, as did Mordecai. Xerxes lifted Esther to himself in a warm embrace, and she kissed him with the gratitude of a queen and the passion of a new bride.

To make a further impression on the people throughout the provinces, Xerxes had his couriers ride his own royal horses and deliver this new edict to each sector in his kingdom. This was done to make it abundantly clear that the king was personally in favor of the Jews and this new law, in place of the previous one. He wanted all of Persia to be reminded of his pluralistic ideals, in order to keep peace in the land and to strengthen his favor in their eyes. By the written laws of the land, Xerxes was not able to completely reverse Haman's previous edict. However, this was a clear display of his current partiality toward the Jews, so much so that his nobles, governors, and administrators helped the Jews during the days of battle.

As the message went out, joyous celebration broke out among the Jews. This was indeed a day to rejoice; the tables had been turned, and the enemy had been thwarted. Esther and Mordecai rejoiced openly. As they enjoyed tea and prayer together later that evening, they could not help but proclaim, *"Praise the Lord. Sing to the Lord a new song, his praise in the assembly of the saints. Let Israel rejoice in their Maker; let the people of Zion be glad in their King. Let them praise his name with dancing and make music to him with tambourine and harp. For the Lord takes delight in his people; he crowns the humble with salvation. Let the saints rejoice in this honor and sing for joy on their beds.*

"May the praise of God be in their mouths and a double-edged sword in their hands, to inflict vengeance on the nations and punishment on the peoples, to bind their kings with fetters, their nobles with shackles of iron, to carry out the sentence written against them. This is the glory of all his saints. Praise the Lord." [3]

A TIME TO CELEBRATE

The enemy was slain. War had been waged and won; the victory belonged to God and His servants. The rescue of a generation was complete, and God's choice servants were clothed in royal garments. It was time to celebrate! A humble queen and a faithful servant who *"worked for the good of his people and spoke up for the welfare of all"* (Esther 10:3) had, in the providence of God, brought to complete fruition the power of a surrendered life.

We should never be surprised when the downfall of an enemy comes to pass before our eyes. While we should pray for our enemies that their hearts would be turned toward righteousness, at the same time, we should anticipate that the Lord will deal ruthlessly with those who remain sworn enemies to Him and His people. There are rewards for those who earnestly

> *"There are rewards for those who earnestly serve the Lord, and there is judgment for those who harden their hearts against God and His people."*

serve the Lord, and there is judgment for those who harden their hearts against God and His people.

- *"The evil deeds of a wicked man ensnare him; the cords of his sin hold him fast"* (Proverbs 5:22).

- *"A scoundrel and villain, who goes about with a corrupt mouth ... who plots evil with deceit in his heart—he always stirs up dissension. Therefore disaster will overtake him in an instant; he will suddenly be destroyed—without remedy"* (Proverbs 6:12-15).

- *"The fear of the Lord adds length to life, but the years of the wicked are cut short"* (Proverbs 10:27).

- *"The righteous will never be uprooted, but the wicked will not remain in the land"* (Proverbs 10:30).

- *"The righteousness of the blameless makes a straight way for them, but the wicked are brought down by their own wickedness"* (Proverbs 11:5).

- *"When the righteous prosper, the city rejoices; when the wicked perish, there are shouts of joy"* (Proverbs 11:10).

There is a time to do battle and a time to celebrate. When the Jews in Persia won their battles, they had a celebration called "Purim," a national celebration of victory. It was so named because "pur" meant "lot," referring to the lot that Haman had cast against the Jews and the king's edict that cast it back to defeat him. This was not a religious holiday; it was simply a holiday to rejoice in God's providential care in giving them victory against their enemies. Contemporary Jews still celebrate Purim today.[4] Many nations have such holidays, expressing joy and thankfulness for freedom and victory.

THE COST OF FREEDOM

The freedom that Americans experience today was birthed out of battles that our forefathers fought. It was birthed when a parent-nation, England, usurped its authority and, rather than blessing and releasing this new American nation to develop on its own, attempted to keep it under its dominant rule. Much like the Jews of Persia, the colonists had to fight for their freedom; but before the fight, there were voices, like that of Mordecai, heard in the land, voices calling for unity and humility among the people, beseeching God's grace while proclaiming His divine authority.

William Prescott made a call for unity in August of 1773. William was the leader of a group of men from Massachusetts that was sending relief food supplies to the people of Boston, and he wrote this in a letter to the men of Boston:

> . . . Let us **all be of one heart,** and stand fast in the liberty wherewith Christ has made us free. And may He, of His infinite mercy, grant us deliverance out of all our troubles.[5]

John Hancock made a call for humility and God's grace in October of 1773. John was the president of the Massachusetts Provincial Congress at the time. He said this:

> We think it is incumbent upon this people **to humble themselves before God** . . . [and] also to implore the **Divine Blessing** upon us, that by the assistance of **His grace** we may be enabled to reform whatever is amiss among us, that so God may be pleased to continue to us the blessings we enjoy . . . by causing harmony and union to be restored between Great Britain and these Colonies.[6]

Patrick Henry, while in the Virginia House of Burgesses, made a proclamation of God's authority on March 23, 1775. He said this:

> "God presides over the destinies of nations. . . the battle is not to the strong alone; it is to the vigilant, the active, the brave . . ."

*. . . We shall not fight alone. **God presides over the destinies of nations**, and will raise up friends for us. The battle is not to the strong alone; it is to the vigilant, the active, the brave . . . Is life so dear, or peace so sweet, as to be purchased at the price of chains and slavery? Forbid it, almighty God! I know not what course others may take, but as for me, give me liberty or give me death![7]*

John Adams wrote this statement in a letter to his wife, Abigail, in 1776, referring to the day when the Declaration of Independence was passed:

> *. . . will be the most memorable . . . in the history of America. I am apt to believe that it will be **celebrated by succeeding generations**, as the great anniversary festival. It ought to be commemorated, as the Day of Deliverance, by solemn acts of devotion to God Almighty. It ought to be solemnized with pomp and parade, with shows, games, sports, guns, bells, bonfires and illuminations, from one end of this continent to the other, from this time forward forevermore . . .[8]*

Americans walk in freedom today in a land paid for with blood that was shed because of a belief that roots itself in the shed blood of Jesus Christ. This belief was that *"all men are created equal."*[9] It is in covenant with Christ that we understand our equality, as Paul says in Galatians 3:28, *"for you are all one in Christ Jesus,"* and again in Ephesians 3:6, *"This mystery is that through the gospel the Gentiles are heirs together with Israel, members together of one body, and sharers together in the promise in Christ Jesus."* We are free today because two centuries ago the leaders of this newly established nation challenged its people to be humble, walk in unity, and to acknowledge God's grace and authority at the roots of its destiny.

The closing statement of the Declaration of Independence, at the birthing of the United States of America says, **". . . for the support of this Declaration, with a firm reliance on the protection of divine Providence, we mutually pledge to each other our Lives, our Fortunes and our sacred Honor."** [10] In other words, being of one heart and mind, care and concern toward one another is pre-eminent.

Upon disbanding his army, General George Washington wrote to the governors of each of the thirteen states:

> *I now make it* **my earnest prayer that God . . . would incline the hearts of the citizens . . . to entertain a brotherly affection for one another, for their fellow-citizens of the United States at large,** *and particularly for their brethren who have served in the field. And finally that He would most graciously be pleased to dispose us* **all to do justice, to love mercy, and to demean ourselves with the charity, humility and pacific temper of mind, which were the characteristics of the Divine Author of our religion,** *and without an humble imitation of whose example in these things, we can never hope to be a happy nation.* [11]

As a free nation and a free people in Christ, we have a call to serve, to reach out to the harvest. As it was for the Jews of Persia and the newborn nation of Americans, there had been a great deliverance wrought, not through the mere strength of men, but rather through the providence of God. It came by His mercy and grace and through the power of surrendered lives. Therefore, each of us bear the responsibility to fulfill Galatians

5:13, *"You, my brothers, were called to be free. But do not use your freedom to indulge the sinful nature; rather, serve one another in love."*

RESCUE THROUGH SERVICE

My friends and colleagues in the ministry, Pastors Danny and Gisselle Bonilla, pastor a church in the heart of New York City in upper Manhattan. Following the September 11, 2001, crisis of mass murder at the Twin Towers and the Pentagon, Pastor Danny, along with many other city pastors, received an invitation to attend a clergy press conference with Mayor Giuliani at city hall. They prayed together for their city on the steps of city hall and stood in solidarity, carrying the burdens of the city to the Lord. Following the press conference, the pastors received a guided escort to the site of the disaster. They spent three hours surveying the site, talking with rescue workers, and praying for the city. Pastor Danny felt shock and desperation in his spirit as he witnessed firsthand the devastation. He felt like he was standing in a massive open grave, a war zone. It was the most unbelievable devastation that he had ever personally witnessed, and he declared that the loss was much worse than television cameras were able to project on the screen.

Along with other city pastors, Pastors Danny and Gisselle determined to take their city on a journey of recovery and hope. As well as ministering to members of their own congregation who were in dire need as a result of the terrorist attacks, they also set up a command center in their church, with volunteers and staff working long hours to meet as many needs as possible. Money from fellowshipping churches throughout the nation began to pour into their church resource fund. They took truckloads of supplies to the rescue workers and displaced families, and they offered counseling and financial assistance to needy families throughout the city. In other words, they got involved, loving their city in practical ways, but their assistance did not end there.

Along with this natural aid, they also held additional prayer and evangelism services in the weeks that followed. Within two weeks of

September 11, they had led almost nine hundred people to the Lord in their services. Although the Lord Jesus loved people and ministered to their natural needs when He walked the earth, His primary motivation was always to lead them to a personal relationship with Him. While earthly help remains here on earth, the salvation of the soul lasts forever. This is the kind of good that the Lord desires to bring out of every disaster that comes our way, both personally and nationally. Along with Esther and Mordecai, the Bonilla's congregation is rejoicing today in the goodness of God to have led so many people to Himself.

Out of victory and rejoicing must come service, or the reason for the sacrifices will be short-lived. Does this not bring us full-circle? Christ laid down His life that we might be saved and, in turn, lay down our lives for others. Esther, Mordecai, and so many others in nations around the world have laid down their lives in surrender, not to man, but to God, that we might live.

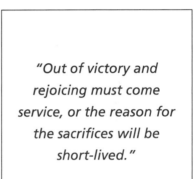

"Out of victory and rejoicing must come service, or the reason for the sacrifices will be short-lived."

May the same be said of us; we are blessed to be a blessing and rescued to be rescuers of others. His voice speaks to each of us today to first deal with the prejudice in our own hearts and then reach out and touch those who are being persecuted for righteousness' sake. It is when we choose to lay down our prejudices and surrender our wills to the will of the Master that there can be a rescue of a generation. **That** is the power of a surrendered life.

The Lord, Our Rescuer

THE LORD'S RESCUE THROUGHOUT THE GENERATIONS

EX. 18:10   *"He said, 'Praise be to the LORD, who rescued you from the hand of the Egyptians and of Pharaoh, and who rescued the people from the hand of the Egyptians.'"*

NUM. 10:9   *"When you go into battle in your own land against an enemy who is oppressing you, sound a blast on the trumpets. Then you will be remembered by the LORD your God and rescued from your enemies."*

1 SAM. 11:13   *"But Saul said, 'No one shall be put to death today, for this day the LORD has rescued Israel.'"*

1 SAM. 14:23   *"So the LORD rescued Israel that day, and the battle moved on beyond Beth Aven."*

2 SAM. 3:18   *"Now do it! For the LORD promised David, 'By my servant David I will rescue my people Israel from the hand of the Philistines and from the hand of all their enemies.'"*

NEH. 9:27   *"So you handed them over to their enemies, who oppressed them. But when they were oppressed they cried out to you. From heaven you heard them, and in your great compassion you gave them deliverers, who rescued them from the hand of their enemies."*

DAN. 3:28 *"Then Nebuchadnezzar said, 'Praise be to the God of Shadrach, Meshach and Abednego, who has sent his angel and rescued his servants! They trusted in him and defied the king's command and were willing to give up their lives rather than serve or worship any god except their own God.'"*

DAN. 6:27 *"He rescues and he saves; he performs signs and wonders in the heavens and on the earth. He has rescued Daniel from the power of the lions."*

ACTS 12:11 *"Then Peter came to himself and said, 'Now I know without a doubt that the Lord sent his angel and rescued me from Herod's clutches and from everything the Jewish people were anticipating.'"*

GAL. 1:3-4 *"Grace and peace to you from God our Father and the Lord Jesus Christ, who gave himself for our sins to rescue us from the present evil age, according to the will of our God and Father."*

COL. 1:13 *"For he has rescued us from the dominion of darkness and brought us into the kingdom of the Son he loves."*

2 TIM. 3:10-11 *"You, however, know all about my teaching, my way of life, my purpose, faith, patience, love, endurance, persecutions, sufferings—what kinds of things happened to me in Antioch, Iconium and Lystra, the persecutions I endured. Yet the Lord rescued me from all of them."*

PETITIONS FOR RESCUE

PS. 25:20   *"Guard my life and rescue me; let me not be put to shame, for I take refuge in you."*

PS. 31:2   *"Turn your ear to me, come quickly to my rescue; be my rock of refuge, a strong fortress to save me."*

PS. 43:1   *"Vindicate me, O God, and plead my cause against an ungodly nation; rescue me from deceitful and wicked men."*

PS. 71:2   *"Rescue me and deliver me in your righteousness; turn your ear to me and save me."*

PS. 82:4   *"Rescue the weak and needy; deliver them from the hand of the wicked."*

PS. 140:1   *"Rescue me, O LORD, from evil men; protect me from men of violence."*

PS. 143:9   *"Rescue me from my enemies, O LORD, for I hide myself in you."*

PS. 144:11   *"Deliver me and rescue me from the hands of foreigners whose mouths are full of lies, whose right hands are deceitful."*

PROV. 24:11   *"Rescue those being led away to death; hold back those staggering toward slaughter."*

PROMISES OF RESCUE

PS. 18:47-48 *"He is the God who avenges me, who subdues nations under me, who saves me from my enemies. You exalted me above my foes; from violent men you rescued me."*

PS. 35:10 *"My whole being will exclaim, 'Who is like you, O LORD? You rescue the poor from those too strong for them, the poor and needy from those who rob them.'"*

PS. 91:14 *"'Because he loves me,' says the LORD, 'I will rescue him; I will protect him, for he acknowledges my name.'"*

PS. 107:20 *"He sent forth his word and healed them; he rescued them from the grave."*

PROV. 11:8 *"The righteous man is rescued from trouble, and it comes on the wicked instead."*

JOB 5:19-26 *"From six calamities he will rescue you; in seven no harm will befall you. In famine he will ransom you from death, and in battle from the stroke of the sword. You will be protected from the lash of the tongue, and need not fear when destruction comes . . . You will come to the grave in full vigor . . ."*

ISA. 46:4 *"Even to your old age and gray hairs I am he, I am he who will sustain you. I have made you and I will carry you; I will sustain you and I will rescue you."*

JER. 1:19 *"'They will fight against you but will not overcome you, for I am with you and will rescue you,' declares the LORD."*

JER. 15:20 *"'I will make you a wall to this people, a fortified wall of bronze; they will fight against you but will not overcome you, for I am with you to rescue and save you,' declares the LORD."*

JER. 39:17 *"But I will rescue you on that day, declares the LORD; you will not be handed over to those you fear."*

ACTS 26:17-18 *"I will rescue you from your own people and from the Gentiles. I am sending you to them to open their eyes and turn them from darkness to light, and from the power of Satan to God, so that they may receive forgiveness of sins and a place among those who are sanctified by faith in me."*

2 PET. 2:9 *". . . the Lord knows how to rescue godly men from trials and to hold the unrighteous for the day of judgment, while continuing their punishment."*

NOTES

1   Esther 8:5-6

2   Esther 8:8-14

3   Psalm 149

4   "*Pur* is a Persian word signifying a part, and thence denoting a lot. With the Hebrew plural termination it becomes *purim*, 'lots.' This is the name by which the feast is known which is kept to commemorate the deliverance of the Jews from the plot of Haman. It is called the Feast of Lots because Haman in his superstition resorted to divination for the purpose of ascertaining when he could most effectually destroy the Jews. See Esther iii, 7. Some think that the name was given in irony, as denoting the contempt in which the Jews held Haman and his divination.

   "There is a tradition that the introduction of this feast among the Jews met with some opposition, though it afterward became generally observed. The day before the feast is kept as a solemn fast. On the day of the feast the people assemble in the synagogue, where the book of Esther is read amid clapping of hands and stamping of feet, as demonstrations of contempt for Haman and of joy for the deliverance of the Jews. After leaving the synagogue there are great feasts at home, which have been sometimes carried to such excess that some writers have called the Feast of Purim the Bacchanalia of the Jews." James M. Freeman, *Manners and Customs of the Bible* (Plainfield, N.J.: Logos, 1972), 207.

5   George Bancroft, *Bancroft's History of the United States*, 3d ed., 10 vols. (Boston: Charles C. Little & James Brown, 1838), 99; originally found in Peter Marshall and David Manuel, *The Light and the Glory* (Old Tappan, N.J.: Fleming H. Revell, 1977), 268.

6   Bancroft, Bancroft's History, 229; originally found in Marshall and Manuel, *The Light and the Glory*, 269.

7   Bancroft, Bancroft's History, 274; originally found in Marshall and Manuel, *The Light and the Glory*, 269.

8   L.H. Butterfield, *Adams Family Correspondence*, Vol. 2, (Cambridge: Harvard Univ. Press, 1963), 28, 30-31; originally found in Marshall and Manuel, *The Light and the Glory*, 310.

9   *The New Book of Knowledge*, Vol. 4, (Grolier, 1976), 64.

10 Ibid., 65.

11 From *The Washington Papers*, Saul K. Padover, ed.; as quoted in *Decision* (February 1976); originally found in Marshall and Manuel, *The Light and the Glory*, 339.

The Surrendered Life

As we have attempted to identify with Esther and walk in her shoes throughout these pages, we have learned some very valuable lessons through her surrendered life. As we have endeavored to make this leap in time and connect in perspective with Esther, Mordecai, and the other players on this page of history, as well as the one true God Himself, one message has become clear—powerful influence comes to those who surrender themselves humbly and purposely to the will of God. It has also been implicitly clear that, many times, surrendering to God translates into submission to another person. Another message that has been repeatedly obvious is that God never wastes anything, whether it is a beauty pageant, a gallows, or the prayers of a city in urgent need.

As we have seen in Esther's life and so many others, influence comes, not only through moments, but also throughout a lifetime. It comes through the most insignificant situations as well as the most amazing proposals. Opportunities for yielding to God's will and intent come to our doorstep each day. Hidden within those repeated opportunities, a surrendered life can radiate like a brilliantly cut diamond on a black velvet backdrop.

In Esther, we found a young woman who continually bent her will to the will of others and to the wisdom of God. This continual yielding must have worked an internal brokenness in her, for she was neither unable nor incapable of thinking intelligently on her own. Her intelligence, cloaked in wisdom, is easily seen through her deeds of discretion. However, through her brokenness, purpose was discovered, and destiny was fulfilled. Through bowing her knee to the one true God, a generation was rescued from the clutches of death. Through this brokenness, she was able to nourish her generation, rather than deplete it of its resources.

> *". . .through her brokenness, purpose was discovered, and destiny was fulfilled."*

Is it not through a yielded life that many are sustained? Is it not through humility that hearts are won, that enemies are brought down and the lowly lifted up? Is it not through wisdom that minds are changed and lives are spared, and is it not God who knows all and sees all?

God set the stage; He chose a yielded vessel and planted her in the garden of His choosing. He purified her heart as she humbled herself to His purposes. He set a faithful watchman on the wall to watch over her and foresee the storm that was brewing. He chose her and partnered together with her in the conquest of a king's heart, the downfall of an enemy, and the liberation of a people. Esther's part was laid out in simple fashion; it carried a singular repetitious theme of surrender. If she did her part, He would do His.

God's theme is much the same today as it was in Esther's day, simple surrender. The outworking of such humility in a person's life produces much fruit, personally and in the lives of others. The equation for such humility and fruitfulness was similarly acknowledged in a pattern that Jesus used when He shared bread with others. In fact, every time Jesus handled bread during His time here on earth, He always used the same pattern. In His example is a message about our lives, not just a mere mealtime pattern.

At His last supper with the disciples, we read, *"and he took bread, gave thanks and broke it, and gave it to them. . ."* (Luke 22:19). In this particular

> *". . .do this in remembrance of me."*

passage, He told the disciples to *"do this in remembrance of me"* (Luke 22:19). In other words, He wanted them to pay particular attention to the manner in which He was about to break bread with them. One Greek word for "time" meant "that which blots out all things." As the old adage goes, "out of sight, out of mind," Jesus knew the human tendency to forget whatever is not within view. He wanted to tell the disciples something about His life and about their lives that they would remember through this illustration, so He used this same pattern every time He handled bread.

This was not an unusual pattern to the disciples; they had seen Him do it many times before, when feeding the multitudes on the hillsides or when eating together at previous Passover meals. The method was always the same, but this time, Jesus was telling them that when they shared bread with each other in the future, they were to remember Him and the life message that He had carried to them. What was the message in the pattern? What was it that Christ longed for them to remember in this illustration of bread, and what does it hold in store for us? It was a message very much like that of Esther's life.

CHOSEN

First, he **chose it**. He took the bread in His hands. The reminder in this act is that the Father chose Jesus to come to earth. The one true God selected Him, took Him from heaven's realm, and placed Him on earth for our sake. Matthew quoted the prophet Isaiah's proclamation, *"Here is my servant whom I have chosen, the one I love, in whom I delight..."* [1]

Esther also was chosen. She was not merely taken by the king's soldiers, selected by Hegai, and then chosen by the king; she was chosen by the Lord to influence a king, slay an enemy, and rescue a generation. God had a plan for this young maiden from the time that she was in her mother's womb, and He was with her in every ensuing season thereafter. Whether she was orphaned and raised by a single cousin or swept up into the pageantry and palace of a heathen king, God had chosen her and ordered her steps.

The message tucked away for us in this reminder is that the Lord has also chosen us for a specific work. Jesus said to his disciples, *". . . I chose you and appointed you to go and bear fruit—fruit that will last."* [2]

Later Paul wrote, *"In him we were also chosen, having been predestined according to the plan of him who works out everything in conformity with the purpose of his will."* [3]

Then Peter proclaimed to us all, *". . . you are a chosen people, a royal priesthood, a holy nation, a people belonging to God, that you may declare the praises of him who called you out of darkness into his wonderful light."* [4]

Clearly, you are chosen and have been personally selected by the Lord to make an impact on the generation in which He has placed you.

> *"You look the way you do and are planted where you are because you have been uniquely designed for a specific purpose, time, and place. You are chosen."*

Esther was chosen to do a work, and so are you. That work has been uniquely designed by your heavenly Father to fit you. Just as David could not wear Saul's armor and Esther was not allowed to marry just any Jewish man, you must recognize that you have been chosen by God for a specific purpose. You look the way you do and are planted where you are because you have been uniquely designed for a specific purpose, time, and place. You are chosen.

ANOINTED

Secondly, Jesus **blessed it**. He gave thanks for the bread, indicating the Father's blessing and anointing in His life. He was chosen for a specific purpose and was blessed, or anointed, to do a specific task. When He made His triumphal entry into Jerusalem, the crowds proclaimed along with the psalmist of old, *". . . Blessed is he who comes in the name of the Lord!"* [5]

In every place where Esther found herself, she discovered the accompanying blessing of God. God uniquely planted her in the capital city of Susa in the home of her beloved cousin Mordecai, an official at the king's gate. There she was mentored in the ways and wisdom of Jehovah. Next God planted her in the king's palace, in a favored apartment, with the best mentoring eunuch in matters of winning a king's heart. Then God blessed her with a position of influence, like no other woman in the land had had at that time. He had chosen her, groomed her, and anointed her for the greatest task and greatest privilege of her life. Everywhere Esther went, the blessings of God followed her.

On a day when Jesus prophetically spoke in parables to the crowds and to His disciples, He said, *"Then the King will say to those on his right, 'Come, you who are blessed by my Father; take your inheritance, the kingdom prepared for you since the creation of the world. For I was hungry and you gave me something to eat, I was thirsty and you gave me something to drink, I was a stranger and you invited me in, I needed clothes and you clothed me, I was sick and you looked after me, I was in prison and you came to visit me.'"* [6] In other words, you are blessed to be a blessing; you are anointed by the Father to do specific deeds of kindness. Whatever He has called you to do, He will enable you to do it.

> *"you are blessed to be a blessing; you are anointed by the Father to do specific deeds of kindness."*

God has chosen you, just as He did Esther, and He has also blessed and anointed you to serve Him in specific ways in this particular generation. The wonderful promise that comes to you if you believe and surrender your life totally to God is that *"the one who calls you is faithful and He will do it."* [7] In other words, if He chooses you, He will bless you and do the task through you in partnership. You will never be alone in that which He has called you to do. *"He will never leave you nor forsake you."* [8]

BROKEN

Thirdly, Jesus **broke it**. After He chose the bread and blessed it, He broke it. This, of course, was to be a reminder to all of His disciples, both then and now, that He was not only chosen by the Father and anointed to do a task during His time here, but He was also broken in the process for our sakes. He had a task to do that brought Him great joy, but that which was set before Him would come with the expensive price tag of personal breaking. For every crown of joy, there is a task of sorrow; for every great accomplishment, there is a stretching that requires reaching toward the one who has called us to the task. The prophet Isaiah tells us why He was treated in such a manner: *"But he was pierced for our transgressions, he was crushed for our iniquities; the punishment that brought us peace was upon him, and by his wounds we are healed."* [9]

> *"For every crown of joy, there is a task of sorrow;*
> *for every great accomplishment, there is a stretching that requires reaching toward the one who has called us to the task."*

It was for you and me that Jesus endured such brokenness and shame on the cross. The author of Hebrews says, *"Let us fix our eyes on Jesus, the author and perfecter of our faith, who for the joy set before him endured the cross, scorning its shame, and sat down at the right hand of the throne of God. Consider him who endured such opposition from sinful men, so that you will not grow weary and lose heart."* [10] Through Christ's example of brokenness, you are to receive strength during your times of despair. He was broken and crushed that you and I would not grow weary and lose heart in the midst of the journey.

Esther experienced brokenness as she went through the purification process for an earthly king. During this natural process, surely she allowed the Lord to do an inner work for the sake of the destiny to which she was called. She was probably unable to see very far into the distant future, but she endured the cross of broken dreams and placement within a palace that bore all the trappings of God-forsakenness. She embraced the trial of her faith for the sake of the destiny that reigned in her heart.

You too must not reject the personal cost that may be before you, for destiny is just around the corner. The book of James sends this encouragement your way today: *"Blessed is the man* [or woman] *who perseveres under trial, because when* [s]*he has stood the test,* [s]*he will receive the crown of life that God has promised to those who love him."* [11] Through trials, others who are wounded can relate to you. Through these same trials, personal breaking will become food in the Master's hands so that He might use your life to feed others who are in like need.

GIVEN

The last thing that Jesus always did with bread after he chose it, blessed it, and broke it was to **give it** to those who were hungry. This, of course, was to underscore the fact the He was given to us and for us. 1 Timothy 2:5-6 tells us, *"For there is one God and one mediator between God and men, the man Christ Jesus, who gave himself as a ransom for all men—the testimony given in its proper time."*

When Esther came out of her time of fasting and prayer and crossed the threshold out of the safety of her personal world and into the intimidating world of wickedness and deception, she stepped into the very arms of God. Neither Satan nor his toy soldier, Haman, could touch her; the angels of the Lord were 'round about her as she did the bidding of the Lord Most High. She had been blessed to be a blessing, and she offered herself on the altar of sacrifice on behalf of her people. In being given, she gave, and in giving, she received.

> "She had been blessed to be a blessing, and she offered herself on the altar of sacrifice on behalf of her people. In being given, she gave, and in giving, she received."

265

Just as Jesus gave of Himself on our behalf, and just as Esther surrendered her life and offered it bravely on behalf of her people, so are you called to offer up your life. The apostle Paul proclaims with zeal, *"For we are God's workmanship, created in Christ Jesus to do good works, which God prepared in advance for us to do."* [12]

He says in Romans 14:7-8, *"For none of us lives to himself alone and none of us dies to himself alone. If we live, we live to the Lord; and if we die, we die to the Lord. So, whether we live or die, we belong to the Lord."* Fully believing this to be true, we should live bravely and conscientiously before the Lord and the people with whom He has surrounded us. We should freely offer ourselves to the service of the King of Kings and His people.

The next time you sit down to enjoy a piece of bread, remember, the Father has chosen you, and He has anointed you for a task. You may be broken in the process, but you are to give yourself with utmost abandon to that which the Master has placed before you. God chose Esther; He prepared and anointed her to do that which He had called her to do. He then allowed her the privilege of crossing the threshold of self-sacrifice through the avenue of humility. If He would do this for Esther and for His only Son, would He do any less for you?

The palace that the Father had prepared for Esther had destiny engraved on its walls; that place which He has prepared for you has these same etchings of destiny. Your pathway may not lead to palace halls, like Esther's did, and your future may not include a beauty pageant or nearby gallows, but your destiny will cost you everything. Destiny's price will be more than you had anticipated, yet will give you more than you had ever hoped. Your sacrifice may not cost you a crown, but your surrender will award you influence.

> *"Destiny's price will be more than you had anticipated, yet will give you more than you had ever hoped."*

If you are struggling with any hesitation about giving your life fully to Jesus Christ in complete surrender, I hope that you are encouraged by Esther's example and the example of Christ. Whether you decide to walk with Him personally or not, that choice is yours. However, along with opportunities to give of yourself to others, seasons of brokenness will come into your life, as well. People will demand humility and sacrifice, whether you respond willingly to their demands or not. If you should choose to be become a recluse, nature itself will demand sacrifice. You cannot escape surrender and sacrifice, but you can choose to whom you will surrender and sacrifice.

> *"You cannot escape surrender and sacrifice, but you can choose to whom you will surrender and sacrifice."*

It is only through a surrendered life to Christ that your influence will penetrate cultural barriers and the hearts of generations to come. Just as the message of Esther's life reaches across the generations to you today and sings a sweet melody of victory and praise, so too can your story penetrate the hearts of children, grandchildren, friends, and friends of friends. It can affect businesses, neighborhoods, cities, and nations. Truly, this is the *power of a surrendered life.*

My prayer for you today is one that the apostle Paul prayed many years ago: *"I pray that out of His glorious riches **He may strengthen you with power through His Spirit** in your inner being, so that Christ may dwell in your hearts through faith. And I pray that you, being rooted and established in love, may have power, together with all the saints, to grasp how wide and long and high and deep is the love of Christ, and to know this love that surpasses knowledge—that you may be filled to the measure of all the fullness of God. Now to Him who is able to do immeasurably more than all we ask or imagine, **according to His power that is at work within us, to Him be glory in the church and in Christ Jesus throughout all generations, for ever and ever! Amen."* [13]

The "I Will" of Psalms

PS. 3:6 *"I will not fear the tens of thousands drawn up against me on every side."*

PS. 4:8 *"I will lie down and sleep in peace, for you alone, O Lord, make me dwell in safety."*

PS. 5:7 *"But I, by your great mercy, will come into your house; in reverence will I bow down toward your holy temple."*

PS. 9:1 *"I will praise you, O Lord, with all my heart; I will tell of all your wonders."*

PS. 13:6 *"I will sing to the Lord, for he has been good to me."*

PS. 16:7 *"I will praise the Lord, who counsels me; even at night my heart instructs me."*

PS. 18:3 *"I (will) call to the Lord, who is worthy of praise, and I am saved from my enemies." (KJV)*

PS. 18:49 *"Therefore I will praise you among the nations, O Lord; I will sing praises to your name."*

PS. 23:4 *"Even though I walk through the valley of the shadow of death, I will fear no evil, for you are with me; your rod and your staff, they comfort me."*

PS. 26:11 *"But I (will) lead a blameless life; redeem me and be merciful to me." (KJV)*

PS. 27:3 *"Though an army besiege me, my heart will not fear; though war break out against me even then will I be confident."*

PS. 30:1 *"I will exalt you, O Lord, for you lifted me out of the depths and did not let my enemies gloat over me."*

PS. 39:1 *"... I will watch my ways and keep my tongue from sin; I will put a muzzle on my mouth as long as the wicked are in my presence."*

PS. 45:17 *"I will perpetuate your memory through all generations; therefore the nations will praise you forever and ever."*

PS. 52:9 *"I will praise you forever for what you have done; in your name I will hope, for your name is good. I will praise you in the presence of your saints."*

PS. 56:3 *"When I am afraid, I will trust in you."*

PS. 57:1 *"... I will take refuge in the shadow of your wings until the disaster has passed."*

PS. 57:2 *"I (will) cry out to God Most High, to God, who fulfills his purpose for me." (KJV)*

PS. 59:9 *"O my Strength, I (will) watch for you; you, O God, are my fortress." (KJV)*

PS. 63:4 *"I will praise you as long as I live, and in your name I will lift up my hands."*

PS. 63:7 *"Because you are my help, I (will) sing in the shadow of your wings." (KJV)*

PS. 71:14 *"But as for me, I will always have hope; I will praise you more and more."*

PS. 71:16 *"I will come and proclaim your mighty acts, O Sovereign Lord; I will proclaim your righteousness, yours alone."*

PS. 75:11 *"I will remember the deeds of the Lord; yes, I will remember your miracles of long ago."*

PS. 75:12 *"I will meditate on all your words and consider all your mighty deeds."*

PS. 85:8 *"I will listen to what God the Lord will say; he promises peace to his people, his saints—but let them not return to folly."*

PS. 86:11 *"Teach me your way, O Lord, and I will walk in your truth; give me an undivided heart, that I may fear your name."*

PS. 89:2 *"I will declare that your love stands firm forever, that you established your faithfulness in heaven itself."*

PS. 101:4 *"...I will have nothing to do with evil."*

PS. 116:2 *"...I will call on him as long as I live."*

PS. 116:14 *"I will fulfill my vows to the Lord in the presence of all his people."*

PS. 119:7 *"I will praise you with an upright heart as I learn your righteous laws."*

PS. 119:15 *"I (will) meditate on your precepts and consider your ways." (KJV)*

PS 119:16 *"I (will) delight in your decrees; I will not neglect your word." (KJV)*

PS. 119:32 *"I will run in the path of your commands, for you have set my heart free."*

PS. 119:45 *"I will walk about in freedom, for I have sought out your precepts."*

PS. 119:46 *"I will speak of your statutes before kings and will not be put to shame."*

PS. 122:8 *"For the sake of my brothers and friends, I will say 'Peace be within you.'"*

PS. 122:9 *"For the sake of the house of the Lord our God, I will seek your prosperity."*

PS. 139:14 *"I (will) praise you because I am fearfully and wonderfully made; your works are wonderful, I know that full well." (KJV)*

PS. 145:5 *"... I will meditate on your wonderful works."*

PS. 145:6 *"... I will proclaim your great deeds."*

PS. 146:2 *"I will praise the Lord all my life; I will sing praise to my God as long as I live."*

N O T E S

1   Matthew 12: 18; Isaiah 42:1 (NIV)

1   Ephesians 1:11 (NIV)

2   John 15:16 (NIV)

2   Mark 11:9; Psalm 118:25-26 (NIV)

3   Matthew 25:34-36 (NIV)

4   1 Peter 2:9 (NIV)

5   Psalm 118:26; Matthew 21:9 (NIV)

6   Matthew 25:34-36 (NIV)

7   1 Thessalonians 5:24 (NIV)

8   Reference to Hebrews 13:5

9   Isaiah 53:5 (NIV)

10   Hebrews 12:1-2 (NIV)

11   James 1:12 (NIV)

12   Ephesians 2:10 (NIV)

13   Ephesians 3:16-21

Bibliography

Arnold, Duane W.H., *Prayers of the Martyrs*, Grand Rapids: Zondervan, 1991.

Bancroft, George, *Bancroft's History of the United States*, 3d ed., 10 Vols., Boston: Charles C. Little & James Brown, 1838.

Baxter, J. Sidlow, *Explore the Book*, Vol. 2, Grand Rapids: Zondervan, 1973.

Bodine, Dave, *PNWP Ministries*, December 10, 2001 <http://www.pnwp.net> (December 10, 2001), Northwest Revival News.

Butterfield, L.H., ed., *Adams Family Correspondence*, Vol. 2, Cambridge: Harvard Univ. Press, 1963.

Carter, Dr. Les, *The Prodigal Spouse, How to Survive Infidelity*, Nashville: Nelson, 1990.

Cook, F.C., ed., *Barnes Notes: The Bible Commentary*, Heritage ed., 14 Vols. Grand Rapids: Baker, 1996.

Elliott, Charlotte, "Just as I Am, Without One Plea," *The Methodist Hymnal*, Nashville: Methodist, 1966.

Freeman, James M., *Manners and Customs of the Bible*, Plainfield, N.J.: Logos, 1972.

Gentile, Ernest, *Worship God!*, Portland, Ore.: City Bible, 1994.

Green, Michael, *Tyndale New Testament Commentaries, The 2nd Epistle General of Peter and The General Epistle of Jude*, Leon Morris, ed., 2d ed., Grand Rapids: Eerdmans, 1987.

Jamieson, Fausset, and Brown Commentary, PC Study Bible, Nashville: Nelson, 1998.

Keil & Delitzsch, *Commentary on the Old Testament*, PC Study Bible, Nashville: Nelson, 1998.

Kendrick, Larry S., pub., Tonya Eichelberger, ed., *World Christian* (June 1999), 17.

Kent, R.G., *Old Persia*, 2d ed., New Haven: American Oriental Society, 1953.

Konig, F.W., *Der Burgbau zu Susa nach dem Bauberichte des Konigs Dareios I*, Leipzig: J.C. Hinrichs, 1930.

Lee, Laurel, *Walking Through The Fire*, Dutton, N.Y.: Henry Robbins, 1997.

Lucado, Max, *God Came Near, Chronicles of the Christ*, Portland, Ore.: Multnomah, 1987.

MacDonald, William, *Believer's Bible Commentary*, Nashville: Nelson, 1995.

Marshall, Paul with Lela Gilbert, *Their Blood Cries Out*, Dallas: Word, 1997.

Marshall, Peter and David Manuel, *The Light and the Glory*, Old Tappan, N.J.: Fleming H. Revell, 1977.

Matthew Henry's Commentary, PC Study Bible, Nashville: Nelson, 1998.

McConnell, William, *Parables, etc.*, LaGrange, Ky.: Saratoga, 1982.

Maxwell, L.E., with Ruth C. Dearing, *Women in Ministry*, Wheaton, Ill.: Victor, 1987.

Morrison, J.G. *Satan's Subtle Attack on Women*, Kansas City, Mo.: Nazarene.

Nelson's Illustrated Bible Dictionary, PC Study Bible, Nashville: Nelson, 1998.

New Unger's Bible Dictionary, Chicago: Moody Press, 1988.

Northern Ireland: the Background and the Facts, June 1995, <http://www2.nio.gov.uk/p_history.htm> (January 16, 2002), Brief History of Northern Ireland.

Osbeck, Kenneth W., *101 More Hymn Stories*, Grand Rapids: Kregel, 1985.

Ross, Bette M., *Our Special Child, A Guide to Successful Parenting of Handicapped Children*, Old Tappan, N.J.: Fleming H. Revell, 1984.

Smith, Harold Ivan, *A Singular Devotion*, Old Tappan, N.J.: Fleming H. Revell, 1990.

Swindoll, Charles R., *A Woman of Strength & Dignity*, Esther, Nashville: Word, 1997.

Tenney, Merrill C., ed., *The Zondervan Pictoral Encyclopedia of the Bible*, Grand Rapids: Zondervan, 1977.

The New Book of Knowledge, Vol. 4, Grolier, 1976.

The Washington Papers, Saul K. Padover, ed., as quoted in Decision (February, 1976).
Tucker, Ruth A., and Walter Liefield, *Daughters of the Church, Women and Ministry from New Testament Times to the Present*, Grand Rapids: Zondervan, 1987.

Vredevelt, Pam W., *Empty Arms, Emotional Support for those who have Suffered Miscarriage or Stillbirth*, Portland, Ore.: Multnomah, 1984.

Whiston, William, trans., *Josephus Complete Works*, Grand Rapids: Kregel, 1960.

Whitcomb, John C., *Esther: Triumph of God's Sovereignty*, Chicago: Moody Press, 1971.

Wiseman, D.J., ed., *Peoples of Old Testament Times*, London: Oxford Univ. Press, 1975.

Wycliffe Commentary, PC Study Bible, Nashville: Nelson, 1998.

Yamauchi, Edwin M., *Persia and the Bible*, Grand Rapids: Baker, 1990.

Young, Amy Ross, *By Death or Divorce . . . It Hurts to Lose*, Denver: Accent, 1976.